Freaks in Late Modernist American Culture

Yoshinobu Hakutani
General Editor

Vol. 47

PETER LANG
New York • Washington, D.C./Baltimore • Bern
Frankfurt am Main • Berlin • Brussels • Vienna • Oxford

Nancy Bombaci

Freaks in Late Modernist American Culture

Nathanael West, Djuna Barnes, Tod Browning, and Carson McCullers

PETER LANG
New York • Washington, D.C./Baltimore • Bern
Frankfurt am Main • Berlin • Brussels • Vienna • Oxford

Library of Congress Cataloging-in-Publication Data

Bombaci, Nancy M.
Freaks in late modernist American culture: Nathanael West, Djuna Barnes,
Tod Browning, and Carson McCullers / Nancy Bombaci.
p. cm. — (Modern American literature; v. 47)
Includes bibliographical references and index.
1. American fiction—20th century—History and criticism. 2. Modernism
(Literature)—United States. 3. West, Nathanael, 1903–1940—Criticism and
interpretation. 4. Barnes, Djuna—Criticism and interpretation. 5. Browning, Tod,
1882–1962—Criticism and interpretation. 6. McCullers, Carson, 1917–1967—Criticism
and interpretation. 7. Difference (Psychology) in literature. 8. Identity (Psychology)
in literature. I. Title. II. Modern American literature (New York, N.Y.); v. 47.
PS374.M535B66   813.'5209112—dc22   2004027475
ISBN 0-8204-7832-6
ISSN 1078-0521

Bibliographic information published by **Die Deutsche Bibliothek**.
Die Deutsche Bibliothek lists this publication in the "Deutsche
Nationalbibliografie"; detailed bibliographic data is available
on the Internet at http://dnb.ddb.de/.

Cover art: *Pip and Flip* (1935) by Pavel Tchelichew (1898–1957). Oil on canvas.
1943.38
Reprinted courtesy of Wadsworth Atheneum Museum of Art, Hartford, CT.
The Ella Gallup Sumner and Mary Catlin Sumner Collection Fund.

The paper in this book meets the guidelines for permanence and durability
of the Committee on Production Guidelines for Book Longevity
of the Council of Library Resources.

© 2006 Peter Lang Publishing, Inc., New York
275 Seventh Avenue, 28th Floor, New York, NY 10001
www.peterlangusa.com

All rights reserved.
Reprint or reproduction, even partially, in all forms such as microfilm,
xerography, microfiche, microcard, and offset strictly prohibited.

Printed in Germany

Contents

Acknowledgments	vii
Introduction	1
Chapter One: Degeneration, Anti-Semitism, and the Enfreakment of Modernism	9
Chapter Two: Nathanael West's Aspiring Freakish *Flâneurs*	25
Chapter Three: "Well of Course, I *Used* to Be Absolutely Gorgeous, Dear": The Female Interviewer as Subject/Object in Djuna Barnes's Journalism	49
Chapter Four: Heredity, Transvestism, and the Limits of Self-Fashioning in *Nightwood*	65
Chapter Five: Horror, Melodrama, and Mutable Masculine Identity in Tod Browning's Films	81
Chapter Six: "This Thing I Long For I Know Not What": Carson McCulllers and the Melodrama of the Domesticated Freak	109
Conclusion: Deviance, Defiance, and the Problem of "Weirdness"	133
Notes	139
Bibliography	161
Index	173

Acknowledgments

I extend special thanks to Philip Sicker from Fordham University for providing the clarity, insight, and support necessary for the development of this book. I also extend gratitude to Lenny Cassuto, Christopher GoGwilt, Moshe Gold, Yvette Christianse, and Nicola Pitchford, all from Fordham. I would like to thank Jean Walton, now at the University of Rhode Island, whose seminar on postmodern fiction and theory led me to develop the ideas that became the basis of this project.

I wish to acknowledge the Walsh Library at Fordham University, the New York City Public Library, the Raether Library and Information Center at Trinity College in Hartford, and the Mitchell College Library in New London for their invaluable resources. I am grateful to Ruth Higgins of Mitchell College for her meticulous proofreading.

I wish to express special gratitude to my parents, Lucian and Ann Bombaci, whose confidence and support made possible my years of graduate study.

Chapter One is a revised and expanded version of an article published in the April-June 2004 edition of *LIT: Literature/Interpretation/Theory*.

Chapter Two was previously published in the Spring 2002 edition of *Criticism*.

The cover image of "Pip and Flip"(1935) by Pavel Tchelichew has been reprinted with permission of the Wadsworth Atheneum in Hartford.

Introduction

During the late modernist period of the 1930's and early 1940's, a number of American artists displayed a fascination not only with the distortion of conventional verbal and visual media, but with bodies, which, from an essentialist perspective, had been deformed by nature. In exploring "freakishness," these artists locate the similarities and differences between those who are born freaks and those who, through strenuous effort, aim to become freaks by identifying with human oddities. Characters in narratives by Nathanael West, Djuna Barnes, Tod Browning, and Carson McCullers not only exhibit a fascination with the genetically maimed and distorted, but fetishize this difference. This fetishization, as we will see, is based not on a prurient objectification of freakish bodies, but on a desire to know and experience the subjectivity of marginalized others. In a period of American culture beset with increasing pressures for social and political conformity and with the threat of fascism from Europe, narratives that fetishize the freak defy oppressive norms and values as they search for an anarchic and transformational creativity. Influenced by high modernism, but not encumbered by it, the artists in question developed a "freakish aesthetics" by combining "high" and "low" (i.e. popular) forms. In doing so, they challenged the avant-garde, apolitical elitism of high modernism and remade it in ways that initiated postmodern aesthetics. This movement towards postmodernism in the works of Nathanael West, Djuna Barnes, Tod Browning, and Carson McCullers is marked by an acceptance of the disteleology, anarchy, and degeneration associated with racial and ethnic outsiders, rather than the high modernist nostalgia for order, progress, and grand narratives.

Using Benjaminian, Foucaldian, and psychoanalytic theoretical contexts, this study will explore the aesthetic and ideological challenges posed by

West's, Barnes's, Browning's and McCullers' late modernist "freakish" aesthetics—a creative vision that fuses "high" and "low" themes and forms in relation to distorted bodies. All of these artists are fascinated by the sphere of "low" culture which they find in Hollywood, freak shows, circuses, and rural towns filled with eccentrics. Except for Barnes's late work, all use forms that are accessible to a reading public unfamiliar with high modernist habits such as proliferating allusion, syntactical inversion, and self-conscious difficulty. All of these artists employed themes and forms that put them in dialogue with high modernism, which according to Andreas Huyssen created a "great divide" between high and mass culture. Nevertheless, Huyssen notes that the number of "high" appropriations of the popular (as in Joyce, Eliot, and Williams) suggests an unacknowledged symbiotic relationship between high modernism and popular forms:

> [This] opposition [between high and low art]—usually described in terms of modernism vs. mass culture or avant garde vs. culture industry—has proven to be amazingly resilient. Such resilience may lead one to conclude that perhaps neither of the two combatants can do without the other, and their much heralded mutual exclusiveness is really a sign of their secret interdependence.[1]

The interrelation that Huyssen points out raises questions regarding similarities and differences between modernist and postmodern appropriations of "low" culture. Can high modernist uses of popular forms be characterized by ironic condescension towards mass culture? Do the modernists typically exoticize popular forms? Is the postmodern use of "low" forms typified by a greater acceptance of popular tastes? What is the relation of such appropriations to modernist notions of progress and degeneration? Standing at the intersection of high modernism and postmodernism, the works of West, Barnes, Browning, and McCullers give particular point and focus to these questions.

Most important, this study explores causes underlying the fetishization of freakishness in American narratives of the 1930's and addresses the following questions: To what extent does artistic identification with distorted bodies reflect a desire to enact, and perhaps, parody, high modernist distortions of the textual body? How fully were these artists aware of the social construction of freakishness? How do their representations of freaks both draw upon and differ from those found in the popular culture of the 1930's? What scopophilic mechanisms come into play as these artists fetishize freaks? How do these mechanisms compare with those that the spectator of the popular freak show experiences? How do the aestheticizing and scopophilic mechanisms of viewing freaks differ for male and female artists? Finally, what roles do the social, political, and scientific ideologies of 1930's America play in these artists' construction and representation of freaks, and how does this relate to the construction of race and ethnicity? Since most of the artists in this study are especially interested in the construction of Jewish identity, this last question requires a complex historical frame, since several of the most distinctive cultural ideologies of the 1930's have their origins in earlier decades.

The fascination with freakish spectacles in the American popular imagination was spurred in part by eugenic ideologies, which had paved their way into American culture by the 1870's. At this time, institutions for the poor and "feebleminded" developed in order to segregate acceptable from unacceptable human populations.[2] The influx of immigrants during the early twentieth century led members of the Anglo-American majority to condemn these outsiders as intellectually and morally inferior. In the freak show, eugenicist ideology was evident in the presentation of some freaks as the exotic natives of distant or unexplored lands whose bodies differed radically from those of northern Europeans. One of the most racist of these exhibits was the display of Saartje Baartman, a member of a tribe from South Africa whose large buttocks made her the aesthetic and sexual antithesis of the normative white woman. During the early nineteenth century, Baartman was displayed throughout France and England as "the Hottentot Venus," an anthropological "missing link" characterized by grotesquely overdeveloped genitalia and secondary sexual characteristics. Also, retardates were often exhibited as riveting creatures from exotic lands who functioned as subhuman, anthropological curios. A late nineteenth century American freak show, for example, displayed two undersized and developmentally disabled Caucasian brothers as "the Wild Men of Borneo," "uncivilized" specimens who combined human and animal characteristics.[3]

By the late 19th century in Europe and America, eugenics, the pseudo-scientific study of the genetic improvement of the human race, became a dominant ideology among scientists and cultural commentators. Based loosely on Darwinism, the eugenic ideas of Sir Francis Galton, Karl Pearson, and Charles Davenport corresponded with the early modernist progress narratives that gained great cultural favor during the industrial revolution and remained influential well into the twentieth century. However, a number of medical historians have established that by the early 1930's, eugenicist discourses began to decline as powerful social forces. American writers began to challenge eugenic assumptions and, as Donald K. Pickens suggests, the implication of the Great Depression effectively shattered eugenicist ideas in America:

> The decade of the depression questioned the permanence of the capitalist environment; many conservative-progressives, like the eugenicists, did not understand the New Deal changes in American society. The elitist and ethical judgements of conservative progressivism—eugenics—were not part of the changing forms of American democracy. Galtonian genetics was a victim of unemployment.[4]

Although scientific discourses at this time began to question eugenicist elitism, serious artists of the 1930's went further, inverting this racism and snobbery by glamorizing and fetishizing deviance.

While the ideology of progress gained cultural force during the late nineteenth and early twentieth centuries, the biological and social sciences at this time gave rise to equally influential discourses on degeneration. Thus, the idea of progress and its opposite became linked inextricably to form a dichotomy in which the significance and even the existence of the one term was absolutely dependent on the other. As Sander Gilman explains, degeneration "was on the one hand an element of dialectic thought which became in the Hegelian heyday of the second half of the nineteenth century a nice balance to the idea of progress. On the other hand, degeneration embodied something of the structure of an evolutionary reality in which everything moved not towards an advanced state but also towards death."[5]

Skepticism about progress and anxiety about human devolution are evident in quintessential high modernist works from *The Heart of Darkness,* to "Sweeney Erect," and Pound's early poetry. While these works promote the notion that history is essentially anarchic, they incorporate formal innovations that pose a radical aesthetic challenge to traditional literary values. Thus Pound's dictum to "make it new," and Woolf's assertion that after 1910 both history and cultural forms changed radically, both suggest an inherent faith in an aesthetic, if not historical manifestation of progress. Above all, Eliot's insistence on an evolving literary "tradition" propelled by innovative productions reveals an evolutionary foundation in modernist thought. While these writers may not have actually espoused the idea of historical progress, their attempts to create new, radically different literary forms demonstrates that the idea of progress for them could exist within the imaginative space of art. In this vein, Fredric Jameson states that "in art, at least, the notion of progress and telos remained alive and well up to very recent times indeed, in its most authentic, least stupid and caricatural form, in which each genuinely new work unexpectedly but logically outrumped its predecessor."[6]

Barnes, Browning, McCullers, and West subvert theories of progress in a way different from their high modernist predecessors. Whereas Woolf, Pound, and Eliot write from the anguish of post-war cultural disillusionment, their descendants seem never to have had much faith in progress to begin with. Their wholesale dismissal of the ideology of progress, with its distinctly postmodern implications, helps to explain their fascination with freakishness, with the morbidly imperfect born in an age of progress.

While oppressive dominant narratives celebrating normality and progress have inevitably constructed oddity as marginal and undesirable, freakishness has emerged, nonetheless, as a competing (albeit marginalized) discourse of power. The notion that freakishness often constitutes such power may initially seem surprising given the term's pejorative associations. However, modern literature has often presented the freak as the embodiment of erotic and aesthetic power. High modernist European novelists such as Mann, Kafka, and Lagerkvist created deformed characters who often exert sinister force over others. For example, in Mann's "Mario and the Magician," the hunchback Cipolla is a malicious hypnotist who can subject even the most resistant individuals to his will. As a homosexual who avidly pursues a young subject, Cipolla represents Mann's view that the artist, as one who is inherently deviant, often is freakish and dangerous. Cipolla's physical deformity is emblematic of his psychic oddity. While "Mario and the Magician" uses the context of popular entertainment to dramatize the modernist theme of the artist as an outsider, the work retains a high modernist style. By contrast, in most of the late modernist works that I will consider, the representation of deformity often mimics "low" (i.e. popular) forms, replacing the aesthetic complexities of high modernist discourse. A possible explanation for this is that the display of oddity in American literature is so inextricably linked to popular culture, that the late modern artists inevitably invoked popular styles when representing human oddity.

The terms "freakishness" and "human oddity" suggest that certain individuals display grotesque ugliness and suffer social marginality based on their deviance from medically and aesthetically defined standards of normality. Popular discourses have also used these terms to label those whose psychological predispositions or intellectual abilities fall outside of institutionally delineated norms. Freakishness, therefore, has come to denote not only the physically deformed, but the insane, the retarded, the idiot savant, and conceivably, the genius. However, despite the relevance of these psychological definitions of human oddity, the term "freak" is most closely associated with physical deformity and inherited difference. It is the visual impact of physical difference based on an accident of birth that stuns, repels, and ultimately seduces the gaze of the "normals." Therefore, even when one who does not display physical deformity is labeled a freak for psychological reasons, the born freak—the dwarf, the giant, or the pinhead—is still being invoked.

The notion that one can be born "that way"—whether "that way" refers to truncated legs, insanity, or retardation—elicits horror mixed with horrified pity, because such abnormality arises from biological processes over which we have little control. Although contemporary ultrasound and amniocentesis can, to some extent, prevent a "freak" from being born, it still cannot prevent mutations from occurring in utero. While science has ordained the notions of genetic normality and abnormality as incontrovertibly real conditions that occur in nature, science does not consider the extent to which it continues to participate in the social construction of these terms. From a Foucauldian perspective, the distinction between normal and abnormal genetics is constructed at a discursive level and does not pre-exist it. From this point-of-view, the concept of normality functions not as a natural, totalizing truth, but as a socially ordained discourse of medicine and psychology. The erotic and aesthetic constructions of freakishness in late modernist literature have served as powerful counter discourses to rigidly "objective" and "scientific" constructions of abnormality. Through appropriating images of freaks from popular culture, all of the writers in this study examine the ways in which racial and ethnic difference as well as physical disability emerge primarily through rhetoric and performance.

An important line of critical commentary generated by social historian Robert Bogdan suggests that the sideshow freak was constructed more through theatrical performances and social discourses than through actual physical deformity. Bogdan explains, "'Freak' is a frame of mind, a set of practices, a way of thinking about presenting people. It is not the person but the enactment of a tradition, the performance of a stylized presentation."[7] Rosemarie Garland Thomson also views the freak show as an important site of cultural production which enabled working class spectators, especially, to determine their place within American society.[8] From this perspective, the American freak show played a constructive role in making visible cultural tensions relating to constantly shifting economic and class conditions. Other theorists, however, are skeptical that the freak show had positive value, and emphasize that many of the people put on display in these spectacles suffered from obvious disabilities and deformities that the carnival owners exploited shamelessly. David Gerber, for example, suggests that the freak show's main appeal is a based on a revolting sadism that degrades deformed people. [9] Similarly, Susan Stewart observes that even when the sideshow performer presents his or her own spiel, the spectacle of bodily difference usually upstages the rhetorical performance, thus emphasizing the freak's lurid objectification. [10] When discussing recent approaches to the culture of spectacle, Robin Blyn cautions that some contemporary critics naively equate the freak show with the Bakhtinian carnival, a site associated with the subversion of hierarchical values. In light of persuasive Marxist and psychoanalytic critiques of the spectacle, she differentiates the degradation of freakish bodies from Bakhtin's more positive appropriation of the grotesque.[11]

More in line with Bogdan's approach, this study emphasizes that the freak show often transcended its reactionary definition of normality by mediating conflicts that were vital to the development of American identity. In this sense, the freak show functioned as a heterotopia—a modern cultural space which, like the Bakhtinian carnival, brings into play diverse and often conflicting forms and values. Heterotopia, however, are defined more in terms of reordering conventional hierarchies and values than with fostering transgression in a manner associated with the Bakhtinian carnival, a form which has generated much critical skepticism during the past decade. Sociologist Kevin Hetherington, for example, differentiates heterotopia from the carnivalesque:

> . . . in Bakhtin, as well as in the work of more recent geographies of transgression and resistance, the marginal site becomes a free site, celebrated as a

space apart in which people can be and act out difference in ways that challenge the social order. What is missing in such accounts is a recognition that such spaces and such practices have their own way of ordering. The identities that are produced in these spaces, while they may be different and somewhat unsettling and challenging to the many who are happy not to challenge cultural norms, have their own logic, their own symbols, their own rituals and their own ordering.[12]

The heterotopic space of the freak show inverted the mainstream social hierarchy as it played out Americans' desire to render social categories visible. Some of the freak show's exhibits, for example, satirized the racist view that human beings can be scientifically bred to create a perfected bourgeois social order. In this inversion of eugenic ideology, the highest social category in freak shows was occupied by deviants who were born with visible defects, such as retardates, Siamese twins, and hermaphrodites. Those who successfully altered their bodies by growing excess body hair, or getting numerous tattoos, were the next highest category, known as "made freaks." The lowest category was occupied by "gaffed" freaks—those who faked abnormalities such as a "legless" man who hid his legs within a chair-like contraption.[13]

Although the freak show granted a higher status to "born freaks," the carnival culture was still a testing ground for a notion of selfhood based on self-construction. As the freak show inverted and restructured the conventional social hierarchy, it engaged working class subjects to identify with freaks, thus narrowing the distance between the spectators and spectacles emphasized by some Marxist and psychoanalytic critics. In the show business world where hype reigned supreme, rhetorical and theatrical self-fashioning was especially evident in freaks presented in the aggrandized mode. This form of display emphasized that the performers had hereditary ranks or accomplishments that strongly contrasted whatever physical difference they may have had, if any. Of the many aggrandized freaks presented as titled aristocrats, geniuses, and military leaders, the best known is General Tom Thumb, a late nineteenth century midget who gained fame in P.T. Barnum's circus. As Bogdan explains, the most economically successful of the aggrandized freaks began to live the myths they promoted on stage by spending money lavishly and by associating with rich, famous, and powerful people (*Freak Show* 148). One can only speculate that for working and middle class spectators, the public personae of the aggrandized freaks served as reminders that upward mobility is a definite possibility, despite physical and social limitations.

The narratives central to this study appropriate the freak show's function as a heterotopia which inverts and restructures conventional values.[14] Through acts of self-fashioning, however, some characters in these narratives aim for a kind of self-advancement different from that of aggrandized freaks. Rather than aspiring towards upward mobility, they seek expanded consciousness through the emulation of marginalized people. Their most important goal is to challenge reactionary social and aesthetic ideologies from the perspective of cultural outsiders. All hope to appropriate the role and the subjectivity of "freaks" through acts of gazing at them, thus conflating the spectator and the spectacle in surprising ways which construct heterotopic modes of consciousness. In this case, spectatorship is not an act of capitalist oppression or psychological dominance, but a means of identifying with those rejected by the cultural mainstream.

In his well-known study of human anomalies, Leslie Fiedler argues that the perusal of freaks is always eroticized by the viewer or reader, even in discourses that promote "normality":

> All freaks are perceived to one degree or another as erotic. Indeed, abnormality arouses in some "normal" beholders a temptation to go beyond looking to *knowing* in the full carnal sense the ultimate other. That desire is itself felt as freaky, however, since it implies not only a longing for degradation but a dream against breaching the last taboo against miscegenation.[15]

For Fiedler, the desire to gain carnal knowledge of this "ultimate other" is based on a need which is akin to masochism. Fiedler implies that those attracted to what society has constructed as the ultimate other may want to inflict pain on themselves out of a pre-existent self-hatred. On the other hand, he also suggests that those who eroticize freaks may have a secret or unconscious longing for sexual union with deviant bodies—a desire that is rooted in sadism. Contrary to Fiedler, the authors considered in this study all suggest that the desire to know that which has been socially constructed as deviant, horrific, and ugly may lead to a kind of enlightenment: the self-conscious observer may identify with the freak so fully that he or she begins to question the very foundations of normality, itself. While this quest to know the other is not necessarily motivated, as Fiedler suggests, by self-hatred and sadomasochistic tendencies, it often leads the subject to a painful self-awareness. A fundamental problem with Fiedler's sadomasochistic model is that it fails to consider the extent to which the "seeker of human oddity" becomes aware of the social construction of freakishness. In short, we need to consider the attraction to freaks not merely as an erotic pathology but also in relation to various historical attitudes towards the remaking of norms and knowledge.

CHAPTER ONE

Degeneration, Anti-Semitism, and the Enfreakment of Modernism

The fascination with deviant bodies displayed by late modernist American authors is, to a large extent, a reaction against the enfreakment of modern culture and art forms in European discourses.[1] For some late nineteenth and early twentieth century European commentators, modern cities as well as modern art and literature promote deviance and immorality by challenging traditional values and social roles. This enfreakment of modernity and modernism is closely linked with the fear of degeneration displayed especially by reactionary social critics, particularly Max Nordau (1849–1923), the author of *Degeneration* (1895). A German Jewish physician, Nordau censures many *fin-de-siécle* social practices and artistic forms as vulgar, immoral, and conducive to insanity. Nordau's association of late nineteenth century cultural forms with ugliness and degeneration later appealed to the Nazis' reactionary sensibilities, as they used his ideas to promote both their racism and their conservative aesthetics. Ironically, the Nazis appropriated Nordau's writings to bolster their cause despite the fact that he was a Jew and a Zionist. Since the late modernist writers central to this study are particularly concerned with the image of Jews in modernism and modernity, it is necessary to explore these reactionary European discourses and critical responses to them.

Degeneration condemns late nineteenth century cultural trends that threaten notions of decency, order, and stable identity fostered by a staid and moralistic Victorian bourgeoisie. Nordau, for example, is harshly critical of theatricalized methods of self-presentation that were becoming common among the Parisian upper-middle classes who frequented public places such as "the Paris Champs de Mars Salon, or the opening of the Exhibition of the Royal Academy in London."[2] Nordau finds especially troublesome the upper bourgeois women who frequent these places mainly to display their historically allusive clothing[3]. As he disapproves of the transvestism evident in women who wear "masculine" cloth coats, Nordau finds particularly annoying men of his time who engaged in self-fashioning through fashion. He chides that these men "hide their real idiosyncracies" as they "try to present something that they are not" (*Degeneration* 9). Nordau's disparagement of theatricalization extends to his condemnation of the ways that upper bourgeois homes in Paris became the sites of spectacles where "everything . . . aims at exciting the nerves and dazzling the senses" (*Degeneration* 11). Nordau dubs upper middle class Parisians as "folk in masquerade," who have made the interiors of their houses resemble spectacles in the arcades (*Degeneration* 10).

From an early twenty first century perspective, Nordau's distaste for ostensibly innocuous fashion and interior design trends seems laughably alarmist and even paranoid. Yet given the popularity of postmodern theories which draw a relation between identity and performance, we can raise interesting questions about Nordau's reactionary fears, as we view them within a broader historical context.[4] Nordau frequently displays what Jonas Barish terms "the antitheatrical prejudice"—a longwithstanding suspicion of theatricalized forms in Western culture.[5] As a physician who viewed himself as a man of science, Nordau, like others of his time, advocated utopian "ordered progress"—the view that the most natural and beneficial course of history is the improvement of the human race.[6] For Nordau, the late nineteenth century's culture of artistic experimentation and public spectacle impeded this progress, as he perceived theatricalization as inherently dystopian. Nordau judges harshly the theatricalized elements of *fin-de-siécle* high culture as exhibitionistic, overly emotional, and excessively stimulating to the senses (*Degeneration* 14). Using carnival imagery, Nordau describes the French symbolist poets M. Stéphane Mallarmé and Paul Verlaine as "circus-riders" or inveterate attention seekers who cared little for "mockery or praise . . . so long as they got noticed" (*Degeneration* 103). Nordau also ridicules (and enfreaks) romantic poets who declare themselves to be artists by comparing their literary skills to that of a freak performer who imitated a "wild man" in a sideshow (21). In an ironic aside, he explains that this unfortunate "artist" ended up an inmate in the Salpêtrière, a renowned nineteenth century mental institution in Paris (21). Nordau's anti-theatrical critique of *fin-de-siécle* literature extends to his condemnation of Oscar Wilde as an eccentric exhibitionist who displayed "a hysterical craving to be noticed" (317). Even Henrik Ibsen, a playwright noted for his complex explorations of character, does not escape Nordau's censure. For Nordau, Ibsen's excessive theatricalism is evident in his charming Wagnerian tableaux which "[force the audience] into moods, and [bind] them by his spell in the circle of ideas, through the pictures which he unrolls before them" (338–339).

Degeneration, Anti-Semitism, and the Enfreakment of Modernism | 11

Despite the fact that he was a Zionist and a defender of Jewish culture, Nordau never discusses inveterate anti-Semitic discourses which associated Jews with theater and deceit. Jonas Barish explains that "hard-line, fundamentalist antitheatricalism . . . goes back to a day when Jews and actors were lumped together as undesirable members of society, like prostitutes" (Barish 464). However, according to Jay Geller, "[s]ome essential relationship between Jewishness and mimesis was disseminated not only in anti-Semitic discourse but also by the Zionist critique of assimilated Jewry."[7] From this perspective, Jews who conformed strenuously to the social dictates of dominant gentile cultures risked losing their Jewish identity. The acculturated Jew often attempted to conceal his difference by adopting the mannerisms and mores of the dominant culture, and through rhinoplasty—the surgery designed to impose a normative European profile on anyone willing to pay the price. However, despite some Jews' attempts to pass as "normative Europeans," there was a deep suspicion during the nineteenth century of this cosmetic transformation. Gilman also suggests that some Jews's attempts to look like northern Europeans was, in fact, a reminder of an identity from which one, in essentialist terms, could never escape (*The Jew's Body* 192). These essentialist terms, however, emerge from anti-Semitic ideologies rather than from inherited characteristics. Yet even Freud believed that while Jews could appear normative "[they] could never be at peace with the sense of [their] own invisibility" (*The Jew's Body* 192).

Long before the nineteenth century, the malleable, theatricalized identity that various discourses attributed to Jews was associated with bodily difference that resulted from hereditary degeneration.[8] The pathologization of physical characteristics deemed "non northern European" resembles the transformation of the disabled into freaks by the proprietors of freak shows. In the twentieth century freak show, the category "freak" served to emphasize the relative normality and social unity of its observers. Similarly, the anti-Semitic enfreakment of Jews was a cultural attempt to imagine gentiles, particularly northern Europeans, as healthier, physically superior, and more powerful. With reference to *The Dwarf* (1921), an opera by the Jewish Viennese composer Alexander Zemlinsky, Leon Botstein comments on the grotesque identification of Jews with freaks in extremely offensive anti-Semitic discourses from Western Europe: "The dwarf has always been the emblem of the Jew since Rumplestiltskin, who wove gold from straw, had an unpronounceable name and charged a price that was the murder of the gentile baby. The Jew-as-dwarf metaphor was a particularly nasty one."[9]

Reactionary discourses eventually associated the stereotypical Jewish bodily difference, intelligence, and immorality with the emergence of modernism, itself. The Nazis labeled modern art *entartete kunst* or "degenerate art," and associated it with all that they considered unhealthy, ugly, and therefore contrary to their eugenic agenda. The Nazis' 1937 display and vilification of modernist art in an exhibit titled "*Entartete Kunst*" reserved particular ire for the work of Jewish modernists, as it ridiculed paintings by Kandinsky, Grosz, Klee, and others. Different modernist styles such as dadaism, German expressionism, Bauhaus architecture and constructivism were all singled out as unacceptable and debased forms by the Nazis.[10] Hitler posed the following question to modern artists regarding what he viewed as the hideous freakishness of their works: "And what do you create? . . . Misshapen cripples and cretins, women who can only arouse revulsion . . . as the expression of all that molds and sets its stamp on the present age."[11] Unlike Nordau, the Nazis had no fear of theatricalization, as public spectacle was a hallmark of fascism. Ironically, while Nordau viewed theatricalization as threatening to normative identity, the Nazis used their highly theatrical and satirical displays to enforce their eugenic agenda. The Nazi curators designed the *Entartete Kunst* exhibit by placing derogatory and satirical captions by the modernist works of art. As Georg Bussman suggests, this inflammatory commentary was meant to goad a sense of moral indignation in the viewers, as it spurred them to prefer the aesthetic and political values endorsed by National Socialism (quoted in Zuschlag 89). The curators exhibited the works under headings such as "Revelation of the Jewish Racial Self;" "The Ideal—Cretin and Whore," and "Madness Becomes Method," in order to exaggerate and theatricalize the purported deviant nature of these modernist works of art.[12] In order to provoke outrage in the ostensibly normative German citizens who attended the exhibit, the curators even went as far as to hire actors who performed as "indignant and wildly gesticulating visitors" before unsuspecting spectators (Zuschlag 89).

The Nazi curators found especially ugly and threatening modernist forms that emulate the artistic styles of native art works from non-Western cultures, namely Africa. By juxtaposing photographs of physically and developmentally disabled people with celebrated modern "primitivist" works, the Nazi curators tried to draw a clear visual parallel between modernist abstraction and deformed bodies.[13] In an odd conceptual leap, they equated what they regarded as the African or "Negro" ideal of early twentieth century art with a "specific intellectual ideal" that is evident in the "idiot" and the "cretin."[14] They also viewed the artists' creative engagement with such unconventional forms as a serious moral and aesthetic lapse based on a fascination with animality:

> Be that as it may, one thing is certain: to the "moderns" represented here a mindless, moronic face constituted a *special* creative stimulus. This is the only possible explanation for the sheer abundance of sculpture, graphic work, and painting contained in this section of the exhibition. Here are human figures that show more of a resemblance to gorillas than to men ("Facsimile of the *Entartete Kunst* Exhibition," 376 and 378).

Degeneration, Anti-Semitism, and the Enfreakment of Modernism | 13

In contrast, the American freak show often aimed to tantalize audiences with spectacles which combined human and animal characteristics.

Parallels between the *Entartete Kunst* exhibit and the American freak show are striking since both pathologized and theatricalized spectacles of bodily difference. In both cases the freak stands as the inverse of the normative national body. Yet the Nazi exhibit differed sharply from the American freak show in that it also functioned as art criticism which prescribed the "right" aesthetic tastes and values. Numerous critics have described the Nazis' preference for realistic landscapes and idealized images of blonde, Nordic beauty as kitsch or vulgar, mass produced trash. On the contrary, German nationalist ideology viewed glamorized representations of Aryans as images of morality and stable identity.[15] In contrast, as a far more extreme example of kitsch or bad taste, the American freak show frequently investigated the relative instability of social hierarchies and cultural values. Yet while the American freak show often mediated notions of racial and class difference by functioning as a culturally productive heterotopia, the exhibit of degenerate art in Nazi Germany rigorously aimed to suppress any such mediation. Questions remain, however, regarding whether the Nazi curators merely "put on a good show," or engaged in more sophisticated uses of parody and satire.

The curators of the *Entartete Kunst* exhibit tended to perceive all modernist art as inherently dadaist—a view that is reductive in light of the multifaceted nature of modernist visual art. As Christoph Zuschlag explains, "Dada served as a paradigm of 'degenerate' art: the organizers were simply out to exploit the material available, and it was certainly not in their own interests to encourage their visitors to perceive subtleties" (Zuschlag 89). In turn, the Nazis equated the ambivalent, heterotopic nature of dadaism with Jewishness, homosexuality, sexual licentiousness, and all that they regarded as deviant and threatening. At the same time, the Nazis were interested enough in dadaism and its reputation for fostering subversion, to satirize it. Richard Burt demonstrates that while these curators tried "to make the complex nature of [modern] art and its reception simple," they did this through a sophisticated process in which the imitation of modern art worked to clarify its difference from Nazi art."[16] This "sophisticated process" did not, however, significantly challenge the Nazis' enfreakment of Jews, non-Western people, and modernism since their aesthetics was firmly based on their obsession with physical perfection.

Surrealism, an artistic and literary movement that emerged from dadaism, was also the *bête noir* of Clement Greenberg (1909–1994), the influential twentieth century American champion of abstract painting. With reference to art instructor Hans Hoffman, he criticizes the emphasis on content in surrealist painting as aesthetically retrograde: "Surrealsim in plastic art is a reactionary tendency which is attempting to restore 'outside' subject matter. The chief concern of a painter like Dali is to represent the processes and concepts of his consciousness, not the processes of his medium."[17] Greenberg viewed abstraction in modernist writing and painting as aesthetically superior to surrealism and its literary predecessor dadaism, which he dubbed "artificial nonsense."[18] During the 1910's and the 1920's in France and Switzerland, dadaists such as Tristan Tzara and Hans Arp responded to the cultural tumult of World War I by rejecting bourgeois values through their radical experiments with language. Through their disavowal of logic and their theatricalized celebrations of insanity, the dadaists challenged accepted notions of what is beautiful, moral, and necessary for the maintenance of middle class culture.

While many Jews created dadaist and surrealist works, Greenberg, himself a Jew, defined a Jewish literary and aesthetic sensibility as one that favors the highly intellectualized aspects of abstraction: "There is a Jewish bias toward the abstract, the tendency to conceptualize as much as possible, . . ."[19] The Nazi curators viewed both dadaism and modernist abstraction as inherently degenerate and ugly. In a 1954 defense of abstract painting, Greenberg argues that while some commentators view abstraction as "a symptom of cultural, and even moral decay," the most significant works of this time are abstract. Although Greenberg's defense of abstraction is at times overzealous, his argumentative rigor enabled him to develop a sophisticated justification for work that others had deemed freakish and ugly.

> Not that most of recent abstract art is major; on the contrary, most of it is bad; but this still does not prevent the very best of it from being the best art of our time. And if the abstract is indeed impoverishing, then such impoverishment has now become necessary to important art.[20]

In her biography of Greenberg, Florence Rubenfield describes this champion of high modernism as an elitist whose defense of abstraction was wedded to evolutionary cultural goals.[21] Similarly, art critic Darby Bannard praises what he regards as Greenberg's ability to perceive Darwinian forces at work in the sphere of visual arts: "Art has evolved. In the last hundred years, the changes have been more evident and describable than ever before. Greenberg did for art what Darwin did for life: he saw what was happening when no one else saw it, and told us about it."[22] Greenberg even believed that the abstract artist could galvanize socialistic ideals through his "heroic individualism."[23] For Greenberg, progress is evident in abstract modernist paintings that emphasize the aesthetic process, as well as in a "highbrow" rejection of kitsch and its concomitant notions of beauty. Greenberg's tendency to link abstraction with socialist utopianism in "Avant Garde and Kitsch" is also characteristic of his predominantly Jewish contemporaries known as the New York Intellectuals, writers for *The Partisan Review* who believed "a more politicized modernism might provide the best frame through which to analyze society and art."[24]

Degeneration, Anti-Semitism, and the Enfreakment of Modernism | 15

The Nazis' denigration of abstraction seems intellectually unsophisticated in light of the complex and innovative nature of modernist aesthetic theories. Greenberg's formalism, for example, is based largely on the novel approaches to literature characteristic of his contemporaries T.S. Eliot and the British and Anglo-American "New Critics."[25] Despite the innovative aspects of his work, Greenberg's ideas, like those of Eliot, are often characterized by an ideological rigidity based on utopian values that link intellectual elitism with progress.

While Nordau and eventually the National Socialists claimed that modernist aesthetics lead to degeneration, several formally innovative Anglo-American modernists feared cultural forces commonly viewed as degenerate during their time. For these modernists an important paradox emerged: while they produced literary idioms and structures with the textual characteristics of modern heterotopia, their work was often based on reactionary ideologies. For these writers the figure of the Jew, the disabled, and other cultural outsiders is often profoundly threatening. Much has been written about the blatant anti-Semitism evident in the high modernist Anglo-American tradition championed by T.S. Eliot and Ezra Pound. (Eliot is of greater importance to this study since Nathanael West and Djuna Barnes produced critical responses to his ideas on modernism and modernity). Drawing from anti-Semitic ideas perpetuated during the nineteenth century, Eliot, himself, often represented Jews as physically grotesque and rapacious subhuman creatures. We see this denigration of Jews in "Sweeney Among the Nightingales" (1920), where "Rachel nee Rabinovich / Tears at Grapes with murderous paws," an image that conflates Jewishness with femaleness and animality.[26] Eliot's Jewish landlord who "squats on a window sill" in "Gerontion" (1920), represents Jews as bestial by associating them with public squatting or defecation.[27] In "Burbank With a Baedker: Bleistein With a Cigar," Eliot represents Bleistein in stereotypical terms as a Jewish money monger and Sir Ferdinand Klein as a socially ambitious Jew who has bought his was into the aristocracy.[28]

In his persuasive analysis of Eliot's anti-Semitism, Anthony Julius cautions readers that although Eliot based his problematic representations of Jews on common racist ideologies prevalent in Europe and America, he did not merely repeat these ideas nonreflectively. Rather, Eliot "put anti-Semitism to imaginative use" by making it a driving force of his poetic idiom and ideological context.[29] Julius suggests that Eliot's hideous Jews, unlike other grotesques, do not emanate from the supernatural world. Instead, they are far less powerful, but nonetheless base, freakish creatures, who dwell within the social realm of the real world. (Julius 121).

Eliot's Jews are figures of a dystopian modern world that stands as the antithesis of the aristocratic, Christian utopia that this poet persistently glorifies. His utopian ideology exhibits longing for the social hierarchy characteristic of pre-World War I European culture—a time less threatened by the emergence of cities and the presence of racial and ethnic others. Many of Eliot's contemporaries have a more ambivalent attitude towards forms of racial difference and cultural hybridity that are characteristic of modern cities. Modernists such as Virginia Woolf, James Joyce, Karl Lagerkvist, and Franz Kafka view the presence of Jews and the physically disabled as more culturally productive.

Performing as an urban spectator or *flâneur* in her essay "Street Haunting" (1927), Woolf displays a fascination with the lower class denizens of London, especially when encountering a dwarf and a Jew. Woolf advises her readers not to get mired in unnecessary details when taking in various sights. Instead, she advises us to "be content with still surfaces only. . . ."[30] She believes that these surfaces present the kind of beauty that the eye always seeks: "For the eye has a strange property: it rests only on beauty; like a butterfly it seeks colour and basks in warmth" ("Street Haunting" 249). At the same time, she argues that most sensibilities cannot make these things of beauty more interesting by "compos[ing] these trophies in such a way as to bring out the more obscure angles and relationships" (249). For Woolf, most people cannot represent common things of beauty in ways that are intellectually provocative and she believes that when bored with conventional beauty, the *flâneur* will seek novelty, often in the form of human beings who embody difference:

> Hence after a prolonged diet of the simple, sugary fare of beauty, pure and uncomposed, we become conscious of satiety. We halt at the door of the boot shop and make some little excuse, which has nothing to do with the real reason, for folding up the bright paraphernalia of the streets and withdrawing to some duskier chamber of the being where we may ask, as we raise our left foot obediently upon the stand: "What, then, is it like to be a dwarf?" ("Street Haunting" 249).

Woolf describes the female dwarf as having a haughty aristocratic manner when buying shoes. But once she returns from the store back to the streets, she becomes a humble dwarf once again: "she had changed the mood; she had called into being an atmosphere which, as we followed her out into the street, seemed actually to create the humped, the twisted, the deformed" ("Street Haunting" 158).

For Woolf, the street, itself, appears to construct the deviance associated with cultural outsiders. As a member of a high bourgeoisie often associated with high bohemia, Woolf is fascinated less with the street's negative transformational powers than with the dwarf's potential for malleable subjectivity.

Degeneration, Anti-Semitism, and the Enfreakment of Modernism | 17

The dwarf vacillates from quasi-aristocrat when engaged in an act of consumerism to deformed other whose physical difference becomes more intensified when she walks the streets. Earlier, Woolf states that "the average unprofessional eye" cannot adequately "compose trophies as to bring out the more obscure angles and relationships" (157). However, she discovers later that the very presence of the dwarf on the streets of London has the ability to compose a scene, and initiate different forms of ordering:

> Indeed, the dwarf had started a hobbling grotesque dance to which everybody in the street had now conformed; the stout lady tightly swathed in shiny seal-skin; the feeble minded boy sucking the silver knob of his stick; the old man squatted on a doorstep as if, suddenly overcome by the absurdity of the human spectacle, he had sat down to look at it—all joined the hobble of the dwarf's dance (159).

At this point, London is an urban heterotopia that fosters fascinating forms of human difference. While Woolf is intrigued by the subjectivity of these cultural outsiders, she still maintains her distance as an anthropologist/*flâneur* who seems unwilling to subject herself completely to the street's power of enfreakment. Woolf's sense of distance becomes more obvious when she perceives a Jewish man affixed in a scene of hideous poverty:

> They do not grudge us, we are musing, our prosperity; when suddenly, turning the corner, we come upon a bearded Jew, wild, hunger-bitten, glaring out of his misery, or past the humped body of an old woman flung abandoned on the step of a public building with a cloak over her like a hasty covering thrown over the head of a donkey. At such sights the nerves of the spine seem to stand erect; a sudden flare is brandished in our eyes; a question is asked which is never answered (251).

While Woolf, the *flâneur*, later declares that she aspires to "put on briefly for a few minutes the bodies and minds of others," her encounter with the "hunger bitten" Jew causes her to snap back into her dominant role as an educated bourgeois woman (258). With reference to this scene, Bryan Cheyette comments that Woolf's uneasy identification with the poor Jew is comparable to that of other modernist writers who fail to "transform" the image of the Jewish outsider into anything more than a menacing unconscious figure.[31] While Woolf attempts to envision an urban space characterized more by human diversity and different methods of creating order, her vision is not large enough to encompass this.

In his major work *Ulysses*, James Joyce rejects the vision of utopian modernism that tends to view cities and cultural outsiders as degenerate and dystopian. His representation of the union of Stephen Dedalus and Leopold

Bloom demonstrates a fruitful linkage of Christian and Jewish elements in a heterotopic vision of the West.[32] However, as a man of his time, Joyce was not completely immune to cultural discourses about race and degeneration. Joyce, for example, subscribed to some of the beliefs of the reactionary sexologist Otto Weininger, as he unquestioningly accepted the notion that Jewish men are inherently feminine and that women are innately "passive" and "illogical."[33] Nonetheless, Joyce displays skepticism towards popular biologistic views of heredity and identity in *The Portrait of the Artist as a Young Man*. Stephen Dedalus finds problematic the Darwinistic notions that equate aesthetics and eugenics. In a discussion with his classmate Lynch, Stephen states that while different cultures have different notions of female beauty, marks of beauty in most cultures are correlated with a woman's reproductive potential.[34] At the same time, Stephen nonreflectively repeats the essentialist ideology of his time when he meets a dwarf whom he perceives in terms of a degraded aristocratic lineage. When Stephen notices that the dwarf's upper class enunciation is marred by poor grammar, he wonders if this man is the illegitimate descendent of a noble line (248). Yet despite this lapse into essentialist thinking, Joyce eventually has Stephen question these biologistic notions in *Ulysses*.

Explorations of freakery in relation to utopian ideologies are also evident in early to mid-twentieth century works outside of the Anglo-American modernist canon in writers such as Par Lagerkvist and Franz Kafka. In *The Dwarf* (1944), Swedish modernist Lagerkvist explores the consciousness of an anomalous misanthropic outsider who rejects the progress narratives of his day. Less concerned than many of his contemporaries with problems posed by racial and cultural hybridity, Lagerkvist uses this character to question utopian visions of humanity that emerged during the Renaissance and continued to develop well into the twentieth century. Set during the Italian Renaissance, the dwarf, Piccolino, describes himself as a member of a "race" that has "no homeland" and "no parents."[35] (*The Dwarf* 151). In contrast to Piccolino is the Prince, a stereotypical Renaissance man who seeks intellectual and spiritual enlightenment through art and science. The Prince tends to objectify Piccolino by subjecting his body to various "scientific" inspections which the dwarf finds abhorrent (*The Dwarf* 37). Disdaining members of the court, Piccolino declares, "They think they can read the book of nature, that is lying open before them. They even believe that they can look ahead in the book and read the blank pages where nothing is written. Heedless conceited lunatics! There is no limit to their shameless self-sufficiency" (*The Dwarf* 42). This is an indictment of the utopianism evident in Renaissance notions of science and human nature. Piccolino makes the case for the view that nature is neither benevolent nor predictable, especially when it gives rise to anomalies such as himself:

> Who knows what nature carries in her womb? Who can even guess at it? Does a mother know what she has conceived? How could she? She bides her

time, and eventually we see the thing to which she has given birth. A dwarf could tell them about that (*The Dwarf* 42).

Sounding like a Nietzschean nihilist, Piccolino concludes that life is meaningless (43). Yet unlike this Nietzschean dwarf, other of Lagerkvist's characters do not easily disavow a longing for meaning and spirituality. This is especially evident in *The Death of Ahasuerus* (1960), where Lagerkvist considers in detail the legend of Ahasuerus or the wandering Jew. Towards the end of the novel, Ahasuerus asks God, "Why do you persecute me? Why do you never leave me in peace? Why do you never forsake me? . . . Why do you force me to think of you continually?"[36] At the end, Ahasuerus declares that a greater force beacons to humanity, and our inability to grasp it increases our desire for it (114–115). For Lagerkvist, the dwarf and the wandering Jew are figures of modern alienation and solipsism rather than dystopian creatures of cultural decline.

For Franz Kafka, the freakish conflation of the animal and the human represents racial and cultural hybridization—heterotopic modern forms towards which he displays ambivalence. In *The Metamorphosis* (1937), Kafka's best known late modernist novella, the young businessman Gregor Samsa transforms into a huge insect who must stay confined within his room and in a sense remain physically immobile and disabled. The narrative's ambivalence towards his subhuman state is evident in the contrast between its sordid details and the languid pace that seems to revel in describing Gregor's effect on others. This is especially obvious in Gregor's evasion of male authority figures such as his father and his employer, where he seems to enjoy eluding and transgressing their socially validated masculine power.[37] Critics have viewed Gregor Samsa's transformation as representing a rejection of bourgeois mores, since his extreme difference makes him unable to participate in the rigorous work ethic celebrated in nineteenth century German culture. Sander Gilman reads Samsa's metamorphosis as Kafka's comment on the anti-Semitic view that Jews could never fully assimilate into European culture no matter how hard they try. With reference to both Gregor in *The Metamorphosis* and Red Peter, the talking ape in "Report to the Academy," Gilman argues that Kafka, as a Jew, demonstrates a painful awareness that for anti-Semites, "Jews see and represent the world differently from Germans; their sexuality, their bodies remain as different as the bugs or the apes."[38] From this perspective, Kafka internalized the hostile attitude towards racial and cultural difference held by reactionary Germans.

While Kafka may well be dramatizing anti-Semitic perceptions of the Jewish body in his representation of Gregor Samsa, he also aestheticizes this figure by presenting this character's experience as anti-bourgeois and transgressive. Mark Anderson presents a more positive reading of Gregor Samsa's transformation by associating it with a heightened mode of perception that can be associated with the "Utopian space of play, distraction, and childlike innocence that is curiously consistent with late nineteenth-century definitions of aesthetic experience. In fact, Gregor's metamorphosis fulfills the dream of every serious *fin-de-siécle* aesthete: to become not just an artist, but artwork, the visual icon, itself."[39] While Kafka attempts to conflate beast and human in The Metamorphosis, he is unable to negotiate a method of keeping these disparate elements in balance, thus commenting on the difficulty for artists and cultural outsiders such as Jews to assimilate into an increasingly reactionary German society.

At the same time, Kafka's harsh judgement of a conventional, unimpressive singer in "Josephine the Singer, or the Mouse Folk" (1924), can be read as a warning to Jews of the pitfalls of assimilation. Josephine, the mouse, "pipes" rather than sings; that is, she goes through the motions of vocalizing, rather than singing with a combination of passion for her art and dazzling technique. The narrator often suggests that Josephine's piping is characteristic of those of her "race," and identifies her as one of them through the use of "we":

> . . . we are too old for music, its excitement, its rapture do not suit our heaviness, wearily we wave it away; we content ourselves with piping; a little piping here and there, that is enough for us. Who knows, there may be talents for musing among us; but if there were, the character of our people would suppress them before they could unfold.[40]

Mark Anderson reads this story as Kafka's negative response to Jews who conform too readily to dominant social forms and ideologies in an effort to assimilate.[41] The bland quality of Josephine's "piping" resembles Clement Greenberg's notion of kitsch as popular pseudo-art that fails miserably in its aspiration towards high seriousness. Greenberg's analysis of avant-garde and kitsch can be read as an exploration of Jewish difference that parallels Kafka's investigation of the problem of assimilation for Jews.

Clement Greenberg expanded the definition of the German word "kitsch" to mean not only popular commercial art, but all that he found contemptible about images that are mass produced and easily consumed. Thus, the adjective "kitschy" describes what for Greenberg is "ersatz culture . . . destined for those who, insensible to the values of genuine culture, are hungry nevertheless for the diversion that only culture of some sort can provide" ("Avant Garde and Kitsch" 10). Greenberg cites both Nazi aesthetics and Hollywood movies as examples of kitsch ("Avant Garde and Kitsch" 13, 19–20). The intellectual rigor and utopian sensibility characteristic of Greenberg derive from both Eliot's and the old New Critics' preference for aesthetic formalism and the Jewish emphasis on logical rituals and moral laws. Greenberg identifies Kafka as a quintessential modern Jewish writer, one who represents the horror that emerges when his characters experience absurdity and illogic. Providing this faith in logic with a

Jewish theological context, Greenberg associates it with Jewish moral laws known as the Halacha.[42] However, we have seen that Kafka's representation of disorder, especially in The Metamorphosis, cannot be reduced to a simple defense of logic and order, as the narrator at times seems to revel in Gregor's deviance. Greenberg claims to have rejected the quest for order that he associated with Jews who longed for assimilation into the American bourgeoisie. Complaining about this tendency among Jews, Greenberg stated, "No people on earth are more provincial, more commonplace, more inexperienced; none observe more strictly the letter of every code that is respectable; no people do so completely and habitually what is expected of them: doctor, lawyer, dentist, businessman, school teacher, etc., etc...." ("Under Forty" 178–179).

On the one hand, the young Greenberg turned his back on the expectations of his culture by pursuing the financially insecure, "bohemian" sphere of art and literary criticism. Also, the avant-garde works that he championed often left conventional bourgeois sensibilities in a state of anger and confusion. At the same time, both Greenberg's rigid insistence on the primacy of abstraction and the lucid, sober quality of his rhetoric demonstrate *halachic* tendencies towards logical rigor. When Greenberg makes a case for modern painting, he emphasizes with nearly scientific precision the painter's use of the artistic medium. This is evident in his discussion of Klee's desire to incorporate elements of three dimensionality into his work, at a time when abstractionists were experimenting more with the representation of two dimensional space.[43] Holding to his rigorous religion of abstraction, Greenberg was quick to admonish painters who strayed from this ideal: "Organic objects have replaced the mechanical ones and the abstract forms—Leger was never a consistently abstract painter—and they are used to attain a stale, poster prettiness.... When the abstract artist grows tired, he becomes an interior designer—which is still, however, to be more creative than an academic painter."[44] While Greenberg claims that the abstraction that he lauds has associations with Jewish intellectualism and Jewish difference, his ideological and rhetorical rigidity prevent a more thorough exploration of these aspects.

In contrast to Greenberg's more conservative and *halachic* vision of modernism, his German Jewish contemporary Walter Benjamin (1892–1940) developed a more flexible approach to different aesthetic styles that emerged at that time. Most notably, Walter Benjamin developed theories that challenged the cultural power of "high art," and imagined a sophisticated method of spectatorship that is open to both elite and popular forms. In "The Work of Art in the Age of Mechanical Reproduction" (1935), he calls into question aesthetic ideologies that glorify coherence and what he defined as a work's "aura," or the essential essence linked inextricably with the original version of it.[45] Benjamin's rejection of the aura entails a resistance to notions of beauty promoted by German idealists such as Goethe and Schiller, writers who believed that beauty is the "semblance" or outward manifestation of an "idea" or of truth.[46]

While Greenberg never uses the term "aura," he invests the creative processes that foster modernist abstraction with spiritual qualities akin to what Benjamin defines as the aura. In fact, he locates the very notion of originality (the antithesis of kitsch) in this creative process.[47] Benjamin differs radically from Greenberg not only in his rejection of the aura, but in his faith in the power of mass art forms. For Benjamin, mechanical reproduction need not necessarily lead to tawdry art and passive receptivity, as he believed that a non-auractic art form such as avant-garde cinema could engage its spectators at a more active intellectual level. He explains that those inclined to free objects of their aura demonstrate "the mark of a perception whose sense of 'the universal equality of things' has increased to such a degree that it extracts from a unique object by means of reproduction" ("The Work of Art in the Age of Mechanical Reproduction" 223). From this perspective, art need no longer be limited to upper class contexts that celebrate the uniqueness of creative works, as it is now more accessible to the masses.

Jay Geller suggests that when questioning the value of auractic works of art in the modern world, Benjamin aims to set free a different kind of aura—one that is associated with the masses and with social outsiders. While Benjamin defines the aura in terms of the spiritualization of bourgeois art objects, Geller explains that the Greek term "aura" originally defined the sense of smell and associations attached to various odors. Geller describes "aura" in terms of the stench associated with Jews and the lower class masses in nineteenth century discourses.[48] By focusing on the positive universal qualities of mass culture that the enlightened spectator could perceive, Benjamin challenged the "utopian" aspects of aura evident in works by Baudelaire and Proust as he unleashed a less valued aura associated with Jews (Geller 207). Geller states, "[c]ontributing to the redemptive possibilities of the aura, then, is a transfiguration of Jewish otherness. And *aura*, in particular, represents a redemptive moment in which olfaction, as the sense of materiality and as the character of that which the dominant class fears and thus seeks to foreclose, escapes the optics of discipline and control" (Geller 247). From this perspective, Benjamin's anti-auractic aesthetic is a means of articulating the otherness of the Jew in early twentieth century western Europe. Greenberg, on the contrary, makes Jewish difference intelligible through a more Kantian based auractic aesthetic that is also immersed in the elitism of the New York intellectuals.

For Benjamin, the antithesis of the aura is "profane illumination"—a variation of transcendence that the sophisticated spectator can find in common or even tawdry things. Benjamin discovered examples of profane illumination especially in surrealist works that represent dated cultural artifacts or seedy urban areas. He admired the poet André Breton's ability" to perceive the revolutionary energies that appear in the 'outmoded,' in the first iron constructions, the first factory buildings, the earliest photos, the objects that have begun to be extinct . . ."[49] Breton's images of Paris remind Benjamin of early twentieth century photographs that poignantly capture the mood of this city: "It makes the streets, gates, squares of the city into illustrations of a trashy novel, draws off the banal obliviousness of this ancient architecture to inject it with the most pristine intensity towards the events described . . ." ("Surrealism" 183). Benjamin describes Paris as a locus of surrealism since the city, itself, constantly engages seemingly unrelated forces connected to the unconscious: "There, too, are crossroads where ghostly signals flash from the traffic, and inconceivable analogies and connections between events are the order of the day" ("Surrealism" 183). Thus, profane illumination has the astonishing power to draw connections between disparate things.

Benjamin's profane illumination, the inverse of aura, can be viewed as an idealization of the Jewish difference that anti-Semites regarded as threatening to cities and to Western culture. For Benjamin, the very tawdriness that reactionaries projected onto Jews and seedy urban areas is instead a spiritualized force that mediates the strange and ambivalent aspects of the West's cultural unconscious. The rest of this study will show that late modernist Americans such as West, Barnes, Browning and McCullers reveal a more Benjaminian bent in their openness to forms of cultural difference which mark the twentieth century. In their explorations of people and cultural practices labeled as deviant or freakish, they challenge the reactionary enfreakment of modernism.

CHAPTER TWO

Nathanael West's Aspiring Freakish *Flâneurs*

Critical commentary on Nathanael West since the 1950's has often characterized the writer as a self-hating Jew whose internalized anti-Semitism shaped his portrayal of sadomasochism and other assorted forms of deviance. The centrality of psychosexual disorder and degeneracy to West's fictive and cultural vision is indisputable. His fascination with physical and behavioral anomalies, as well as with scatology and sexual eccentricities borders on fetishization. However, the relation of West's prurient interests to his self-conception as a Jew needs further analysis since his attitude towards his ethnicity was, at best, complex. While the sadomasochistic elements in West's works may suggest a tendency towards self-hatred, he never uses these aberrations to enforce *bourgeois* standards of normality and decency. That is, West never creates a dichotomy between the normal and the deviant, in which the former is the dominant and preferred condition. Rather, West associates deviance with a strange power that can disrupt and corrupt all that is normal, acceptable, and respectable. In his attempt to understand the nature of this power throughout his oeuvre, West represents ostensibly normal Anglo-American male characters who attempt to gain a vicarious awareness of various freaks, both born and made. Within this search for vicarious experience, the freak, and by extension the Jew, who has been pathologized by anti-Semitic discourses, is not an anathema, but an exotic object to be emulated on a path towards expanding self-knowledge.

West was not alone among American writers of the first half of the twentieth century in his tendency to associate Jewishness with a unique intellectual perspective. Both Jews and gentiles who wrote for the *Partisan Review* from the 1930's to the 1950's often argued that Jews are gifted with incisive literary and historical insight based on their position as simultaneous insiders and outsiders within modern cultures. In his study of these writers, Alexander Bloom explains that they aimed to combat anti-Semitism by arguing for the importance of a Jewish point of view in American letters: "To demonstrate the fallacies of the anti-Semites' claims, they argued for a reversal of conceptions. These intellectuals posited that Jews had a central place because of their Jewishness. They now felt that Jewishness, once a source of scorn among some writers, offered a special sight, useful in the analysis of the modern condition" (*Prodigal Sons* 150). While West was not closely affiliated with the New York Intellectuals, he considered in fictional form similar concerns about the role of the Jewish American writer by performing a comparable reversal. When making a Jewish perspective the supreme object of desire for Anglo-American male characters, West aims to broaden the definition of American literature by making central a position associated with an ethnic and religious minority.

As West aims to invigorate American literature by making it more cosmopolitan and Jewish, he also works within an American tradition that tries to define the possibilities and limits of an expansive Emersonian vision.[1] West's Anglo-American male characters aspire to a Semitic perspective which they associate with creative talent and a more penetrating awareness of modern American culture. For West, the modern American visionary must know the social marginality associated with Jewish experience in order to see from the Semitic dual perspective of simultaneous insider and outsider. However, as his characters begin to confront elements of marginality within themselves, they fearfully turn away from this potentially enlightening vision.

West evokes the title character of *The Dream Life of Balso Snell* (1931) as a picaresque bungler whose ineptitude is evident not so much because of social stupidity as his inability to understand his own fantasies. In parodying surrealistic conventions of mystical self-discovery, West evokes Balso Snell's journey as ultimately futile. Yet later in *Miss. Lonelyhearts* (1933) and *The Day of the Locust* (1939), West maintains an important motif that he sets forth in his first novel: the figure of the voyeuristic wanderer or *flâneur* in search of self-knowledge and knowledge of history. In his later novels especially, West makes clear that these observer figures are gentiles from the American Protestant tradition—Anglo-American men in search of spiritual transcendence through artistic expression and sensationalistic experiences.

The *flâneur*, a figure that Walter Benjamin exlores in his extended analysis of late nineteenth century urban spectators, resembles the wandering Jew of legend in his penchant to roam from place to place, seeking knowledge and identity.[2] As a Jew, Benjamin could well have revised this figure in order to present him as an astute urban spectator who is also a powerful representation of modernist consciousness. The *flâneur* was fascinated by crowds and attempted to peruse them with the objectivity of a cameraman. Yet this ostensible objectivity was compromised by his extreme fascination with faces in the crowd.[3] From his boyhood, West appropriated the perspective of the solitary observer, or *flâneur*. His biographer Jay Martin notes that as a high school student, West "defined the self by what he could observe yet remain untouched by. He would be [. . .] a 'lonely spy,' watching but never participating. He was interested in society only as a foundation for fantasy, hardly as an area for action."[4] As he evolved as a writer in college, West engaged in "the accurate and pitiless observation of others," and later he further developed this stance in his short story, "The Adventurer," where the main character approaches his subjects "knowing the signs and habits of our quarry, trailing, observing carefully" (Martin 50).

Martin attributes West's preoccupation with observing others' values to his sense of confusion over determining the religious beliefs and social ideologies that would have been most suitable for him. Like the rest of his immigrant family, West disavowed Judaism, but he also refused to follow their pursuit of the material comfort and social conformity characteristic of the American dream.[5] Throughout his life, West maintained an ambivalent relationship to both his Jewish heritage and to the upper class Anglo-American culture that socially mobile immigrants often tried to emulate. When he was a student at Brown University in the 1920's, West rejected his Jewish background outright and attempted to take on a parodic form of an idealized gentile persona. He would constantly doodle the aristocratic "von" before his name, and he wore Brooks Brothers suits—the stereotypical uniform of preppie men. He even insisted on associating with forbiddingly snobbish fraternities that would not allow Jews to become full members.[6] In Groucho Marx's terms, West pined to belong to clubs that would not truly accept him—a tendency that ostensibly shows masochism and self-hatred. Yet despite his fascination with socially established Anglo-Americans, West's intellectual interests leaned more towards European aestheticism and decadence—artistic movements antithetical to the genteel but often menacing conformism characteristic of upper class Anglo-American culture. The young West, for example, was particularly interested in "mysticism, magic, medieval Catholicism, Joyce and Nietzsche" (Hyman 12). He was also drawn to late nineteenth century Symbolists, aesthetes and decadents such as Baudelaire, Verlaine, and Arthur Marchen (12).

At the same time, West attempted to synthesize both American and Jewish elements into his persona and his work. It is telling that Nathanael Wallenstein Weinstein changed his name to West. When discussing his choice of name with William Carlos Williams, West stated "Horace Greeley said, 'Go West young man.' So I did" (Hyman 12). This Anglo surname deliberately suggests Western culture and consciousness, as well as the American Western frontier. While West's first name has Hebraic origins, it was also a common name in Colonial America, thus denoting both West's American identity and Jewish origins. As a Jewish-American writer whose aesthetics are informed by a high modernist and surrealist ideology that celebrates decadence and deviance, West produced his version of a "degenerate art." In most of his works, West dramatizes the condition of deviance and marginality, especially as it relates to Anglo-American men in search of non-mainstream identities and cultural experiences

※ ※ ※

Upon encountering a Jewish guide who will lead him through the surrealist dreamscape of the novel, Balso Snell quotes an oft cited passage from C.M. Doughty's *Travels in Arabia Deserta*: "The Semites are like to a man sitting in a cloaca to the eyes, and whose brows touch heaven."[7] Doughty, an orientalist who traveled throughout the Arab world in the late nineteenth century, uses the term "Semites" to refer to all Middle Eastern peoples. West, however, uses the quote primarily in relation to Jews, whom he characteristically defines as spectators. The image of a man "sitting in a cloaca" or opening to the eyes as his "brows touch heaven" literally means one who sits in an opening to the eyes of another as he gazes into them. Doughty, according to Stephen Ely Tabachnick, uses this quote to disparage what he believes is the inferior spiritual nature of the Semites.[8] While their brows "touch the heavens," their eyes never look beyond the cloaca to someone else's gaze. Doughty regards the Semites as limited and debased observers who narcissistically seek their reflection in an ahistorical gaze. Like the Baudelairean and Benjaminian *flâneur* in an early state of his trajectory, they are akin to infants grounded in the pre-mirror stage who never enter the symbolic order, although they forever seek it. While this observer desires knowledge, desire, according to Lacan, can only emerge once one has entered the symbolic order—the "realm" where language produces meaning, and meaning, in turn, constructs subjects.

In his wanderings throughout a surrealist dreamscape, Balso Snell displays a fascination with epistemological processes, particularly the nature of artistic perception. West initially locates this surrealist *flâneur's* perceptions not in a major city, but within the large intestine of the Trojan horse. When Balso Snell offends his guide by shouting "What a hernia! What a hernia!" when he believes he has encountered such an aberration, he tries to pacify the guide: "What a pity childish associations cling to beautiful words such as hernia, making their use as names impossible. Hernia! What a beautiful name for a girl! Hernia Hornstein! Paresis Pearlberg! Paranoia Punz! How much more pleasing to the ear (and what other name should please) than Faith Rabinowitz and Hope Hilkowitz!"[9] By connecting feminine sounding words to Jewish surnames, West creates a grotesque caricature of Jewish women as aberrant. West himself often made derogatory comments about Jewish women, whom he referred to as "bagels" (Hyman 12), and he reproduces both his social self-contempt and his guilt in Balso's exchange with his guide. The guide takes offense at Balso's ridicule of Jewish women and shouts, "I am a Jew! and whenever anything Jewish is mentioned, I find it necessary to say that I am a Jew. I'm a Jew! A Jew!" (8). Victor Commerchero explains that West, who took pride in the cultural assimilation of his family would never have made the guide's declaration of his Jewish identity. Indeed, he would have "felt ashamed and disgusted by such a person."[10] Commerchero adds, however, that this "passage reflects West's sensitivity to the entire Jewish question, to the complex play of identification and alienation often felt by Jews who have lost their faith" (17).

While some anti-Semitic discourses constructed Jews as freakish spectacles, others represented them as voyeuristic spectators. Jewish eyes and the gaze that they hold were the subjects of quasi-medical and anthropological discourses of the late nineteenth century. For example, the eugenicist Sir Francis Galton constructed photographic composites of Jews' faces in which he searched for the cold, calculating stare that some European cultures had attributed to them. With reference to Galton, Sander Gilman explains that both "the eyes of the Jew and his gaze are pathologized" (*The Jew's Body* 68). As a Jew, Walter Benjamin understood entrenched European stereotypes that represent those of his ethnic group as specifically masculine voyeurs whose voracious desire for knowledge poses a threat to the dominant culture. Benjamin is in a sense revising the Jewish stereotype as he universalizes it. Benjamin's conception of the *flâneur* as an intellectually voracious male who silently pervades urban spaces both echoes and revises vulgar anti-Semitic stereotypes of Jews as all-pervasive and economically rapacious.

Given that Western culture frequently constructs Jews as deviant outsiders who are nonetheless endowed with incomparable powers of perception, Jewish observer figures often occupy the role of what I term the freakish *flâneur*. This figure brings together the stereotypical Jewish penchants for freakery and voyeurism. While the performing freak may have compromised his dignity and subjectivity, the freakish *flâneur*, I propose, embodies a complex, heterotopic consciousness that combines poignant epistemological insight with an identification with deviance. The freakish *flâneur* maintains his creative duality by functioning simultaneously as a performer who exaggerates his deviance for all the world to watch, and as an observer who casts his gaze on those who enfreak him.

On the one hand, the Baudelarian *flâneur* of Benjamin's model was fascinated by crowds and attempted to peruse them with the detachment of a cameraman. Yet this ostensible objectivity was compromised by his personal fascination with "faces in the crowd" (Benjamin 30). When engaged in the act of perception, the *flâneur* wants to respond, in Lacanian terms, as if he were an infant who had not yet experienced the mirror stage. In his nostalgia for the malleable state of consciousness where the possibilities for identification are endless, the *flâneur* fantasizes that he can become one with everything he sees. He aspires to be a formidable singular consciousness who can not only take possession of all elements of the dominant culture, itself, but eventually mimic and "reproduce" its signifying function. In his narcissism and grandiosity, the pre-mirror stage *flâneur* wants simultaneously to be an infant who has not yet entered the symbolic order, and one who can successfully appropriate all of its images and meanings. Yet as a predominantly male consciousness, he also identifies with the mirror, itself—the dominant mechanism that imposes a culture's values on its subjects. Arguably, the *flâneur*'s privilege as a quintessentially masculine consciousness gives him the creative license to identify with both roles. As a masculine objectifier, he wants to go back to a polymorphuous pre-mirror stage of consciousness in order to increase his possibilities for identification, thus to see and know more.

The Baudelarian *flâneur* of Benjamin's model never relinquishes his status as a male objectifier of images and maker of culture. Benjamin explains that the *flâneur*'s obejctivity is based on bourgeois notions of an artistic prerogative that writers during the late nineteenth century began to attribute to artistic creativity and idealized notions of masculine objectivity. However, the *flâneur*'s ecstatic statement that he "become[s] one flesh with the crowd" as he remains hidden from it, reveals his penchant for voyeurism and fetishization—tendencies that are stereotypically associated with masculinity.[11] These masculinized observer figures who construct images and spectacles primarily for their epistemological or financial gain function as what I term "*flâneur* colonizers or commodifiers." In this sense, the object is not "possessed' or "colonized" in the way that Columbus possessed the Indies, but through a process of intellectual appropriation.

West represents the Anglo-American male's quest to experience the freakish *flâneur*'s deviant role in his major works *Miss Lonelyhearts* and *The Day of the Locust* where the title characters function more as *flâneur colonizers*. Questions remain as to whether or not West's ideal of the freakish *flâneur* is more or less epistemologically empowered than the non-ethnic *flâneur* who chooses his own estrangement. In his novels, West considers the extent to which a strong identification with one's difference from the cultural mainstream can, conceivably, be a form of empowerment, particularly if one uses this difference to challenge oppressive and intellectually narrow norms and values. A number of West's characters, most notably Miss. Lonelyhearts and Tod Hackett in *The Day of the Locust*, aim to go beyond the role of *flâneur* colonizer in order to experience the freakish *flâneur*'s empowerment through deviance. As they aim to appropriate the Jewish gaze, they aspire to a marginalized but more sophisticated perspective on Western culture.

The stereotypical Jewish gaze often presents a threat to westerners precisely because it transforms Western consciousness, itself, into an object of observation. This other, who can simultaneously function as subject and object, challenges the ideal of hegemonic Western specularity. Thus, in West's novel, Doughty's dictum has ironic significance. The Semite who gazes into the eyes of Western consciousness wishes to identify with it. Yet this identity will not be the

Jew's sole identity, since he possesses an essentially malleable consciousness. Between the gentile and the Jewish subject there is sometimes an open contest of specularity to determine which gaze is the most powerful. Within this contest the Jew, whose body and consciousness have been pathologized in the West, may choose to perform as an epistemologically empowered freak. By the same token, the freakish *flâneur* may perform the culturally imposed role of exoticized other as he observes life from the margins. The Jewish guide, while comically rendered, embodies the idealized specularity that Nathanael West valorizes throughout his oeuvre, and that Balso never attains.

After the guide expresses his offense at Balso's play on Jewish names, Balso repeats C.M. Doughty's dictum. Although Balso Snell's (and West's) use of this epigram suggests a stereotypical judgement of Jews, he takes a favorable view of modernist distortion, an artistic method that is sometimes associated with Jewish consciousness. Jay Martin explains that West's fascination for high modernism was characteristic of many New York Jewish intellectuals of the 1920's and 1930's (80). As Stuart E. Rosenberg states, "Those Jews who accepted modernism did so most radically" and "brought with them the intellectual vitality, the moral perplexity, the religious optimism, the sound and the fury of a great awakening [. . .]" (*Jewish Identity* quoted in Martin 80). While West embraced modernism, he also used his penetrating vision to call into question its values. When the guide says "Art is a sublime excrement," Balso Snell replies, "Picasso says there are no feet in nature"—a statement which suggests that ideal forms of the human body reside only in art, never in the natural world (9). When discussing the relation between art and nature, the guide constructs reality as diverse and prone to subjective interpretation, rather than monolithic and discernable through the lens of ideology. Picasso's rejection of ideal forms is based on a view that reality is multifarious and prone to diverse interpretations, particularly through artistic mediums. According to the guide, however, Picasso transforms this ostensible defense of pluralism into a monistic, totalizing discourse. Throughout his oeuvre, but especially in *The Dream Life of Balso Snell*, West is concerned with the extent to which high modernist vision can become unyieldingly hegemonic. When the modernist *flâneur* aims to impose his singular vision of the world, he engages totalizing discourses that could become authoritarian and fascistic. Averse to the implications of fascist modernism, West turned more towards surrealism, an aesthetic ideology that more forcefully calls into question the validity of aesthetic coherence and unified selfhood (Genova 86).[12] However, despite his greater affinity for surrealism throughout his career, West is still critical of what he regards as its more pretentious manifestations in *Balso Snell*.

From an essentialist's perspective, the freakish body, which deviates from medical or quasi-medical norms, also appears to be a surrealistic, decontextualized object. The surrealists' frequent representation of objects removed from their normal contexts also resembles the postmodernists' similar experiments with the decontextualization of objects. As Pamela Genova explains: "It is the calling into question of the object of representation, that is, of the object itself, that establishes a link between Surrealism and Postmodernism, and one can uncover in much postmodern thought the pervasive surrealist influence, focused on the question of mimesis, of the depiction of art in concrete reality" (91). As a surrealist and a proto-postmodernist, West was fascinated by decontextualized objects and bodies, and as a Jew whose physical characteristics were pathologized by racist discourses, West both understood and identified with freaks. From this perspective, Balso's reference to feet is particularly significant. Debates regarding natural and unnatural feet concerned not only visual artists, but physicians with eugenic visions. In their effort to construct a freakish body, racists of this period defined the "Jewish foot" as flat, "crooked," and "cloven" like that of a medieval devil.[13] This frightening foot, whose satanic origin indeed renders it unnatural, is "a sign of the primitive and corrupt masked by the cloak of civilization and higher culture" (*The Jew's Body* 39). The Jewish foot was therefore a symbol of the "overcivilized oriental" whose intelligence and deviance posed a threat to the cultural mainstream.[14] In such medical discourses, the stereotypical Jewish foot takes on the surrealistic role of the decontextualized object. It represents what anti-Semites regard as the innate unnaturalness of Jews, or at its most paradoxical, their natural deviance.

The first spectacle that Balso Snell encounters is that of Maloney the Areopagite, a self-mutilating fanatical Catholic who is an obvious parody of James Joyce. Maloney is an Irish Catholic mystic in Bloom's dress who attempts to crucify himself using thumbtacks. Balso Snell finds this enfreaked Christ a distasteful exhibition of navel gazing, and at this point he begins to rethink the aesthetic tenets of Joycean and Eliotic modernism. As he calls into question the high modernist preoccupation with consciousness, distortion, and abstraction, he also finds repulsive those who maim and enfreak themselves for mere effect. Instead, he prefers to view spectacles of those who are born distorted, such as physically malformed freaks, or those who, like Jews, are "innately" distorted by their birth into a stigmatized ethnic culture. West eventually develops an aesthetic which appears to discover freakish reality, rather than create it. Balso shares this preoccupation, but exhibits none of West's discernment. In representing this quest for the freakish through a blundering and comically inept *flâneur* colonizer, West demonstrates that Balso's spectacles are, in fact, projections of his own mind. The bizarre exhibits that he finds so titillating are not, in fact, part of the "natural" world, but instead are "natural" manifestations of his dream life. West's aesthetic consciousness differs from Balso Snell's primarily in his ability to see cultural myths for what they are and to transform them into parodic spectacles, even when they are the esteemed narratives and artistic methods of the elite culture By parodically distorting high modernist techniques in *The Dream Life of Balso Snell*, West attempts to divest high modernism of its elitist implications and reduce it to a freakish spectacle. For West, however, high modernism is itself a freakish spectacle that the wise and perceptive late modernist *flâneur* only needs to discover. By contrast, Balso Snell, in his desire to be like Joyce and Eliot, takes seriously the spectacles of high modernism that West exposes as freakish cultural fictions. By ridiculing and putting Balso's fetishization of high modernist elitism on display, West enfreaks the dominant cultural tradition.

Throughout West's oeuvre, we can perceive a supple ironic narrative stance that identifies with both the observer and the spectacle, combining these roles in a way that his characters cannot. This becomes especially evident in Balso Snell's second vignette, an episode in which he encounters and defines himself against a spectacle of true physical distortion. When projecting himself as John Gilson, a youngster who fills his diaries with strange sexual fantasies, Balso immediately declares that the search for reality is futile (14) and that "order is vanity" (15). As Balso resigns himself to unknowable reality and unattainable order, he risks relinquishing his tendency to appropriate images as a *flâneur* colonizer. Rather, he behaves more like a freakish *flâneur* who revels in his self-projection as a deviant other. If the *flâneur* colonizer identifies too closely with what he sees, rather than maintain his ostensible distance and power as a fetishizer, he may lose his dominant sense of himself as a quintessentially masculine appropriator of discourses. Balso takes this risk when he reads John Gilson's account of slaying a freakish idiot. Yet at this point, West's narrative sensibility avoids this risk through his ironic identification with both roles, which correspond respectively with dominance and passivity.

John Gilson develops animosity towards Adolph, a freakish mentally retarded man who laughs constantly and uncontrollably. Adolph is the antithesis to all that is healthy, beautiful and conventionally powerful. Dwelling above John in a dingy Manhattan apartment building, Adolph "was a fat pink and grey pig of a man, and stank of stale tobacco, dry perspiration, clothing mold, and oatmeal soap. He did not have a skull on top of his neck, only a face—a face without side, back, or top like a mask" (18). Adolph's mask-like countenance makes him seem like a surreal, decontextualized object. Unlike the freakish *flâneur*, who understands the figural or performative nature of all discourse, Adolph lacks this awareness. Devoid of any selfhood beyond his mask-like performance, Adolph's very existence can be reduced to a masquerade devoid of consciousness. While those who become aware of the masquerade of gender can consciously remove the mask, Adolph cannot take off the accouterments of his oddity. Unmanned by his disability and his deformity, Adolph is also feminized by his tendency to seduce the gaze of others by performing as a spectacle.[15]

Balso Snell, in his various projections, fails to adequately acknowledge the "freakishness" within himself, which is manifested in latent homosexuality. Nonetheless, he is consumed with discovering the nature of this oddity in others, as if by doing so he could drive out what he fears within himself. Balso never relinquishes his ideal of "normality," yet he remains a *flâneur* colonizer of his own mindscape. West, on the other hand, grapples with the freakish elements of high modernism in *Balso Snell*—its structural dislocations, its moral and sexual ambiguities, its manifold ironies, and its broad associations with Jewish intellectuals—as he tries to determine its meanings in relation to his role as a Jewish male artist.

In the fourth vignette, Balso Snell gains a sense of epistemological power by taking the role of the chivalrous male who loves to seduce women. However, in this case, the women are not conventional beauties, but possessors of what he regards as exotically freakish bodies. Balso Snell becomes fascinated with "the many beautiful girl-cripples who congregate" in the lobby of Carnegie Hall "because Art is their only solace" and because "most men look upon their strange forms with distaste" (37). In keeping with the Jewish guide's preference for forms that embody variation rather than ideality, Balso Snell "preferred the imperfect[ions] of these women, "knowing well the plainness, the niceness of perfection" (37). He becomes infatuated with Janey Davenport, a "tall and extraordinarily hunched humpback" who "looked like some creature from the depths of the sea" (37). Overwhelmed with desire for the beauty of her imperfections, he cries, "O deviation from the Golden Mean! O out of alignment!" (38).

Balso Snell maintains his fascination with oddity, yet he can only peruse it without distress if he denies it first within himself. As a woman who embodies deviance, it is particularly significant that Janey's name is "Davenport," and that she has been wronged by a man named "Beagle Darwin." Both of these names allude to the progenitors of evolutionary and genetic theories. Charles Davenport, a protégé of the eugenicist Sir Francis Galton during the early twentieth century, identified "good human stock" with intellectuals who were part of "the native white Protestant majority" and believed that those whom he deemed genetically inferior should undergo "forced sterilization."[16] When Balso Snell's dream logic (and West's narrative wit) transform the stereotypical WASP queen into a freak, he inverts the role that Davenport would have attributed to her. Janey Davenport, as West constructs her, has been dealt a cruel hand by her genetic fate. Although she was born to wealth, status, and WASP identity, she is still viewed as a freak. Nonetheless, Balso Snell transforms this freakish Anglo-American woman into an alluring creature who "had never before known the thrill of being subdued by a male from a different land from that of her dreams" (38). By taking the role of the gallant man who objectifies and seduces an exotic queen, Balso Snell gains a sense of power by playing the *flâneur* colonizer. Yet he never occupies the more "Jewish" position of the freakish *flâneur*—a role that West explores more thoroughly in his later works. Daniel Walden identifies West as "a Jew who did not want to be a Jew" but who "became one in spite of himself."[17] By making his male protagonists Anglo-Americans who aspire to the Semitic dual consciousness of the freakish *flâneur*, West constructs this role as a powerful epistemolgical state that provokes envy in those who fail to possess it. West does not make Jewish ethnicity the prime focus of his work, concentrating instead on male sexual anxiety, especially as it is manifested in latent homosexuality. However, this sexual angst may have associations with Jewish identity for West. As Sander Gilman explains, racist discourses have associated circumcision with castration and emasculation (*The Jew's Body* 189). Also, various discourses, dating from the nineteenth century, tended to view Jewish men as physically weak and effeminate. By creating WASP male protagonists in *Miss. Lonelyhearts* and *The Day of the Locust* who also experience male sexual anxiety, West demonstrates that this problem need not be limited to Jews.

❦ ❦ ❦

At the beginning of his sociological study of stigmatized individuals, Irving Goffman quotes from West's *Miss Lonelyhearts:*

Dear Miss Lonelyhearts—

I am sixteen years old and I don't know what to do and would appreciate it if you could tell me what to do [. . .] I would like to have boyfriends like other girls and go out on Saturday nites, but no boy will take me because I was born without a nose—although I am a good dancer and have a nice shape and my father buys me pretty clothes (West quoted in *Stigma: Notes on the Management of a Spoiled Identity* i).[18]

Goffman defines a stigma as a physical, psychological, or social "attribute" that the dominant culture defines as frightening, ugly, or inferior. Stigmas, according to Goffman, include "various physical deformities" and "blemishes of individual character" such as "mental disorders [. . .] addiction . . . homosexuality" and even "radical political behavior" (4). Stigmas, as Goffman explains, serve the function of reinforcing the normality of those who do not possess these negative defining traits. Therefore, the stigmatized and the nonstigmatized constitute a binarism in which both groups depend on each other for definition, but in which the latter constructs more powerful discourses.

Yet the binary relation between the stigmatized and the nonstigmatized becomes more complex when the stigma is hidden, and therefore known only to the subject who possesses it. Stigmas relating to race, ethnicity, religion, and sexual orientation are often easy for a subject to conceal in a symbolic closet. Psychoanalyst David Allen argues that stigmas, particularly those in the form of hidden physical deformity, can be a source of creative power.[19] From this perspective, the creative artist achieves distinction through hidden suffering and produces work that both compensates for and masks the stigma (Allen 118). Early twentieth century writers such as James and Kafka have explored the longstanding myth of the hidden wound as a source of creative power. In Goffman's terms, the closeted homosexuality that Eve Sedgwick attributes to high modernist style, can be viewed as a hidden stigma.[20]

In *Miss Lonelyhearts*, West confronts this hidden stigma of modernism by probing and questioning the dynamic among homosexualized, heterosexualized, and feminized styles that defined the arts during the late modernist period. Through the character *Miss Lonelyhearts*, West questions whether a sensibility that demonstrates homosexualized kitsch and feminized sentimentalism can be based on a keen *flâneurish* gaze.

West's *Miss Lonelyhearts* portrays a creative traveler through the minds and souls of others, who attempts to feminize his consciousness, even as he uses the quintessentially masculine prerogative of the gaze. A fundamental problem for this *flâneur* in the land of freaks is that his feminine empathy prevents him from maintaining a *flâneur's* distance. Instead, the writer who carries the hidden stigma of latent homosexuality, identifies with stigmatized others so fully that he wants to become them. His desire to achieve the dual perspective of the freakish *flâneur*, and his foray into the land of the deviant and the deformed leads him to a creative self-fashioning that rejects *bourgeois* mores. However, like the freakish subject of Allen's study, the feminized part of Miss Lonelyheart's consciousness prevents him from maintaining the distance necessary to achieve the perspective of the freakish *flâneur*.

"Miss Lonelyhearts" is the feminized persona that the title character assumes when answering letters from the lovelorn, the deformed, and the downright suicidal. Although we never learn his real name, since his feminized persona has become a dominant part of his identity, we learn that he is of Anglo-American Puritan stock and that he comes from a long line of Baptist preachers (62). The editor Shrike, who is the ironic and parodic center of the novel, views Miss Lonelyheart's column as a joke and encourages him to "forget the crucifixion" and "remember the renaissance" (71). Yet for Shrike, both art and religion are campy spectacles, and those who invest meaning in either are dolts. Miss. Lonelyhearts also views Christianity as a spectacle, but one that ultimately empowers those possessed of the religious mania that they put on display. When Miss Lonelyhearts tries to amuse himself by chanting "Christ, Christ, Jesus Christ," he feels a surge of excitement, but in a disturbing dream, he imagines that he is a preacher incapable of generating excitement in others (76). Pierced by Shrike's ironic sensibility that views everything in life in terms of parody, Miss Lonelyhearts envisions himself as a dull, unenlightened preacher who sounds like a train conductor (76). Shrike's excessively ironic posture of detached spectatorship constitutes the *flâneur* colonizer's sensibility. His extreme detachment has led to nihilism, as well as the savage exploitation and ridicule of those who do not share his ironic perspective.

In his analysis of the relation between Miss Lonelyhearts and Shrike, David Madden argues that West has inadvertently made the latter's strident voice more dominant in the novel.²¹ Madden proposes that West uses Shrike's disturbingly ironic, detached voice when describing crowds "mov[ing] through the street with a dream-like violence (207). Also, according to Madden, West "strike[s] a Shrikean tone" when he comments on the "idiomatic" and "daily" quality of violence in America (207). West's own attitudes and sensibility, as his biographer Jay Martin explains, often reflect Shrike's trenchantly ironic perspective. West, for example, often exhibited "intellectual brutalism," which was evident in his scathing sense of humor, his overt disdain of those he regarded as stupid, and his tendency to "[mock] the emotions of others" and "suppress all sentiment" (Martin 204). In West, the tension between a tough, intellectualized gaze and sentimental feelings, mirrors a conflict between stereotypically masculine and feminine subject positions that he explores in *Miss Lonelyhearts*. West's trenchant, bitterly ironic wit also resembles the exaggerated masculinity characteristic of a sadomasochistic and proto-fascistic attitude—a position that is based on a fear of effeminization. According to West's brother-in-law S.J. Perelman, West, in his brilliant yet rancorous irony was like a bitter dwarf who wrecks anarchy on what he regards as the foolishness of others.²² The Westian dwarf, who performs his deviance in the narrative by using his penetrating gaze, is the freakish *flâneur*, who is both a spectacle and an observer. West's characters, however, cannot attempt to enact both roles without experiencing trauma.

Ultimately, Miss Lonelyhearts aims to become one whose exhibition of deviance is an authentic representation of psychic reality, especially as it is manifested in suffering. For instance, in a dream where Miss. Lonelyhearts imagines that he and a group of rogues attempt to sacrifice a lamb, the bloody half-dead animal escapes. Yet Miss. Lonelyhearts returns to "put the lamb out of its misery" (77). In search of authentic examples of suffering and social deviance, Miss. Lonelyhearts goes on to create scenarios where dying lambs must be euthanasized. While Miss Lonelyhearts behaves like a *flâneur* colonizer who gains knowledge and power by putting sacrificial lambs on display, his identification with these freakish spectacles prevents him from maintaining his *flâneurish* distance. Moreover, Miss Lonelyheart's drag act as a female advice columnist can be viewed as a freakish performance that connects him with those who offer up their suffering to his gaze. Through the accumulating images of an exotic desert, West constructs Miss Lonelyhearts as a *flâneur* who occasionally gains access to freakish subjectivity. For instance, when writing for his column a kitschy celebration of "the cloud flecked sky" and "the feel of velvet and satin [. . .]," Miss Lonelyhearts daydreams about an "imagined desert where Desperate, Broken-Hearted, and others were building his name" in the sand with common objects such as "faded photographs, soiled fans, time tables, playing cards, broken toys, imitation jewelry—junk that imitation had made precious, far more precious than anything the sea might yield" (98). In his dream of the desert, Miss Lonelyhearts's stigmatized admirers construct her name in terms of sentimentalized kitsch rather than exoticized objects. This suggests that Miss Lonelyhearts wants those who seek his aid to view him within the feminized sphere of feeling and sentimental keepsakes. Immediately after sentimentalizing his role, however, Miss Lonelyhearts imagines himself taking on a more exotic and surreal form in the desert. When thinking about a letter he received from Faye Doyle, a sexually frustrated housewife married to a deformed cripple, Miss Lonelyhearts "thought of [Faye] as a tent, hair-covered and veined, and of himself as the skeleton in the water closet, the skull and bones on the scholar's bookplate. When he made the skeleton enter the flesh tent, it flowered through every joint" (149). This vision of penetration is ostensibly quite different from Miss Lonelyhearts's earlier sentimentalization of his feminine role. In fact, the poles of sentimental kitsch and exotic avant-gardism represent dichotomous aesthetic modes that both West and Miss Lonelyhearts employ and explore.[23]

On the one hand, Miss. Lonelyhearts orientalizes his freaks into strange avant-garde curios, as a *flâneur* colonizer would. On the other, he can only represent them and identify with them through the kitsch medium of the tabloid column. In *Miss. Lonelyhearts*, the boundaries between "high" and "low" culture blur to the point where modernist forms become kitschified and kitsch takes on the erotic, exotic, and intellectualized aspects of high modernist art. For example, the skeleton that flowers inside the flesh tent can also be construed as a grotesque kitsch image reminiscent of cartoon gothicism. This erasure of the distinction between "high" and "low" forms in West is characteristic of surrealism and postmodern art, historicized aesthetic modes that call into question the repressed homosexuality of high modernism through their playful, campy incorporation of kitsch. This conflation of "high" and "low" forms can be defined as "freakish aesthetics"—an approach to art that overrides the boundaries of class, gender, and genre. West's representation of the skeleton in the tent blurs distinctions that pertain to gender as well as aesthetics. West subverts the expectation that the tent of flesh should flower as a result of male sexual entry. Instead, the skeleton flowers, as if it is becoming fecund with its own penetration. This image suggests a consciousness that aspires to androgynous creativity.

When "physically sick and unable to leave his room," Miss Lonelyhearts thinks about the nature of order and disorder and imagines the objects in the windows of a pawnshop as "the paraphernalia of suffering" (104). West represents Miss. Lonelyhearts' Christ complex as an inherently doomed quest for order. In West's postmodern world, Christian teleology is relegated to the absurd and nihilism is the dominant cultural perspective. However, truth and authenticity still exist in the needless sufferings of others. However, in this novel, the most authentic victims are those deformed from birth, since they have entered the world with stigmas that are constantly on display. For Miss. Lonelyhearts, therefore, an understanding of truth and authenticity comes with an identification with freaks.

The only genetic freaks in Miss. Lonelyhearts are the noseless teenager, who signs herself "Desperate," and Peter Doyle, a deformed cripple. In her letter, "Desperate" describes herself as a woman whose noselessness has rendered her sexually undesirable. Her social marginality is reflected not only in her complaint about her deformity, but in her illiterate grammar and spelling. Although putatively about a "real" person, the letter represents an experience so extreme and sensational that it easily lends itself to lurid spectacle. In fact, Miss. Lonelyhearts's column functions for readers as a freak show, where he takes on the roles of a *flâneur* colonizer and carny talker who puts unfortunate people on display. Miss. Lonelyhearts reacts to the letter as nonchalantly as a jaded *flâneur* would: he simply draws on a cigarette. However, he begins to lose this sense of specular detachment when he attempts to apply a *flâneurish* gaze to Peter Doyle. This freakish man, who is emasculated by his deformity, has a problem which Miss. Lonelyhearts identifies with more closely.

After Faye Doyle seduces Miss. Lonelyhearts, she describes her husband as a cripple who is "all dried up" and "much older than she" (101). Aware of his wife's infidelity, Peter Doyle remarks before Faye and Miss. Lonelyhearts, "Ain't I the pimp to bring home a guy for my wife?"(128). When Miss. Lonelyhearts and Peter Doyle first meet in a bar, however, they behave like kindred spirits or lovers who "[sit] staring at each other until the strain of wordless communication begins to excite them both" (124). Their mutual understanding goes beyond language and Miss. Lonelyhearts perceives Doyle as one whose tortured inner nature lies beyond conventional language (124). Doyle's use of language, which Miss. Lonelyhearts feels compelled to interpret, is prone to abstraction. Doyle speaks a language that only he, himself, can understand: he is akin to a difficult self-referential text that begs to be interpreted. The autobiographical letter that Doyle finally hands Miss. Lonelyhearts is similarly jumbled, inarticulate, and illiterate. It is, however, expressed as a kind of stream of conscious discourse (125). While Peter Doyle, as human text, is linked with the techniques of high modernism, he also suggests a riddle from popular culture that calls for interpretation:

> The cripple had a very strange face. His eyes failed to balance; his mouth was not under his nose; his forehead was square and bony: and his round chin was like a forehead in miniature. He looked like one of those composite photographs used by screen magazines in guessing contest (124).

Like Doyle's face and language, the quasi-cubist composite photographs in movie magazines lure the observer to make sense of them. Again, we see a blurring of the distinction between high and low forms in West. In this case, the freak, himself, is emblematic of the loss of boundaries between the realm of modernist abstraction and the world of kitschy magazines. By making Peter Doyle an undecipherable figure with high and low implications, West maintains the formidable enigmatic qualities of the intellectually enticing modernist sign, while at the same time democritizing it. As subject of interpretation, Peter Doyle resembles both composites from movie magazines and figures from Picasso's "Guernica." Thus, West demonstrates the freak's status as a provocative sign can survive the differing frames of high and low culture. Moreover, Doyle's sexual ambivalence stands in relation to his status as both a modernist and kitsch object; he represents the closeted homosexuality of high modernist form, as he functions as a camp figure that would appeal to an openly gay sensibility. By conflating the two, West "outs" the homosexualized basis of high modernist abstraction. Miss Lonelyhearts wants to maintain a *flâneurish* distance from the freak, while still experiencing the freak's performative consciousness. As one who performs as a kitschy religious spectacle who identifies with social misfits, Miss. Lonelyhearts has, to some extent, gained access to freakish subjectivity. Yet his transformation into a freak is never adequate, since his identification is always through the distorted lenses of sentimentality and religious pity. Miss. Lonelyhearts never gains the epistemological status that Western culture has attributed to Jews; he cannot perform simultaneously as freak and *flâneur*. Miss. Lonelyhearts is doubly limited by his ethnic heritage: it is telling that West chooses to make his protagonist an Anglo-American of Puritan stock, a "race" that condemned spectacles and that is stereotypically associated with a harsh, judgmental gaze. A number of critics have argued that Nathanael West's fascination with deformity is essentially a sadomasochistic manifestation of his Jewish self-hatred. For example, Victor Commerchero believes that West "seems to have inherited that mixture of pride and metaphysical unworthiness that is part of his Jewish heritage" (13). While West felt ambivalent about Jewish culture and never identified with it too closely, he nonetheless validates and celebrates a dual mode of consciousness that has been traditionally and stereotypically associated with Jewish ethnicity. That the Anglo-American male protagonist of *Miss. Lonelyhearts* is unable to fully realize this mode of consciousness suggests that West did not completely internalize anti-Semitic beliefs and values. In his later novels, West continues to explore how far WASP male characters can effect psychological transformation on themselves by identifying with freaks.

✺ ✺ ✺

Both *A Cool Million* (1934) and *The Day of the Locust* (1939) stand as scathing invectives against the American dream. In fact, both forcefully represent the American quest for social and economic status as a meaningless farce in which most are freakish performers and few are empowered spectators. Not surprisingly, these works take a dim view of both *flâneurism* and freakishness. West's late novels suggest that in America of the 1930's empowered spectatorship is difficult to sustain and freakishness has emerged as a dominant means of experiencing the world. From West's late modernist perspective, we all have become freaks, and the *flâneur's* epistemological power is unattainable. The kitsch spectacle (with its homoerotic overtones) is the dominant mode of discourse in the fascistic capitalist world of *A Cool Million*, West's least "difficult" work.²⁴ West, however, resumes experimenting with a more complex interplay between high modernist form and kitsch in his last novel, *The Day of the Locust*.

In its ironic appropriation of kitsch forms, including fascist rhetoric, *A Cool Million* stands as a work of campy satire that exposes the reactionary aspects of pure kitsch. However, as Andrew Hewitt explains, there is a complex relation between camp, a homosexualized form, and the ostensibly heterosexual fascist kitsch, since the former often recognizes the latter in its own aesthetics: "If the homosexual can turn kitsch into camp—'mistake' kitsch for camp, in the example of fascist art—then he potentially subverts the kitsch logic of attribution (what we might otherwise call the logic of alienation) with a logic of identification" (208). In this vein, West demonstrates that an elitist parodist can take pleasure in rendering aesthetically reactionary styles that promote politically reactionary content, particularly because he enjoys the performative force of these forms. While West uses a performative "rhetorical" method in order to criticize the narcissistic excesses of high modernism, he also shows how unmediated performative rhetoric, itself, can be used for reactionary ends. Theoretically, a freakish *flâneur*, functioning as an empowered elite observer and a marginalized performer, could keep both rhetorical perspectives in balance. However, the interplay of these perspectives is more developed in West's other works, which combine "high" and "low" styles more effectively. A loss of faith in the ideal of freakish *flâneurism* in *A Cool Million* and *The Day of the Locust* is caused, in part, by what West represents as a virulent strain of capitalism that consumes, digests, and regurgitates American culture in vulgar and debased forms. In fact, West begins *A Cool Million* with a quote that suggests that one needs "a strong stomach" in order to withstand the state of American capitalsim: "'John D. Rockefellar would give a cool million to have a stomach like yours'—Old Saying."²⁵ According to this ironic motto, which West most likely invented, a celebrated venture capitalist would give a million dollars to have the intestinal fortitude of one who was far less successful. Since only the failure understands economic difficulty and endures social marginality, West's shibboleth privileges knowledge over success, setting the tone for a novel that exhibits the financial destruction and physical dismantling of Lemuel Pitkin, an innocent boy from rural Vermont.

The voice that narrates *A Cool Million* performs like a ringleader or carny talker, presenting the gullible Lemuel and his foibles, but offering little psychological insight about this character. West seems more concerned with exposing faulty surfaces than excavating psychological depths. His narrator occasionally uses sarcastic "one liners" to evoke characters. For example, he offers a comic platitude to sum up the fascistic right wing ideologue, Shagpoke Whipple:

> One of his favorite adages was "Don't teach your grandmother to suck eggs." By this he meant that the pleasures of the body are like grandmothers; once they begin to suck eggs they never stop until all the eggs (purse) are dry (147).

As the narrator explains Whipple's aphorism, which lays bare his greed and sexism, he seems to take pleasure in his sarcasm, which impersonates and ridicules Whipple. He offers a more searing parody in describing the Chinese pimp Wu Fong and his racist attitudes:

> The reader may be curious to know why he wanted an American girl so badly. Let me say now that Wu Fong's establishment was no ordinary house of ill forms. It was the more famous one in the Rue Chabanis, Paris, France—A "House of All Nations." In his institution he already had a girl from every country in the known world except ours, and now Betty rounded the collection.
>
> Wu Fong was confident that he would soon have his six hundred dollars back with interest, for many of his clients were from non-Aryan countries and would appreciate the services of a genuine American. Apropos of this, it is lamentable but a fact, nevertheless, that the inferior races greatly desire the women of their superiors. This is why the Negroes rape so many white women in the Southern states (169).

Up until the final sentence, the narrator mimics and performs Wu Fong's internalized racist view that white women are prime objects of desire for non-white men. In the final sentence, however, the narrator goes beyond the pimp to mimic American racist views in their most vile and unmediated form. The narrator in *A Cool Million* is both an observer and a campy impersonator whose use of irony enables him to engage both roles.

For West's ringleader narrator in *A Cool Million*, the enactment of both specular and performative roles is relatively simple and free of angst. In this novel, the enactment of both subject positions is free of the identity issues that plague Balso Snell and Miss. Lonelyhearts. While this narrator poignantly exposes greed, racism, and sexual exploitation in America's late capitalist culture, he appears to have safely appropriated the role of pre-mirror stage *flâneur* who can briefly inhabit the minds of others simply to amuse himself, rather than a freakish *flâneur* who is more concerned with identity issues. Yet this narrator in *A Cool Million* does take a critical moral stance against the American tendency to create colonizing spectacles. Such spectacles, which abound in the American capitalist hell of *A Cool Million*, encase people within cultural stereotypes and blight their dreams. The narrator exposes some of the most blatant colonizing spectacles in Wu Fong's house of prostitution, where all of the women are displayed and commodified through kitsch, as stereotyped representations of their

American places of origin.²⁶ For example, the woman from Bucks County, Pennsylvania, lives in an apartment "filled with painted pine furniture and decorated with slipware, spatterware, chalkware and 'Gaudy Dutch'" (203). Through the narrator's performative irony, West feigns "worldly admiration" for these whorehouses where bootstrap individualists from colonized ethnic groups now function as colonizers and producers of fetishes. Wu Fong is "a very shrewd man" who knows how to "turn his establishment into a high percentum American place, and the Jewish interior decorator Asa Goldstein creates the visual spectacles that confirm this.²⁷ Both function as colonizers and objectifiers, not as *flâneurs* in the Baudelarian and Benjaminian sense. For Benjamin, the *flâneur's* penchant for consumption is really a metaphor for intellectual appropriation in an extended quest for knowledge and power. When describing Wu Fong and Asa Goldstein, West represents both the democritization and debasement of the *flâneur* colonizer's gaze into that of an appropriative kitsch monger. Confronted with contrived spectacles and commodity fetishes, observers need no longer be intellectuals and artists. West's satiric narrative voice expresses dissatisfaction with the demise of the elitist *flâneur*, which he seems to associate with the venerated high modernist tradition that he satirizes and exposes in his earlier novels.

West further explores the degeneration of observer figures in *The Day of the Locust*, where he represents a group of lower class gazers:

> [. . .] they loitered on the corners or stood with their backs to the shop windows and stared at everyone who passed. When their stare was returned their eyes filled with hatred. At this time, Tod knew very little about them except they had come to California to die (*The Day of the Locust*).²⁸

The *flâneur* in *The Day of the Locust* has declined from empowered spectator to *badoud* or gaper, a term that Benjamin uses to define lower class spectators who lose their sense of self when gazing at spectacles (Benjamin 69). West's gapers, who are neither self-conscious pre-mirror stage *flâneurs* nor *flâneur* colonizers, are from economically marginal classes, and feel intense animosity towards the spectacles that they see. As Gerald Locklin explains, "[t]his group is volatile because it is most sensitive to the dreams churned out by Hollywood reality: West called the first draft of the novel, considerably different, *The Cheated*, and the cheated have survived as the starers."²⁹ Commodity culture, which can only be fully indulged and enjoyed by those who have money, inscribes epistemological differences between the rich and the poor, even as it tries to entice members of all social classes.

Unlike the cheated *badouds* of West's novel, the modernist *flâneur* never, at least overtly, succumbs to mass culture's seductive promises of power, success, and money. Ironically, however, the *flâneur's* bohemian rejection of middle class values and affectation of aristocratic snobbery positions him squarely as a burgher who hankers to be a prince. West's youthful intellectual posturing as a French symbolist and as Nathanael *von* Wallenstein Weinstein demonstrates his intense early desire to be both a social aristocrat and an aristocrat of the intellect. Susan Sontag redefines the *flâneur's* aristocratic posturing in postmodern terms. The contemporary spectator relishes objects that the elitist spectator would damn as vulgar: "The old style dandy hated vulgarity. The new style dandy, the lover of camp, appreciated vulgarity. . . . The dandy held the perfumed handkerchief to his nostrils and was liable to swoon; the connoisseur of camp sniffs the stink and prides himself on his strong nerves."[30] West's protagonists in *The Dream Life of Balso Snell, Miss. Lonelyhearts,* and *The Day of the Locust* are akin to Sontag's "new style dandy" who is fascinated by deviance, decadence, and kitschified spectacles. In fact, they all represent a fascinating inversion of the ethnic intellectual whom those with social power fail to accept. Miss. Lonelyhearts and Todd Hackett are, in fact, from idealized Anglo-American backgrounds, yet they identify almost exclusively with those who have been marginalized and enfreaked. One could go as far as to say that West makes these characters long to experience the ethnic role that Western culture has constructed as Jewish. Yet for West's characters, this potentially glamorous outsider position becomes complicated not only by sexual identity confusion, but by socioeconomic problems. The late capitalist depression era in which these novels are set threaten the culture that makes *flâneurism* possible. In a world where the rich can become bankrupt, the possibilities for self-fashioning that capitalism offers may fade away forever.

The conspicuous absence of the bourgeois WASP male who seeks and identifies with freakery and marginality is notable in *A Cool Million*. Unlike Miss. Lonelyhearts, Lemuel Pitkin does not actively seek these things, but they somehow find him. Pitkin's first name and his blind optimism bring to mind Lemuel Gulliver and Voltaire's Candide—two of literature's most famous satiric naifs. After losing his teeth, his eye, his finger, his leg, and his scalp in a number of symbolic castrations, Lemuel Pitkin becomes the "star" of a freak show masterminded by the demagogic Shagpoke Whipple:

>   FREE   FREE   FREE
>
>   Chamber of American Horrors
>   Animate and Inanimate
>   Hideosities
>   also
>   Chief Jake Raven
>   Come One   Come All
>   S.Snodgrass
>   Mgr.
>
>   FREE   FREE   FREE (237).

A Cool Million demonstrates that the late capitalist depression era culture disables and enfreaks even those with the purest backgrounds and the best intentions; one need not be a genetically constructed freak to become a grotesque spectacle. In fact, it is not only this culture, but Lemuel's inability to "debunk" its myths of progress, self-advancement, and self-reliance that get him into trouble.

At the end of *A Cool Million*, an "assassin's bullet" kills Lemuel as he performs his freakish spectacle for Whipple's fascist "national revolutionary party" (253). As in *Balso Snell* and *Miss. Lonelyhearts*, the enfreaked character ultimately dies, but with a difference. Freaks die in *Balso Snell* so that the protagonist can assert his heterosexualized *flâneurish* gaze, and in *Miss. Lonelyhearts*, the freak and the *flâneur* become one in death. But in *A Cool Million*, the freak does not exist in tension with an observer figure who sees himself as a freak, yet feels ambivalent about this identification. Rather, the would-be observer, Pitkin, has become the freak—but without any understanding of *flâneurism* and freakish performance. While the narrative voice in *A Cool Million* performs as an ironic observer, there is no tension between spectatorship and enfreaked character as their are in West's other works. The lack of *flâneurish* gaze in this novel is a cultural statement in itself. West represents a world where "low" forms have supplanted the "high" and uses a narrative style that turns away from the alienated but perceptive observer figure of high modernist fiction. In all of West's works, his use of "low" themes and forms anticipates the postmodern appropriation of kitsch. In *A Cool Million*, however, we see only the specter of low culture, so reduced to a series of grotesque clichés.

In *The Day of the Locust*, we see the fall of the American capitalist dream and the demise of the empowered spectator whose very existence is based on the ideology of high modernism. For West, these are parallel but separate developments that signal the end of empowered spectatorship. As *The Day of the Locust* charts the demise of the *flâneur* and the rise of the freakish spectacle, it also demonstrates that no individual can attempt to embody both roles without angst. Tod Hackett, a young Anglo-American who had attended the Yale School of Fine Arts, has come to paint what West regards as the ersatz and kitschy milieu of Hollywood. While Tod is intrigued by the filming of a reenactment of a battle that took place during the French Revolution, he is also disgusted by houses in the Hollywood hills that were built to look like Rhine castles and palaces with "domes and minarets out of the Arabian nights" (262). The Western gaze that transforms any kind of difference into a grotesque spectacle need no longer seek strange sights in the near and far East; the vast desert of the American West has now become the site of a lurid exhibition. The seductive spectacle of Hollywood and the gapers who are drawn to it, have so seduced Tod that he no longer wants to represent staid New England scenes. Instead, the spectacle of Hollywood inspires Tod to become a satirist like Goya or Daumier (261). In fact, since the world that he walks through is characterized by grotesque exaggeration, it would be difficult not to represent its scenes satirically. When Tod views Hollywood palaces he find them comically exaggerated, "but he didn't laugh" (262). Nonetheless, as a nascent *flâneur* colonizer, Tod is drawn to monstrously exaggerated kitsch and to the pathetic people who know no other world.

Tod is especially fascinated by Abe Kusich, a Jewish dwarf who seems plagued by an excess of testosterone. In fact, Abe Kusich provides "an important figure in a set of lithographs called "The Dancers," which Tod hopes to transform into a complex and provocative work of art (263). The lithographs, which depict a group of gapers dazedly watching grotesque performers, not only represent a scene of scopophilia and exhibitionism, but suggest Tod's idealized conception of himself. He is neither a gaper nor a freak, but a quintessential *flâneur* colonizer. Tod does not, at least ostensibly, identify with Abe Kusich's freakish difference, but feels compelled to paint and objectify him:

> Despite the sincere indignation that Abe's grotesque depravity aroused in him, he welcomed his company. The little man excited him in a way that made him feel certain of his need to paint (264).

Tod, who is excited by the spectacle of Abe's oddity, feels an attraction for the freak that borders on the erotic. The inverse of Tod, Abe is physically grotesque and poorly educated. While Abe Kusich embodies the enfreakment of Jews in the West, he fails to demonstrate the observational and intellectual powers that have been stereotypically associated with members of this group and make so many freakish *flâneurs*. A pure performer, Abe is concerned only with defending and exhibiting his masculinity, particularly by "talking tough."

Abe symbolically affirms his masculinity by his boisterous spectatorship at a cock fight involving two birds named Jujutala and Herman. Abe identifies strongly with the former, whom he is determined will win the match.[31] While Abe Kusich is clearly intent on proving his masculinity and heterosexuality, Tod Hackett is also concerned with his manhood. After he views a drag act with the naive Homer Simpson and the would-be actress Faye Greener, the latter remarks that she despise homosexuals:

> "I hate fairies," Faye said.
> "All women do."
> Tod meant it as a joke, but Faye was angry.
> "They're dirty," she said.
> He started to say something else, but Faye turned her head towards Homer again. . . . (371).

Tod's glib and knowing response to Faye may indicate feelings of latent homosexuality, but other instances more clearly suggest his inability to perform effectively as a heterosexual male. Tod's sexual insufficiency is not only reflected in his voyeuristic tendencies, but in his inability to strike a balance between voyeurism and exhibitionism. That is, he is not sufficiently attuned to his own oddity to turn his *flâneurish* gaze towards his own psyche. While he aspires to paint the "anarchic powers" that result from the gapers' "fury," he fails to glimpse any anarchy within himself. Beginning as a *flâneur* colonizer, he ends a *badoud*, carried away by the forces of a riot in Los Angeles (421). Long argues that Tod's "paranoic vision of victimization" suggests "the Freudian correlation between the paranoid personality and latent homosexuality—which can be surmised in Tod, and in West himself" (146). Unlike Tod, West lays bare his stigmas of Jewish identity and latent homosexuality in novels whose freakish characters function as objective correlatives for both his psychic state and the state of late modernist Western culture. Tod's limited consciousness does not approach West's authorial voice, which provides a *flâneurish* gaze as it enacts a *freakish* performance. This is most evident in passages where West's narrators and characters vacillate between appropriations of trenchant irony and an observational stance that mimics a placid objectivity which seems to accept things as they are.

Critics have often noted the anomalous, uncategorizable qualities of West's works, which combine "high" and "low" forms. As Deborah Sue Wilson explains, West, like his contemporaries Carl Van Vechten and e.e. cummings, was fascinated "by various modalities of popular culture."[32] Yet the appropriation of popular forms "has a long and even respectable tradition in *avante-garde* movements generally [and] in surrealism particularly" (81). Despite his sometimes horrified fascination with popular art, West was also deeply suspicious of the possibility that 'low" forms and the popular mind that engenders them would eventually overtake the sphere of high art. Although he successfully combines high and low forms in *Miss. Lonelyhearts*, he also represents the destructive nature of "low" prurience and decadence in this novel. His final novel, *The Day of the Locust*, demonstrates that the low perspective of *badouds* cannot compete with that of the elitist *flâneur*, and that the latter is unattainable in the lurid carnival world of Hollywood.[33]

In the hellish Hollywood that West represents in *The Day of the Locust*, everything has become a lurid, freakish spectacle. Racial spectacles such as young Adore Loomis's rendering of an overtly sexual blues song, have become normative forms of entertainment in Hollywood.[34] Since nearly everyone in this Westian world performs in a bizarre act, real freaks, whose bodies have traditionally lured spectators, have lost their distinction. Little Adore Loomis who belts, "Mama don't want no gin/Because gin do make her sin," without understanding the meaning of these lyrics, is as freakish as Abe Kusich. This grotesque conflation of adult sexuality in the body of a child is far from the more positive heterotopic values associated with the freakish *flâneur*. In the burgeoning postmodern world, ubiquitous spectacles are on par with freak shows, and also exhibit dangerous fascistic power over their spectators.

While West's ambivalence about the power and value of popular forms is at odds with postmodernists who welcome the presence of "low" art, West's proto-postmodernism is more evident in his fusion of the observational gaze with the performative impulse in a culturally productive heterotopia.[35] Taken as performances of a specific authorial consciousness, West's novels function as Semitic narratives that present the Anglo-American male's inability to occupy the role of the *flâneur* and the freak simultaneously, since he is incapable of fully appropriating the malleable identity that Western discourses have often deemed "Semitic." Although West may have felt ambivalent towards his Jewish identity, his works inherently celebrate the freakish *flâneur* perspective, one that is closely linked to observational and performative tendencies stereotypically associated with Jews. West's emphasis that freakish *flâneurs* emerge only through rigorous self-confrontation demonstrates that the process of transcending boundaries of identity can be a difficult and serious endeavor fraught with psychological risks.

CHAPTER THREE

"Well of Course, I *Used* to Be Absolutely Gorgeous, Dear"

The Female Interviewer as Subject/Object in Djuna Barnes's Journalism

> The reason that there is something "nasty" about them (the Jews) is because they have been thought nasty . . . In 1945 I had to view thousands of feet of film from Buchenwald and other concentration camps. My first reaction was horror, but after some hours I found myself fascinated by the dream-like insensibility of those walking skeletons and the inhuman beauty of the marmorial dead, attenuated by famine and disease to the shapes of modern sculpture.
>
> —Djuna Barnes, 1962 letter[1]

Djuna Barnes was a woman who was not afraid to look, but she felt profound ambivalence about being looked at. In her life and throughout her oeuvre, she unabashedly appropriated the prerogative of the fetishistic gaze associated with the masculine observer. Yet as her comment on film footage from Buchenwald indicates, her unflinching fascination with these lurid images suggests a potentially anti-Semitic desensitization to the historical reality of Jews dying in the Holocaust. The question as to whether Barnes's blunt and often grotesque descriptions of Jews is based on an anti-Semitic objectification or on a desire to expose and condemn such racism has been a frequent subject of contemporary work on Barnes, most of which tends to praise this writer for her identification with racial and cultural difference. In this vein, Nancy J. Levine and Marian Urquilla describe Barnes's disturbing representation of concentration camp imagery in her later journals as a "polyvalent use of 'the abject' head on," comparable to Julia Kristeva's exploration of similar images in *Powers of Horror*

(1982) (Levine and Urquilla).² From this perspective, Barnes is neither merely engaging in aesthetic fetishization, nor is she perversely reveling in the suffering of Jews, but instead is exposing her identification with those who have been condemned for their "deviant" identities associated with racial and sexual difference.

While Barnes's motives for representing the grotesque differ significantly from those who hate and fear forms of deviance, she seems unaware that the very act of objectifying the images from Buchenwald has anti-Semitic implications. This obliviousness is peculiar in Barnes since she usually displays an acute understanding of the stakes involved in the act of looking. Yet, as an artist, Barnes did not merely want to *be* an embodiment of difference, but she wanted to *see* it from the vantage point of one who will engage in the act of representation. For this reason, she frequently explores and appropriates a subject position associated with male spectatorship—a vantage point based on a tendency to fetishize and objectify. As we will see, she frequently attempts to experience the roles of both the feminized spectacle that carries unconscious associations with castration anxiety and the masculinized gaze that tries to control it.

In her classic essay on male spectatorship, Laura Mulvey emphasizes that paradoxically, the spectacle of female beauty always retains associations with castration anxiety, although the woman's role as fetishized object is to alleviate this fear.³ Until her retreat from public view in the middle of her life, Barnes often engaged in a seductive and ironic spectacle that courted the male gaze. In the 1970's, Barnes told an interviewer, "Well of course, I *used* to be absolutely gorgeous *dear*."⁴ Aware of her considerable charms, Barnes often used her seductive powers as a female spectacle, while simultaneously functioning as a masculine spectator. The fact that Freud deemed woman, the castrated other, as incapable of fetishizing has not deterred feminist theorists from exploring and debating the paradox of the female fetishist—a subject position that Barnes especially embodies through her authorial perspective when taking the role of interviewer in her journalistic work and in her final novel, *Nightwood*.⁵

Before Barnes wrote her formidable experimental works of fiction, she was forced by financial necessity to engage in a more commercial literary endeavor. From 1913 to 1931, she wrote journalistic interviews with some of the most intriguing artists, performers, and theatrical directors of her day. Barnes's interviews, in short, are largely concerned with those who transform either themselves or others into spectacles. While Barnes regarded her interviews as mere "hack work," she nonetheless used these pieces to develop her interest not only in lurid spectacles, but in the relationship between the commodifiers and the commodified. In her interviews with Flo Ziegfield and Arthur Voetglin, for example, she exposes these vaudeville producers as pimp-like procurers of beautiful women.

She does so, however, by using her alluring femme drag persona to elicit their reactions. When interviewing male subjects, Barnes often makes a spectacle of herself by playing the *femme fatale* who deliberately destabilizes the male gaze with her exaggerated and threatening performance.[6] At the same time, she adopts the male role of the incisive masculine spectator, thus conflating masculine and feminine subject positions. In an act which conforms to Joan Riviere's definition of the masquerade, Barnes guards against retaliation from the men from whom she has appropriated the phallus.[7] Yet for Barnes, the masquerade is also an aggressive performance that calls into question male specular power. Barnes's female fetishism tests the structure of gendered looking: does the female's proximity to the feminized fetish object, itself, impede clarity of perception, or does it promote an ability to see power relations with greater insight? Barnes engages in this epistemic "testing" particularly when interviewing Jewish showmen. In these examples, she demonstrates that she can identify with their gaze, even as she simultaneously attempts to undermine it.

At the beginning of her interview titled "Flo Ziegfeld is Tired of Buying Hosiery," Barnes, who is obviously fascinated by her subject's "closed-mouthed and satirical eyed" manner, is far less impressed by what she regards as his kitschy girly show:

> I didn't see anything terrible about it, nor did I see anything glamorous or grand or inspiring or even beautiful. All I did see, all that made a new impression on me, was the number of limbs that a girl manages to secrete about her when she has nothing much on and nothing much to do, and sits down, only to arise at a shriek from the manager. The only high life about it was the dash of a vivid gehenna in the sudden gashed red of a badly painted mouth.[8]

With satirical eyes and an acid tongue, Barnes exposes Ziegfeld as someone akin to the Mormon polygamist Brigham Young. However, given her tendency to embellish her interviews with her own wit, she may have imagined him saying this:

> "You know, he went on presently, "I have to pick out all the shoes and stockings and other things that go with a show, and I'm tired to death of hosiery. It's like being another Brigham Young, only he had an incentive, because stockings were in the family—" He paused ("Flo Ziegfeld 71).

That Djuna Barnes's father, Wald Barnes, was a proud polygamist is surely significant here.[9] Barnes felt ambivalent towards this grandiloquent and sexually nonconforming patriarch of two families. Thus, rather than passing sanctimonious judgement on Ziegfeld's use of women in vaudeville spectacles, Barnes undermines him with brutal satire, speaking from the position of a seductive *femme fatale*. After getting Ziegfeld to admit that he prefers redheads, the auburn tressed Barnes makes him confess his fascination with vampiric women:

> "A vampire," he returned, "is a woman who eats lightly of uncooked things; who walks out between tall avenues of spears to die, and doesn't, and finally spend the evenings in an orgy of virtuous dreams. That's time wasted. A vampire is a good woman with a bad reputation, or rather a good woman who has had possibilities and wasted them" ("Flo Ziegfeld, 73).

With reference to Barnes's effusion about vampires, Philip Herring suggests that the writer seemed at times to "put words into [her subjects'] mouths, since "few could have equaled her wit" (Herring 91). Barnes, who often displays a fascination with seductresses, is clearly projecting herself as a stereotypical dangerous redhead who could put Ziegfeld's star-making machinery into high gear. However, rather than basking in Ziegfeld's troubled gaze, Barnes continues to tease him by asking him to go into further detail about vampiric women. Obviously uncomfortable, Ziegfeld sends a telegram and hums a few songs rather than answer her question directly. Barnes, who is setting out to be as wicked as possible, says, "I hope you are not feeling ill" ("Flo Ziegfeld" 74). With bravado, Barnes projects herself as a vamp who is overwhelming a notorious creator and marketer of female spectacles with her own vampiric eroticism. Unimpressed by these showgirls, Barnes, who has little conventional feminine modesty, believes that she is a far more powerful spectacle of femininity, as well as far wittier and more perceptive about showgirls than Ziegfeld. In this case, Barnes has successfully used her femme drag to expose Ziegfeld as a glorified pimp, demonstrating that the masquerade can be used to facilitate female knowledge and power.

When attempting to exert her subjectivity as an interviewer, Barnes encounters formidable resistance from Arthur Voegtlin, a Broadway producer who enjoys her feminine charm, but who clearly refuses to fall into the trap of her femme masquerade. Obviously peeved by the elusive Voegtlin's refusal to be too self-revealing, Barnes titles the essay, "Interviewing Arthur Voegtlin is like having a Nightmare." She deems him a nice social fraud, the kind that says, "'chase me, because I'm worth catching.'"[10] Ostensibly refusing to play up to him, Barnes proclaims that she "had no reverence for him at all, which he said he liked" ("Voegtlin 78). By repeatedly calling Barnes "Gunga Duhl," a name that she frequently called herself to satirize her reputed toughness, Voegtlin ridicules both her attempts to exert journalistic power and her femme fatale posturing. Barnes, however, refuses to defer to Voegtlin, not only by frequently announcing her lack of admiration of him to her readers, but by making his reticence the theme of the essay. His refusal to tell her the name of an upcoming play he has produced leads Barnes to satirize both his detachment and his refusal to take her seriously:

"All right, don't; but listen, Mr. Voegtlin. I'm going to write about you and I'm going to be honest. I'm going to say that you talked a lot, but didn't say anything."

"That, Gunga Duhl, would be the biggest compliment you could pay me, and I would be sure that even the persuasions of a charming thing with poppies in her hair could not make me divulge. Come along; I'll show you the resurrecting room" ("Voegtlin" 82).

Barnes performs as "a charming thing with poppies in her hair" for both Voegtlin and her readership. While she seeks to unsettle the gaze of the man she satirizes, she also performs for sophisticated women who would find her brazen performance amusing, and who may even want to emulate her. Barnes constructs her female readers as intelligent and sophisticated enough to discern and admire her act. According to Herring, Barnes despised the necessity of having to write popular journalism and regarded the audience for such light, commercial fare as "vacuous, superficial, poorly educated yahoos" (Herring 78). Yet despite her reputed disdain for mass audiences, Barnes never "dumbed down" her artistic intentions and even uses her interviews as fertile ground for artistic experimentation and poignant cultural criticism of popular icons.[11]

Although Barnes nowhere mentions that both Ziegfeld and Voetglin are Jewish, her representation of them as ruthless objectifiers mirrors late nineteenth and early twentieth century stereotypes of Jewish theatrical producers.[12] In his study of Jews in the American theater at this time, Harley Erdman explains that Jews were stereotyped as "vulgar and lecherous" money mongers whose power in the entertainment industry "[threatened] to debase both the art of the stage and gentile womanhood. The anxiety is that gentiles are at the mercy of Jews."[13] The stereotype was so ingrained that the term "theatrical producer" may have been viewed as synonymous with Jewishness. Barnes, who confronts the issue of Jewish cultural power more directly in *Nightwood*, must have been aware of this stereotype, although it is difficult to determine if her interviews with Ziegfeld and Voetglin are intentional responses to it. The sense of her subjects' Jewishness carries over to her response to American vaudeville, as she regards both Ziegfeld and Voetglin as kitsch mongers who hold the masculinized controlling gaze. By contrast, Barnes displays more respect for the Europeanized theatrical producer David Belasco, a son of English Sephardic Jews who, beyond his theatrical talents, was deeply concerned with the invidious representation of Jews on the American stage.[14]

In "David Belasco Dreams," Barnes describes the producer as a thoughtful and intelligent theatrical visionary who even exhibits a penchant for asceticism. Educated in a monastery as a young boy, Belasco, while Jewish, always maintained a fascination for Catholicism and monastic detachment. Throughout his life he collected lavish Catholic icons and even went as far as to wear a clerical collar in public. Far more than merely a showman, the reclusive and contemplative Belasco presents himself as a consummate observer who takes pleasure in using his senses to learn about the world:

> Be conscious always, be alert; have eyes and use them; have a tongue and speak little. If you cultivate your silence, your ultimate sounds will be profitable ("Belasco 192).

Neither Barnes nor Belasco clarifies whether the profits of intense observation are of a cultural or purely economic nature. In his search for cultural capital, Belasco applies his keen gaze to American culture as he walks its streets. Barnes displays reverence and fascination for Belasco's particular kind of self-fashioning, one that is based not merely on objectifiying sexualized spectacles, but on a strong identification with Catholicism, another minority culture.

As Barnes attempted to destabilize the male gaze, she also maintained an identification with spectacles of cultural and bodily difference that have associations with uncanny, feminized others. For example, in *Nightwood* she represents and at times celebrates the role of those at the cultural margins. In what amounts to being a convoluted apologia for *Nightwood* in his editor's introduction to the novel, T.S. Eliot alerts the readers that the work they are about to encounter is not (among other things) "a horrid sideshow of freaks."[15] Obviously uncomfortable with *Nightwood*'s subject matter, Eliot instead characterizes it as a nonjudgemental representation of those who defy "Puritan morality" (*Nightwood* xv). Despite Eliot's timidity regarding "freaks," Barnes represented racial others, homosexuals, and theatricalized spectacles of bodily difference throughout her oeuvre in order to explore "freakish" roles from the perspective of both the observer and the deviant other. Particularly in her journalism, Barnes's performance as a female fetishist resembles that of a masculine modernist figure that I term the freakish *flâneur*—a spectator who is simultaneously an enfreaked object of observation and a voyeur who applies his searching gaze to what he regards as the differences of others. As Barnes embodies both the roles of spectacle and observer in her interviews, she explores the malleability of her own subjectivity in relation to boundaries relating to class, gender, and race. Jews are of particular interest to Barnes, since various discourses have associated them with a malleable subjectivity that enables them to occupy the positions of both observers and performers.

When the *flâneur* transcribes his observations into journalism or fiction that he eventually sells, he becomes both a literary performer and a commodifier, thus demonstrating that the idealized modernist observer can also function as a capitalist spectacle.[16] In her journalism, Barnes calls into question the *flâneur's* tendency towards intellectual consumerism as she combines the roles of spectator and spectacle into that of a freakish *flâneur* cum female fetishist. Priscilla Parkhurst Fergusson explains that while the nineteenth century ideology of *flâneurism* defines the male gaze as capable of uncompromising lucidity and objectivity, this same ethos also suggests that women lack the sense of detachment necessary for *flâneurism*. Instead, it views women as consummate consumers who are prone to compulsive shopping: "No woman is able to attain the aesthetic distance so crucial to the *flâneur's* superiority. She is unfit for *flânerie* because she desires the objects spread before her and acts upon that desire. The *flâneur*, on the other hand, desires the city as a whole, not a particular part of it."[17] As a female fetishist, Barnes goes beyond the mere consumerism attributed to women, as her spectatorship alternately resembles that of the masculinizing colonizing *flâneur* and the freakish *flâneur*. At the same time, Barnes maintains an ironic distance from these roles, as she calls into question the power relations inherent in masculine spectatorship.

The female fetishist's penchant for experiencing antithetical subject roles also parallels the malleable subjectivity that the masculine Baudelarian and Benjaminian *flâneur* aspires to achieve. However, Mary Ann Doane explains that the female fetishist faces obstacles that bar her from experiencing the clarity of perception that is stereotypically associated with the male gaze: "For the Female Spectator there is a certain overpresence of the image—she *is* the image" (Doane 22). Thus, what the female fetishist sees when engaged in the act of perception is herself, and her gaze is, at least narcissistic. Barnes demonstrates in her early work that the female subject can transcend the overpresence of the image through an appropriation of phallic wit—a bitingly ironic use of language associated with masculine power and authority. In blending and blurring the positions of subject and object, Barnes engages in complex gender bending. As interviewer and novelist, she performs as a male transvestite, who combines the female masquerade with the male subject's ability to gaze and speak. This appropriation of subjectivity imitates masculinity, since it is modeled on a male subject who, in turn, pretends to be a female object, while maintaining his ability to function in the realm of language.[18] When Barnes appropriates the phallus by performing in a manner that resembles a man in drag, she attempts to speak from a place that goes beyond all gender essentialisms. In her interviews and her early fiction, Barnes engages in a form of female fetishism that enables her to remain firmly grounded in the realm of language, thus avoiding the pitfalls of narcissism or emasculation that Doane warns about when defining the limits of female desire. The spectacle of femininity, alone, lacks the masculine spectator's ability to see and to know. Yet by conflating the roles of the observer and the observed, the female fetishist, like the freakish *flâneur*, disrupts the power relations inherent in the mind/body, subject/object, male/female dichotomies.

In several of her interviews and later in *Nightwood*, Barnes abandons this competitive impulse to threaten the masculine gaze and to outperform *flâneur* colonizers and freakish *flâneurs* in order to identify with the feminized uncanny—a subject position that she clearly links with women and people of color. Freud defines the "uncanny" in terms of the German word *unheimlich*, which means simultaneously "homely" or familiar, and strange.[19] The preverbal state which Barnes explores in some of her journalistic essays and later in *Nightwood*, takes on the dimensions of the uncanny since it is both familiar and strange to those who have entered the realm of the symbolic. Barnes shares Freud's linkage of the uncanny with femininity, but she regards it not as an abyss, but as a source of power and knowledge.[20] In short, Barnes's approach to the uncanny stands as a challenge to both Freudian and Lacanian views that knowledge must be linked inextricably to language.[21] Experimenting with different epistemological approaches in her interviews, Barnes vacillates from using her keen performative wit, to observing and identifying with spectacles of the uncanny feminine associated with a preverbal state. In both her early and late works, Barnes remains fascinated with performative self-fashioning, yet she also exhibits a countervailing interest in hereditary predestination and the primacy of the inarticulate, uncanny other.

In her interviews of Ziegfeld and Voetglin, Barnes demonstrates intense skepticism towards the conventional male gaze as a means of gaining knowledge. When confronting the innovative photographer and art impresario Alfred Stieglitz, Barnes expresses similar dismay at his self-professed pleasure in voyeurism. Stieglitz, who was notorious for his brutal frankness and verbal pyrotechnics, does not hesitate to tell Barnes that he loves to watch the reactions of potential customers who observe the provocative and "revolutionary" art in his Madison Avenue gallery:

> I knew that there was nothing so calculated as to expose men as art. They are simple before it or they are capital liars. What do I know of pictures? Not a thing. What do I know of cubism and all the other things, line and color? Nothing . . . But, say, I'll tell you, I've reached a spot where I'm about willing to turn down the empty glass. I have had them all here to learn what you Americans are like, and I have learned much. My gallery was only a trap set up for humanity, and the trap has worked, season in and out.[22]

It is unlikely that Stieglitz, who was an ambitious and committed artist and critic, knew nothing about the major artistic movements of his day. In fact, according to art historian Barbara Buhler, Lynes, "the impact of [Stieglitz's] theorizing about modern art was widespread—a testimony to his remarkable powers of persuasion."²³ In fact, some of Stieglitz's major theoretical contributions focused on the connections among gender, culture and creativity in modern art—issues that also concerned Barnes. Fascinated by the idea that the unconscious could be a source of modernist abstraction, Stieglitz was especially interested in work by children, women, and non-Western peoples that resembled high modernist works by western male artists. While his theories often bear the mark of gender and racial essentialisms, they nonetheless participated in important debates regarding the sources of artistic creativity. ²⁴

When interviewed by Barnes, Stieglitz presents himself as ignorant of art theory only to emphasize his predilection for observing what he regards as the callow American mind. He even goes as far as to claim that he can read people's character through their reactions to his art objects ("Alfred Stieglitz" 217). Barnes emphasizes that "all of [Stieglitz's] exhibitions have been revolutionary, cubist, irrationalist, all of them" ("Alfred Stieglitz" 216). Besides presenting *fin-de-sicle* and modernist giants such as Toulouse Lautrec, Picasso, and Rodin, he also displayed a "savage art called 'negro'" and the work of "a woman, Georgia O'Keefe." ("Alfred Stieglitz" 216). Disdainful of American consumerism and anti-intellectualism, he suggests that people are too vulgar, insensitive, and stupid to understand the trap that he has set up for them ("Alfred Stieglitz" 220). When Barnes asks him if his spectators should be angry at his tendency to laugh at them, he replies: "No—for what? There is no love, there is not art, and I learned that there are no people. There is only emotional learning, spectacular ABC's and customers" ("Alfred Stieglitz" 220). From Barnes's ironic perspective, Stieglitz, for all his intellectual sophistication, performs as a huckster who depends on "gut" reactions of gullible crowds in order to earn his living as a gallery owner. Instead, besides being a formidable art critic, Stieglitz was also a clever marketing strategist who knew how to captivate the public.²⁵ In his emotional emphasis on his patrons' folly, Stieglitz illustrates what he regards as his own brilliant and tough minded intellectualism, indicative of idealized masculinity: "One should not be in love, it prevents work; and cool, logical study should follow love" ("Alfred Stieglitz" 220).

When functioning as a gallery owner who observes his patrons' responses to the art on display, and while exhibiting his emotional responses to them, Stieglitz simultaneously occupies stereotypical masculine and feminine subject positions. By simultaneously enacting roles associated with spectatorship and performance, Stieglitz behaves as a freakish *flâneur*, a perspective that is often associated with the assimilated Jew's sense of division between his ethnicity and the culture within which he dwells. Ambivalent towards his Jewishness, Stieglitz once remarked: "I never much thought of myself as a Jew or any other particular thing. But I'm beginning to feel it must be the Jew in me that is after all the key to my impossible make up" (*O'Keefe and Stieglitz* 229). According to Benita Eisler, Stieglitz, who identified "with all things German," often denied his Jewish background (*O'Keefe and Stieglitz* 229).

While a consummate *flâneur* herself, Barnes displays resistance towards Stieglitz's *flâneurish* ways. After he proclaims the necessity of a cold, masculinized gaze to foster his observations, Barnes questions this position in a brazen parody:

> From this place I have been standing eternally, looking out towards the world with my eyes seeing men pass and look back at me. And I cold and lonesome and increasing steadily in mine own sorrow, which is caught like the plague of other men, until I am full and my mouth will hold no more, and my eyes will see no more, and my ears can stand nothing further. Then do I begin the steady, slow discharge which is called "wisdom," but which is only that too much the eyes cannot see, the ears cannot hear, the mouth cannot hold ("Alfred Stieglitz" 220).

In this passage, Barnes ridicules Stieglitz's view of himself as an enlightened seer with pretensions to objectivity and implies that his insistence on an ideal masculine gaze may be a symptom of sexual insecurity. She finds this observational stance narcissistic and solipsistic, and questions his motives: "But often when I ask myself when I think no one will hear me thinking, least of all Stieglitz— what has made it necessary for the man to learn life in this way, and what happened to the lives of others that makes it necessary for them to form a sort of 'public society'" ("Alfred Stieglitz" 222). In questioning Stieglitz's *flâneurish* intentions, Barnes implicitly questions her own, since she, herself, functions as a seer who exposes others' desires with brash and incisive irony. In most of her interviews, Barnes the *flâneur* and female fetishist tries to beat the masculine observer at his own game, but occasionally she stops to question the goals of all ironic, masculine observation.

Barnes's fascination with the Jewish *flâneur* colonizer figures more prominently in *Nightwood*, where she satirizes Felix Von Volkbein, a sycophantic Jewish art collector who gazes longingly at the aristocracy from the position of the cultural margins. The freakish *flâneur*, a cultural role that has many associations with the Jewish intellectual, bears a striking resemblance to Barnes's own position as a female fetishist.[26] Both embody dual roles relating to masculine and feminine subject positions. As Doane explains, the female fetishist, particularly in the form of a woman intellectual, presents a subversive challenge to gender norms:

> The intellectual woman looks and analyzes, and in usurping the gaze she poses a threat to an entire system of representation. It is as if the woman had forcefully moved to the other side of the specular ("Film and Masquerade" 27).

When performing as an interviewer, Barnes, herself, engages in subversion by appropriating the gaze from men who feel entitled to objectify what they perceive in order to gain knowledge, money, or both. Similarly, the Jewish intellectual, particularly of the modernist period, subverts boundaries relating to ethnicity and gender by functioning as both cultural insider and outsider. His ability to produce incisive cultural commentary from the margins of the dominant culture, calls into question the notion that only insiders are privy to knowledge and power about themselves. However, not all Jewish *flâneurs* were alike for Barnes, and she displays a more positive identification with David Belasco, who demonstrates a decidedly feminine sensibility. The others exhibit a coercive masculine gaze that she finds both intriguing and repulsive.

At times skeptical of excessive irony and detachment, Barnes is often attracted to people who display more passionate engagement with life, as well as feminine receptivity. In two interviews with Mimi Aguglia, a Sicilian vaudeville performer noted for her portrayal of Salome, Barnes describes the performer in racial terms that make her an exemplar of the pre-verbal, the animalistic, and the hyper-emotional. According to Barnes, the "wild Aguglia," who gyrates like "undulating spaghetti" before the head of John the Baptist, identifies with her pet monkey.[27] Barnes explored the role of Salome, another common *fin-de-siécle* image of unbridled female sexuality and sadomasochism in her short story "The Head of Babylon."[28] Aguglia, whom Barnes regards as its perfect interpreter, "knows how to menace with the back of her throat; strange, animalistic cries set about the most primitive and civilized of all emotions: love and rare hate" ("The Wild Aguglia" 256). Barnes attributes Aguglia's histrionics, which she admires for its "vulgar . . . coarse . . . and full blooded" sensuality, to the performer's ethnicity: "The Italians view life in their drama like a passionate storm and die only to return again" ("The Wild Aguglia" 260). According to Meryl Altman, Barnes and other modernist writers frequently engaged in "an ongoing European discourse" about the nature of "'race,' 'heritage,' 'heredity,' and 'degeneracy'" (Altman 164). In her interviews, Barnes uses these stereotypes as points of departure that enable her to explore human character in relation to spectacles and spectatorship. Barnes clearly views Aguglia as a cultural other whose intense female passion is the antithesis of idealized Anglo-American masculine coolness. Aguglia is a freak of both race and gender, and in her bestiality and pre-verbal expressiveness, she embodies a "primitive" and non-rational state of being that both fascinates and frightens Barnes. Beguiled by that which seems inarticulate, but unwilling to open herself totally to such forces, Barnes tries, throughout her career, to negotiate a space between the poles of rigorous, controlling intellectualism and vehement abandon to the unknown.

At times, Barnes tries bravely to appropriate the receptivity and irrational knowledge characteristic of uncanny freaks. On one occasion, for example, she willingly undergoes a force-feeding in order to make a compelling journalistic commentary about the ordeal of British suffragists.[29] Barnes loathed any form of medical treatment, so it is a wonder that she agreed to submit to a group of male doctors and nurses in what was a problematic and even sadomasochistic procedure (Herring 89). With extreme clinical detachment, Barnes describes her subjugation to medical technology as she "lay in passive revolt."[30] As she was fed milk through a rubber tube in her nose, Barnes had "unbidden visions of remote horrors," such as "the tentacles of some monster devil fish in the depths of a tropic sea" ("How it Feels to Be Forcibly Fed" 177). While Barnes makes herself receptive to this experience of the uncanny by submitting to a force-feeding, she also displays disgust for this procedure. Aware that she is a medicalized spectacle, Barnes quips "This, at least, is one picture that will never go into the family album" ("How it Feels to Be Forcibly Fed" 176). When filled with "wordless anger" as the "torture and outrage" of the experience "burned [her mind]," Barnes still has enough gumption to engage in a bit of detached, caustic commentary at the end of the scene. Commenting on the resemblance of the operating table to a torture chamber, Barnes asks the doctor, "Isn't there any other way of tying a person up? . . . That thing looks like—." In Barnes's terms, her medical subjugator responds, "Yes, I know" ("How it Feels to Be Forcibly Fed" 179). It is this "gentle" response that Barnes finds especially ironic and horrific, since such "gentleness" can cloak sadism in the culturally approved aim of subduing unruly women.

Taking the role of a freakish *flâneur* who ironically comments on the nature of her spectacle, Barnes clearly does not revel in this particular performance of deviance. In fact, Barnes is far too disturbed by the implications of this performance to allow her acerbic wit to take over completely. In her analysis of "How it Feels to Be Forcibly Fed," Barbara Green argues that in this piece, Barnes displays intense skepticism towards the motives of feminists who make political spectacles out of themselves. Green demonstrates that in another essay, "Seventy Trained Suffragists Turned Loose on the City," Barnes exposes suffragist orators as self-aggrandizing performers who are more concerned with flaunting their rhetoric than engaging political action (Green 62). Green believes that in both essays, "Barnes's charge is that performative activism becomes a kind of fashion statement when women are asked to speak with the body" (Green 82). Yet when criticizing women who make spectacles of themselves, Barnes may well have been engaging in an ongoing and unresolved self-critique, since she, the self-proclaimed "pen performer," frequently made a spectacle of her femininity in her performative journalism.

While Green's analysis of Barnes's distaste for feminist spectacles is perceptive, she fails to acknowledge the extent to which Barnes submitted to a force feeding to find out "how it feels." Barnes felt as ambivalent about her need to perform as a feminine spectacle as she did about her desire to appropriate the masculine gaze. Yet she understood intuitively that in order to gain access to the uncanny, one must not merely look at grotesque things, but experience them directly. It was this search for visceral experience rooted in pre-verbal understanding that led Barnes to undergo the horrific force feeding. Nancy J. Levine explains that Barnes used her journalistic experiences in order to discover a means of "[narrowing] the distance between the freakish unfortunates she encountered in 'odd corners' of the city and the audience who '[looks] down upon these people as they enter the abyss.' One way to do this is to enter the abyss herself" (Levine 33).

While Barnes flirts with becoming a spectacle of the uncanny feminine, she also offers amusing, tongue-in-cheek descriptions of social situations where anyone could become an absurd spectacle. Commenting on scantily clad people who bathe in a municipal bathhouse on Coney Island, she suggests that people seem less civilized when unclothed:

> A really very good person can lose his character out there. There's nothing to prevent him from getting down to his basic impulses. I've seen a lot of nice people who didn't look it. Like the best chairs in the parlor, they are better under linen.

Feigning prissy prudery, Barnes in this journalistic incarnation claims to be above the desire to see anything that is barbarous or prurient. In parodying moral rectitude, Barnes states that a normally cautious person will be tempted to "[try] a hazardous-looking spectacle and end up on [his or her] back [viewing] all the beauty of perspective" (149). Barnes, who often seeks the beauty of strange perspectives, mimics a less adventurous soul, undoubtedly aware of the difference between a more sanctimonious reader and herself.

Coney Island spectators may be tempted to enter the abyss of freakery by doing things out of character, but Barnes demonstrates that the freaks on display in the sideshows have less choice in this matter. When describing freakish performers on Coney Island, Barnes demonstrates the extent to which they are controlled by the carny talker whom she calls the "demonstrator."[31] When presenting a thin man dubbed "the Cigarette Fiend," he prods and pokes the man as "he begins to enumerate [his] misfortunes as though they were rows of precious beads" ("Surcease in Hurry" 279). The freak, who resents being made into a spectacle, maintains "a cool, self-possessed stare—a little uncertain, perhaps, whether to be proud or sorry for the accident that has made him of interest to the gaping throng" ("Surcease in Hurry" 280). Barnes finds the commodification of the freak and of other human and nonhuman wares on Coney Island both grotesquely fascinating and morally upsetting.

Encountering the constant bustle of merchants, customers, spectators, and spectacles, Barnes sees Coney Island as a microcosm of American capitalism. She describes a fierce little girl who loudly parodies a pedlar selling his goods: "There is something incomplete in her great, horrifying completeness; she seems to be an outcome of past cries, curses, shouts, laughter, music, dancing, and merry isolence" ("Surcease and Hurry" 280). For Barnes, the girl is the culmination of all the voices of "a thousand middlemen making a nickel" ("Surcease in Hurry" 280). The child, who should be innocent of the ways of the American marketplace, has become the voice and the grotesque image of the commodifier. However, Barnes, who satirically adopts the male gaze and the carny talker's rhetoric, must see a complex image of herself in the bold little girl. While Barnes in her own journalism courts and commodifies the seductive uncanny and the grotesque, she resents the way that spectacles of difference have been appropriated by acquisitive Americans.

This commodification is not limited to avaricious males. Barnes finds female spectators as exploitative as wealthy theatrical moguls such as Ziegfield and Voetglin in "Dempsey Welcomes Women Fans" and "My Sisters and I at a New York Prize Fight."[32] In these interviews, she demonstrates that female spectators of boxing matches often perversely fetishize spectacles of the male body, and she calls into question their motives for attempting to adopt the masculinized role of spectator and fetishist. She notes that these women are not as interested in these men's athletic skills as they are in "a certain curve of the chin, a certain line from throat to brow" ("My Sisters and I" 173). Disgusted by this objectifying female gaze, Jack Dempsey tells Barnes that most of his female spectators are so invasive that he has posted guard dogs at his gate to keep them from coming to his room ("Dempsey" 287). Barnes, who does not use her acerbic wit during these two interviews, seems to empathize with the male boxers who disdain the women that enfreak them. Critics such as Laura Mulvey, who insist that role of spectator is inherently masculine, would argue that these women are engaging in a form of imitative gazing that is inherently masculine and that there can be no authentic visual pleasure in this ogling. Barnes, herself, suggests that when these women look at the boxers, their gaze is not truly erotic—instead their ostensibly feminine gaze is really fostered by their association with "opulent, portly" vulgar men whose hands "gleam with a flash of diamonds" ("My Sisters and I" 169). Here, Barnes's disapproval of nouveau riche conspicuous consumption prefigures her trenchant representation of pseudo-aristocratic taste in *Nightwood*. Yet despite her ostensible disparagement of these women, she also takes vicarious pleasure in observing these female fetishists:

> Was it, after all, the men in the audience who had been careless and indifferent to pain? Was it the sound of a snapping fan that I had heard? Was it a woman's voice that had murmured, "He had fine eyes?" A woman's hand had gripped my arm in the dark? A woman's hand that had ceased so suddenly?
>
> And whose voice was it that had cried out before the finish—"Go to it and show us that you're men?" ("My Sisters and I" 173).

Once again, Barnes displays ambivalence towards the female appropriation of the male gaze. Barnes knows that these "frail, slender throated" bourgeois women, are commodified objects ("My Sisters and I" 169). Yet they are, themselves, capable of the cheap commodification of others.

In both her early and later works, Barnes demonstrates that she is far more fascinated by an uncanny, pre-verbal otherness that cannot be commodified, but experienced. Disdainful of the commercial basis of many American spectacles, Barnes criticizes the commodification of animals by the Bronx Zoo. She goes as far as to argue that these creatures, for all their beastliness, often seem to possess a subjectivity that enables them to transcend their role as objects on display. For example, Barnes defines a female gorilla as "the gorilla woman, the only living captive of her race" who "has a cold sort of appraising stare that holds neither envy nor malice."[33] This "gorilla woman" resembles Barnes in her resistance to objectification, as she also affixes her evaluative gaze on those who ogle her. Throughout her career, Barnes maintained her fascination with the patriarchal construction of femininity as inherently animalistic. This is especially evident in *Ryder* (1928), where Barnes satirically renders the title character's obsession with both masculine procreation and with subduing what he regards as natural female bestiality.[34] Although Barnes satirizes Ryder's masculine tendency to essentialize female difference, she never repudiates completely the notion of biological gender difference. Rather, she calls into question the heterosexual male's visual appropriation and commodification of this deviance and seeks to figure ways wherein women can own their own difference.

Nevertheless, Barnes tends to essentialize racial and cultural difference, which she associates with female bestiality and the uncanny. While Barnes praises the animal's self-absorption and obliviousness to the gaping crowds, her anthropomorphism is tinged with racist stereotypes about Africa and its natives. As the zookeeper Engleholm walks towards the gorilla, Barnes observes that "Germany [is] gaining upon Africa with difficulty" ("The Girl and the Gorilla" 184). At the same time, Barnes also seems to identify with the female gorillas's unruly defiance of male authority, and with the intractability of the uncanny "dark continent." As one capable of functioning as both a masculinized subject and as a feminized, fetishized object, Barnes fails to examine thoroughly her own inclination towards engaging in lurid forms of objectification. On the one hand, Barnes clearly identifies the female gorilla with a powerful resistance to the male gaze and male authority. Yet while she identifies the "gorilla woman" with this power, she does not question the racist and sexist implications of this image.

Engleholm complains that the gorilla, who is "so darned cussed," is "as nice a little girl when she wants to be, and then so mean—as mean" ("The Girl and the Gorilla" 184). Engleholm cannot find the words to describe the gorilla's occasional beastly nastiness, and Barnes cryptically quips that "Kipling commented that 'The female of the species is more deadly than the male,'" as she alludes to his poem "The Female of the Species." Barnes may also have been referring to a poem called "the Vampire" that Kipling wrote in response to his cousin Phil Burne Jones's Pre-Raphaelite painting of a female embodiment of the living dead:

> A fool there was and he made his prayer
> (Even as you and I!)
> To a rag and a bone and a hank of hair
> (We called her the woman who did not care)
> But the fool he called her his lady fair—
> (Even you and I).[35]

The potentially destructive "woman who did not care," has little regard for her effect on others, just as the female gorilla that Barnes "interviews" is completely indifferent to those who observe and control her. Fascinated by the brazen indifference of a "bad girl," Barnes tries repeatedly to emulate it with her sharp, caustic wit and feigned air of detachment.

When describing animals on display at the Hippodrome Circus, Barnes emphasizes the grandeur of their mysterious nonverbal intelligence. When young male spectators gaze at an elephant's huge smile, they observe "the jeer from the jungle, the hint of a possible knowledge of those corners of the human mind supposed to be secret. Upon beholding such a smile, you feel deeply inadequate."[36] Emphasizing these uncanny elements, Barnes dismisses bourgeois notions of animals as cute and cuddly creatures, and praises a ring leader who condemns the "rabble" who sentimentalize nature. Anti-bourgeois and intellectually provocative, Barnes's elitist impulses, based on an appeal to witty and ironic readers, pervade her representation of a popular form of entertainment. Yet despite Barnes's identification with animalistic and deathly images that she associates with the uncanny, she often fails to question their problematic implications. This is especially evident when she gapes at the grotesque and pathetic spectacles from Buchenwald. Performing as a *flâneur* colonizer, she seems almost to perversely envy "the dream-like insensibility of those walking skeletons and the inhuman beauty of the marmorial dead" as they embody the uncanny (Levine and Urquilla 14). However, throughout her interviews, Barnes calls into question the *flâneur* colonizer's fetishizing impulse by performing as a freakish *flâneur* who casts a critical eye towards those who commodify problematic spectacles. Nonetheless, Barnes, herself, was not beyond fetishizing lurid images, as her comment on Buchenwald suggests. While she identifies with the uncanny, her representation of it consistently retains traces of the male gaze's impulse to conquer it. For Barnes, the desire to fetishize remains constant, notwithstanding its cruel will to overpower forms of difference.

CHAPTER FOUR

Heredity, Transvestism, and the Limits of Self-Fashioning in *Nightwood*

Throughout her oeuvre, Djuna Barnes remained fascinated with the notion that identity is malleable and performative rather than innate and fixed. As she represents characters who could simultaneously occupy the roles of subject and object, she explores their potential for self-transformation. In *Nightwood* (1936), she embodies both positions through her authorial perspective as a female fetishist—a role which defies the Freudian belief that Woman, the castrated Other, is incapable of fetishizing. Particularly in her representation of the transvestite Dr. Matthew O'Connor in *Nightwood*, Barnes also examines the closely related late modernist phenomenon that I term the "freakish *flâneur*." In *Nightwood*, Barnes demonstrates that the freakish *flâneur*'s performativity is linked inextricably with his vision, since his gaze is the basis of his identity formation. While the idea of self-fashioning through performance has gained currency with postmodern gender theorists such as Judith Butler, the late modernist Barnes maintained a kernel of skepticism towards this notion.[1] Especially in *Nightwood*, Barnes demonstrates that heredity continues to exert its force on identity, despite the equally formidable effects of a powerful gaze linked with performance.

In *Nightwood*, Barnes represents a freakish *flâneur* as unable to use his expansive vision to fulfill all of his desires. Barnes calls into question the efficacy of the bi-gendered Tiresian consciousness that Eliot develops in *The Waste Land*, as she demonstrates that this freakish *flâneur*, who aspires to view the world from multiple perspectives, has only limited vision. For Eliot, this blind, bi-gendered seer whom he describes as an "old man" with "wrinkled female breasts"—has access to multiple perspectives.² For Barnes, however, questions remain as to how, exactly, one can attain the transcendent and idealized vision that Eliot develops in *The Waste Land*.³

In developing the Tiresian figure, Dr. Matthew O'Connor, Barnes calls into question what Andreas Huyssen terms the "imaginary male femininity" that has been the basis of several strains of masculine modernist epistemology.⁴ In the process, she suggests that this version of the freakish *flâneur* is too confined within the realm of the symbolic to gain access to the feminine uncanny—a mode of experience which is beyond language. In *Nightwood*, Barnes remains fascinated with identity formation through the gaze and performative self-fashioning, but she also exhibits a countervailing interest in hereditary predestination and the primacy of the inarticulate, uncanny Other. Through her ironic presentation of different spectators, Barnes satirizes the notion of transpersonal vision and delineates the limits of both spectatorship and performance. The ineffable and tantalizing Others in *Nightwood* are immune to the colonizing and commodifying tendencies of reductive rhetoric and the objectifying gaze of the "*flâneur* colonizer."

※ ※ ※

Throughout her career, and especially in her later works, Barnes called into question masculine versions of modernist epistemology, particularly those articulated by T.S. Eliot in *The Waste Land* and advanced by Eliot's mentor F.H. Bradley. As the editor of Barnes's major works *Nightwood* and *The Antiphon* (1958), Eliot exerted considerable influence over her more mature literary style. Nonetheless, Barnes's fascination with Eliot's poetic vision led her to investigate and rework its epistemological assumptions from a feminist perspective When describing *Nightwood* in his editor's preface, Eliot's tone is often apologetic and even condescending. His great difficulty explaining exactly what *Nightwood* is, becomes evident in his frequent explanations of what it is not. Eliot emphasizes that it is "not simply a collection of individual portraits" (xiv); it is "not a psychopathic study' (xv); it is "not a philosophical treatise"; and it is not even "a horrid sideshow of freaks" (xvi).⁵ What *Nightwood* is for Eliot, however, is more acutely disturbing and captivating, as he finds Dr. Matthew O'Connor the work's most important character and rhetorical force (xiii-xiv). *Nightwood's* compelling language aptly represents the musings of this tragic freakish observer figure—a modern Tiresias who performs his own difference as he casts his incisive gaze on others.

Like many of his contemporaries, Eliot prefers a mode of expression that engages in self-reflexivity in order to exaggerate its inherent theatrical qualities.⁶ Similarly, Barnes's O'Connor is a figure whose reflexive and parodic language also displays his aspirations towards self-transformation and transpersonal vision. Through O'Connor's self-reflexive and self-parodic stance, *Nightwood* raises questions about the relation between rhetorical performance and identity. The narrator explains that this obstetrician and Catholic priest cum psychoanalyst frequently engages in self-dramatization because "he consider[s] himself the most amusing predicament" (15). Early in the novel, the narrative voice distinguishes itself from what it seems to regard as O'Connor's vulgar and self-serving performativity. Through his rhetorical and theatrical *tours de force*, O'Connor exerts a force of personality that makes him the center of the European demi-monde. As the narrator retreats itself from O'Connor's charismatic displays of wit, she also satirizes his effeminate manner in an ironic parenthetical aside:

> Once the doctor had his audience—and he got his audience by the simple device of pro-nouncing at the top of his voice (at such moments as irritable and possessive as a maddened woman's) some of the more boggish and bitter of the shorter early Saxon verbs—nothing could stop him (15).

In mocking O'Connor, Barnes's narrator seems to exhibit definite anti-theatrical leanings that parallel the novelist's eventual disavowal of her role as the witty ex-patriot bitch queen.[7] Adrielle Mitchell argues that the narrator often speaks from the place of the crowd's "disembodied voice."[8] When reading *Nightwood*, Mitchell feels as if "groups of people were looking over [her] shoulder, only, oddly, they were able to see more than [she]" (215). By speaking as a representative of the crowd, the narrator seems to identify with the beliefs and the values of the dominant culture. However, in order to criticize the mainstream culture, the Barnesian narrator enters the crowd neither to identify with it, nor to eroticize it, like the Benjaminian *flâneur*, but to mime it. Barnes constructs this narrator as a theatrical presence who ventriloquizes the crowd in order to emphasize the difference between the day world of normative values and the demimonde of the night. This detached narrative voice that sees the marginal night world from the outside may appear to be a formidable alternative to the Tiresian freakish *flâneur*, yet its role is not to replace him, but to delineate his boundaries.

While O'Connor may sound and dress like a "maddened woman," the text raises questions regarding the transformative powers of rhetoric and transvestism. While the Tiresian freakish *flâneur*'s dual masculine and feminine perspective should endow him with preternatural empathy and insight, O'Connor, however, describes himself as "the other woman that God forgot" (143) and feels he should have been born with a "high soprano . . . deep corn curls to [his] bum . . . and "a womb as big as a king's kettle" (91). While O'Connor's transvestism at first seems to challenge the notion of innate sexual identity, his gender ideology is firmly based on essentialist notions. This contradiction mirrors Barnes's own vacillation between biological and rhetorical constructions of the human subject, which she brings into play in most of her works. Meryl Altman explains that during Barnes's time there were few if any alternative discourses to the dominant essentialist ideologies "about race, ethnicity, gender and sexuality."[9] However, Barnes sometimes questions these modes of thinking by rhetorically subverting the idea of essential identity. Ultimately, she draws a distinction between linguistic refutations of biological predetermination and what she regards as the irreducible reality of nature and the body. Mirroring Barnes's ambivalence, Dr. Matthew O'Connor performatively subverts the idea of essential gender, but is not beyond stereotyping various minority groups despite his own marginalized status as a homosexual and a transvestite. For example, O'Connor states with confidence, "All right, Jews meddle and [the Irish] lie, that's the difference, the fine difference" (31). By representing social deviants in Nightwood who try to enact what they aspire to be, Barnes explores the effects of rhetoric and performance on what essentialists regard as inherited identity.

Modern and postmodern artists and literary theorists have consistently questioned the relation between rhetoric and the idea of essential meaning or identity. However, within this larger debate, identity is often construed not only as inherited characteristics, but as transcendental meaning, divine essence, or God. Ronald Schleifer describes "modernism in its symbolist moment" as a "crises of representation" where artists as diverse as Eliot, Conrad, Yeats, and Lawrence represented the inability of language to capture transcendental essence.[10] ("Yeats's Postmodern Rhetoric" 18–19). High modernists lamented the difference between rhetoric and transcendental signifiers, but they still imitated or staged the search for such meaning through the use of rhetorical effects. On the other hand, postmodernists accept language's inability to correspond with divine essence and revel in the theatrical play of signifiers.[11] Nightwood functions more like a postmodern text by representing characters whose self-dramatizing rhetoric often fails to correspond to any genuine self-liberating or transcendental experience. Heredity in Nightwood exists as a powerful idea which several characters try to subvert through rhetoric and performance, but the text never fully undercuts this notion. Instead, heredity and self-fashioning operate in a symbiotic relationship—each derives meaning from the other, thus rendering them co-functional and interdependent. Barnes allows neither to ascend to the status of transcendental signifier of identity, thus rendering each as vexed, uncertain, and indeterminate.

The first chapter of Nightwood presents Felix Von Volkbein, a sycophantic self-hating half-Jew who hankers for an aristocratic lineage and the social status that this would bring him.[12] Through his appropriation of the mannerisms, the garb, and the *objets* of the patrician class, Felix and his father Guido engage in what can be described as an aristocratic drag act.[13] For instance, in his effort to look like one to the manner born, Felix "dressed as if expecting to participate in some great event, though there was no function in the world for which he could be said to be properly garbed" (8). Similarly, Guido Von Volkbein makes an inadvertently comic attempt to appropriate aristocratic symbols by buying portraits of those whom he claims are the progenitors of his lineage. The narrator explains that the gentleman represented in one of these paintings wears garb that is "a baffling mixture of the Romantic and the Religious" (6) and that "The whole conception might have been a Mardi Gras whim" (7).

The sarcastic narrator frequently displays a firm belief in cultural determinism when describing the Jews' marginal position in Europe, and Felix Von Volkbein's internalized anti-Semitism. Early in the narrative, we are told that the melancholic Felix is filled with racial memories of Christian spectators who had made unwilling spectacles of Jews, and that he regards this memory of being a freakish spectacle as "the sum total of what is the Jew . . .—the degradation by which his people had survived" (2). According to this definition of European spectatorship, the Christian *flâneur* colonizer collects, commodifies, and rehabilitates the freakish wandering Jew by endowing his seemingly aimless trajectory with form and meaning:

> It takes a Christian, standing eternally in the Jew's salvation, to blame himself and to bring up from that depth charming and fantastic superstitions through which the slowly and tirelessly milling Jew becomes the "collector" of this own past. His undoing is never profitable until some *goy* has put it back into such shape that it could be offered as a "sign." A Jew's undoing is never his own, it is God's; his rehabilitation is never his own, it is a Christian's (10).

Here, as elsewhere, Barnes's narrator demonstrates an identification with the Christian majority and with unidentifiable crowds that project the gaze of the dominant culture. For instance, while we are told that Felix, who adopts a stance of sychophancy, "bows down" to the Christian populace, members of the majority culture will also "exhibit a slight bend of the head" towards him, perhaps out of feigned deference for his father's aristocratic pretensions (*Nightwood* 8). Meryl Altman takes to task the narrator's use of "us" by asking "Who are 'we'? Does this grudging, ambiguous 'bowing down' on the part of the dominant culture . . . indicate that the novel's stance toward [Felix] and toward Jews generally is a pitying and parodic half-tolerance?" (Altman 161). This semi-circular stare which is "unwilling to greet [Jews] with earthly equality (*Nightwood* 8) may well be the commdifier's act of appraisal. Confronted with signs of the Semitic other who hankers for acceptance, the Christian tries to figure out what they mean in order to capitalize on this difference. The Barnesian narrator mimes the role of the Christian *flâneur* colonizer, not to condone its practices but to demonstrate its omnipresence in Western culture. Both the dominant culture and the demimonde gain meaning by defining each other against each other and in commodifying each other's forms and values. While the former attempts to collect difference and put it on display, the latter parodies and satirizes this impulse.

Barnes's narrator is not alone in miming the perspective of the dominant culture. Dr. Matthew O'Connor, a freakish *flâneur* who humorously indentifies with the Catholic priesthood, often parodies the Christian tendency to appraise and commodify when describing various freaks. O'Connor revels in describing "Nikka the Nigger," a black homosexual bear tamer as a human embodiment of the phallus and the stereotypical wretchedness of the dark continent.[14]

> There he was, crouching all over the arena without a stitch on, except an ill concealed loin cloth all abulge as if with a deep sea catch, tattooed with all the *ameublement* of depravity (16).

As a black male fetish object, Nikka exaggerates his difference by covering his body with tattoos which range from the inscription "Desdemona" to symbols of the Hamburg House of Rothschild and the House of Tudor. Within this representation of European power, Anglo Saxon royalty, and the German Jewish wealth of the Rothschild family are equally as significant—the hereditary elite based on notions of racial superiority is on par with the wealthy Jewish mercantile class that can buy aristocratic titles. Nikka represents a subversive appropriation of power that Felix Von Volkbein would never dream of attaining. As a figure who flaunts his status as an outsider, he lampoons all pretensions to legitimate power and parodically appropriates the white Western phallus in order to deride its overvaluation.

Like the fetishized woman, Nikka simultaneously represents the pre-mirror stage of development and entry into the realm of the symbolic.[15] Jane Marcus locates Barnes's own modernist consciousness in Nikka, a figure who embodies "an aesthetic of the Modernist Grotesque, a delicate and exotic refinement of the gross Rabelaisian realistic grotesque and the romantic intellectual grotesque of E.T.A. Hoffman" (227). However, while Barnes often revels in representing or performing as such transgressive figures who ridicule authority, she also demonstrates the painful limitations of their power. For example, when O'Connor engages in his lurid description of Nikka's difference, he appropriates and commodifies a homosexualized fetish that he, himself, never attempts to embody. As an observer and fetishist of freakish others, and as a transvestite who covets conventional femininity, O'Connor is constantly aware of the distance between what he is and what he aims to be. Unlike the other Dr. Matthew O'Connor in Barnes's earlier work *Ryder* (1928), he is openly homosexual. Yet like his namesake, he adheres to essentialist notions of gender identity, and he also identifies himself as a woman trapped in a man's body (*Nightwood* 143).[16] Kaja Silverman explains that during the late nineteenth century, the German sexologist Karl Heinrich Ulrichs defended the homosexual by defining him as "*anima mulierbris in corpore viri inclusa*"—a female soul enclosed in a male body.[17]

When describing freakish Others in *Nightwood*, O'Connor often suggests that the structure (or rhetoric, so to speak) of one's own body is inescapable.

O'Connor compares Felix Von Volkbein to Mademoiselle Basquette, a woman "damned from the waist up" without legs who longed for love and insisted on viewing herself as whole (26). From O'Connor's point of view, there is at once something missing and whole about Baron Felix and Mademoiselle Basquette because they envision themselves as different from what heredity has made them. This rather conservative vision of social outcasts, which classifies them in terms of lack, can be extended to Nikka, who attempts to appropriate the white Western phallus; to O'Connor, who longs to be a woman but laments his imprisonment within his male body; and even to Barnes, herself, when she performs her drag act when conducting interviews. Within the boundaries of this analysis, which Barnes seems to have accepted, those whose cultural and physical differences disinherit them from the social mainstream can never transform themselves completely into what they want to be, and they remain ghettoized within the demimondaine night world of *Nightwood*. For this reason, I question Jane Marcus's view that *Nightwood* "center[s] the marginal" by strongly "articulating the angst of the abject" ("Laughing at Leviticus" 232). While Barnes makes dominant the sphere of rhetorical and performative transgression, she repeatedly exposes its limitations. Although the characters in *Nightwood* define themselves against the concept of normality, the idea of and yearning for normality is an inescapable part of the binarism that constructs the demimonde. In *Nightwood*, the normal gets relegated to a culturally peripheral space where, like the unconscious, it still exerts force.

Like Judith Butler, Barnes associates transvestism with the transformative powers of rhetoric and performance, yet she does not take this view as far as her successor. In fact, as Barnes is ambivalent towards O'Connor's homosexualized consciousness in *Ryder* and *Nightwood*, she also satirizes female power as embodied in Dame Evangeline Musset, a demagogic and phallogocentric lesbian in *Ladies' Almanack* (1928). Barnes demonstrates that Dame Evangeline is a female fetishist who has lost her proximity to the uncanny, despite her ostensibly freakish, hermaphroditic body. Dame Musset tells her father that although she does not possess the literal "Tools of the Trade," she is as well suited as any man for a position of authority and dominance. In fact, Dame Musset has appropriated the Lacanian phallus through her acerbic wit, yet this appropriation is not limited to wit. She describes her verbal powers in comically phallic terms as "the consolation every Woman has at her Finger Tips, or at the very Hang of her Tongue."[18] After her death and cremation at the age of ninety nine, "all had burned but the Tongue," and her followers kneeled before it in prayer (84). Despite this veneration, Barnes trenchantly satirizes the limits of Musset's phallogocentrism. As Barnes considers the limits of Tiresian bi-gendered vision and phallogocentric language in *Nightwood*, questions remain regarding her own attitudes towards non-heterosexual practices and identities. When she reached old age, she refused to identify herself as a woman who was devoted exclusively to other women. She once remarked, "I am not a lesbian, I just loved Thelma [Wood]" (Michel 53). Comments from different critics and biographers indicate that Barnes's sexuality, which seems to have remained fluid throughout her life, cannot be subjected to the binary logic that categorizes people as either gay or straight.[19] However, for Barnes, the marginal realm that questions gender essentialisms and mainstream values does not replace the dominant culture, but coexists with it. When Barnes demonstrates a preoccupation with dominant medical discourses on sexuality in *Ryder* and *Ladies' Almanack*, she never fully calls them into question. Rather, she defines and tries to figure the place of two specific gender deviants—Dame Evangeline Musset— the woman with a "masculinity complex" and Dr. Matthew O'Connor—the "man trapped in a woman's body." While Barnes does not fully challenge the sexological discourses of her day in *Nightwood,* she tries more rigorously to determine the place of social deviants, particularly in relation to Eliot's modernist aesthetics.

Philip Herring contends that Barnes loathed being ghettoized as a "'lesbian writer' and might have preferred to be known as a 'modernist' in the company of Joyce and Eliot, if she had been familiar with that term" (255). Though she was intimidated by them, she viewed her own talents and sensibility to be strong enough to compete with these male writers. However, her approach to the fathers of high modernism was as critical as it was emulative. By representing O'Connor's role as a decontexualized subject and object, and citing his failure to transform into a woman, Barnes calls into question the epistemological goals of imaginary male femininity. Joyce invests Leopold Bloom with androgynous insight and this bigendered condition is also central to Eliot's version of modernist epistemology. As Brooker and Bentley argue, Eliot's Tiresias functions as a unifying perspective that places different objects within a common context (*Reading the Waste Land* 56–57). In the heterotopic waste land of *Nightwood*, the Tiresian figure Dr. Matthew O'Connor achieves this vision, which nonetheless fails to deliver him from the muck of human desire. While this freakish *flâneur*'s dual identity as observer/spectacle and man/woman provides him with important clues to the nature of desire, it does not enable him to attain everything that he wants or fill his lack. Aware of his limitations, O'Connor parodies the impulse to control and experience by collecting decontexualized objects in a world gone awry.

O'Connor is a collector of sorts who displays diverse objects in his room such as "a rusty pair of forceps, a broken scalpel, half a dozen odd instruments . . . a catheter, some twenty perfume bottles" and various forms of women's underwear (70). Jane Marcus likens O'Connor's strange possessions to a parodic version of "Freud's famous totems, the sacred objects from ancient cultures" (233). The rusty and broken instruments also imply that O'Connor may well be a quack—an imposter to medical knowledge and an untrustworthy or flawed guide to psychoanalytic understanding. O'Connor comes into contact with *flâneur* colonizers who aim to collect and commodify decontexualized objects, the most notable of whom is Nora Flood, an American intellectual who indulges her colonizing impulse by collecting such diverse specimens of humanity as "poets, radicals, beggars, artists and people in love" for her literary salon in New York City (50). A consummate *flâneur*, she attempts to peruse others with detached objectivity: "There was no ignominy about her, she recorded without reproach or accusation, being shorn of self-reproach or accusation" (*Nightwood* 53). The narrator likens Nora's epistemological stance to one that views the world and its history "as if they are 'a ship in a bottle'": she herself was outside and unidentified, endlessly embroiled in a preoccupation without a problem" (53). An observer who "by temperament . . . was an early Christian" and "believed in the word," Nora is firmly grounded in the symbolic. Her penchant for intellectualizing causes her to experience a Cartesian mind/body dualism in which she is more firmly grounded in the former half of this binarism (51). Nora's disembodied consciousness suggests a stereotypical masculine subject who gains epistemological power by defining himself against those who embody sexual or racial difference. However, the narrator pathologizes and challenges this means of empowerment by likening it to "some derangement . . . that kept [Nora] immune from her own descent" (51).

Nora Flood's pretensions to objectivity are compromised when she becomes enamored with Robin Vote, a demimondaine, whose strange hybridity of animality and other worldliness brings together an unusual and tantalizing vision of the sacred and the profane. A lesbian and possibly an hysteric, Vote is a psychosexual freak, according to medical and psychoanalytic discourses of the late nineteenth and early twentieth centuries. In the chapter titled "La Sonambule," Vote encounters the novel's other notable psychosexual freak, O'Connor, who revives her after she falls unconscious in a hotel room. Before Felix Von Volkbein, who functions as an audience of one, O'Connor performs not only as a physician, but as a magician and carny talker who introduces his spectator to Robin's seductive deviance (36). O'Connor theatricalizes his ministrations, exaggerating his ceremonial role as magician and Robin's position as passive deviant Other. However, the narrator ironically identifies O'Connor's flamboyant gestures as sham, thus divesting him of authority and making his own perversity complement his patient's. As the embodiment of a pre-mirror stage mode of consciousness, Robin Vote represents the uncanny—the sphere of nonidentity that provokes both fear and curiosity in those who have entered the symbolic. While Robin resists language, O'Connor is word-drunk and uses his considerable verbal acuity to make sense of his experience. When O'Connor laments that he was not born a woman, he says "The wise men say that the remembrance of things past is all that we have for a future, and am I to blame if I've turned up this time as I shouldn't have been, when it was a high soprano I wanted . . . I've given my destiny away by garrulity, like ninety percent of everybody else—for, no matter what I may be doing, in my heart is the wish for children and knitting" (91).

Analyzing this passage, Judith Lee explains that O'Connor wallows in language in order to obliterate his unconscious memory of his true identity as a woman: "Matthew's speech is a way of suppressing his feminine nature and the desire it represents, just as Robin's silence is a way of rejecting the experience of her own difference."[20] Actually, O'Connor does not so much suppress his feminine nature as much as he dwells on his inability to fulfill his feminine desires. While he tries to satisfy his fractured desire for womanhood by describing this longing, this linguistic substitute is inadequate.

Both the narrator and Dr. O'Connor display contempt for Jenny Petherbridge, whom they characterize as the most egregious colonizer in *Nightwood*. A wealthy middle aged widow, Petherbridge tries to transcend the boundaries of her own ego by appropriating other people's lives: "She defiled the meaning of personality in her passion to be a person" (67). For instance, she adopts a fashionable lesbianism by taking over Nora's role as Robin's lover. The narrator identifies Jenny as a "squatter"—one who takes possession of property without legal claim (68).[21] Although he is a collector himself, Dr. O'Connor disdains Jenny's appropriative sensibility that transforms everything she touches into kitsch:

> And Jenny, what of her now? Taken to drink and appropriating Robin's mind with vulgar inaccuracy, like those eighty-two plaster virgins she bought because Robin had one good one; when you laugh at the eighty- two standing in a row, Jenny runs to the wall, back to the picture of her mother, and stands between the two tortures—the past that she can't share, and the present that she can't copy (124).

While both Jenny and O'Connor display an appropriative impulse, Barnes displays a clear preference for the latter, whose desire to collect is based on a need to intellectualize. For Jenny Petherbridge, who is the worst kind of *flâneur* colonizer, the replication of cheap plastic objects replaces the quest to make sense of meaningful signs. This sensibility, which Walter Benjamin criticized in *The Work of Art in the Age of Mechanical Reproduction*, is the appropriative impulse of consumer culture. Jane Marcus views Jenny as a metaphor for faulty intellectual appropriation, but adds that Barnes's undisguised contempt for her presents a mirror to "the voyeuristic reader or literary critic" (252). However, Jenny lacks the intellectual discernment or even the pretensions of a truly dangerous reader who would take more liberties to impose meanings. We find the sensibility of a more intellectualizing and threatening *flâneur* colonizer in Dr. Matthew O'Connor—a consummate ironist and satirist who parodies the collecting habit rather than placing blind faith in its role as a maker of value.

O'Connor parodies the Western impulse to know and to collect as much as possible, but unlike Jenny, he is aware that his penchant for appropriation is limited. O'Connor learns and eventually teaches Nora Flood that knowledge gained through observation is not equivalent with the kind of possession that she desires. When responding to Nora's desire to learn as much as possible about the "night" or the unconscious, he tells us that the night world or "town of Darkness" is dangerous because it submerges individual consciousness (81) and may cause people to commit strange acts (89). He pontificates that some cultures, most notably the French, have a greater affinity for the decadent and untidy realities of the unconscious. He also holds that Americans (like Nora and himself) tend to be "an excessively clean race," incapable of finding the "road" to the more lascivious parts of the mind (84). As a lapsed Catholic, O'Connor also associates a predisposition for unconscious experience with monastic Catholics and Indian gurus, both of whom valorize "Great Enigmas" or paradoxes (83–84). It is telling that in *Nightwood's* final scene, Nora is united with Robin in a Catholic church where the latter, who gets down on her hands and knees and barks like a dog, becomes one with the instinctual life of an animal. Thus, Barnes unites the unconscious aspirations of transcendent Catholicism with a psychosexually freakish madwoman who identifies with beasts. Attuned primarily to the pre-linguistic depths of her own unconscious, Robin demonstrates that this extreme narcissism predisposes her to knowledge of the uncanny. In the novel's closing scene, Barnes satirizes the principle of the uncanny by demonstrating that it pervades the "high" sphere of religious feeling, as well as the more elemental impulses related to sexuality and fear.

When reflecting on his role as an historian of consciousness and an excavator of minds, O'Connor tells Nora, "There is no truth, and you have it set between you; you have been unwise enough to make a formula; you have dressed the unknowable in garments of the known" (136). Calling into question his own phallogocentrism, as well as Nora's, O'Connor suggests that the unknown can never be known, and that the garments of language are mere coverings rather than substitutes for identity or experience.[22] Commenting directly on Nora's intellectualism and her affinity for "the word," he suggests that language is not a substitute for what we encounter through instinct and the unconscious. This may well be an allusion to his own unconventional sexuality, since when O'Connor performs as a transvestite, he transforms his desire to be a woman into "the garments of the known." By relegating rhetoric and transvestism to shadow plays of real experience, O'Connor divests both of their potential to subvert dominant values and renders them mute and inert. O'Connor's views about language parallel Paul De Man's argument that rhetoric merely mimes thought and experience: "To the extent that language is a figure (or metaphor, prosopopeia) it is indeed not the thing itself but the representation, the picture of the thing, and as such, it is silent, mute as pictures are mute."[23] Yet De Man further defines the inherently "privative" and "mute" nature of language as inherently lubricious and prone to deformation: "Death is a displaced name for a linguistic predicament, and the restoration of mortality by autobiography (the prosopopeia of the voice and the name) deprives and disfigures to the precise extent that it restores" (80–81). By this definition, language is inherently freakish and mutable since its forms and meanings are prone to what De Man terms "defacement."[24]

De Man devotes his article on "defacement" most specifically to the deformations characteristic of autobiography and defines this genre as a performance which fails "[to reveal the author's] reliable self-knowledge . . . but . . . demonstrates in a striking way the impossibility of closure and totalization . . . of all textual systems made of tropological substitutions" (71). By extension, just as language is inherently unstable, so is the self. Equally suspicious of autobiographical impulses, T.S. Eliot argues in "Tradition and the Individual Talent" that artists must strive to transcend their personal idiosyncrasies in order to articulate universal truths. While Eliot praises *Nightwood* for its resemblance to what he constructs as the impersonal universality of Shakespearian drama, he fails to realize that this work is an autobiographical novel in which Barnes represents her passion for Thelma Wood, a doomed alcoholic artist.[25] Given her autobiographical inclinations, Barnes challenges Eliot's modernist creed of authorial invisibility by showing that the performing and desiring self is unavoidable. For Eliot, art should be an "escape" from personality and desire, and in Tiresias he creates a performative speaker whose transcendent vision precludes him from being a desiring subject.[26] While the Benjaminian and Baudelairean *flâneur* gains this vision through his desire to identify with his subjects, the removed Tiresias merely transcends his desires through his androgyny. Barnes reintroduces desire to the Tiresian figure by showing that despite Matthew O'Connor's heightened vision, he tends to project and enact his desiring self constantly.

Nora Flood is powerfully drawn to O'Connor's transvestism, which she associates with heightened vision and psychoanalytic acumen. When she visits him in his flat on one occasion at three in the morning, he greets her in dingy drag wearing heavy make-up and a wig of long blond curls. Viewing the strangely attired O'Connor, Nora thinks, "God, children know something they can't tell; they are like Red Riding Hood and the wolf in bed!" (79). Responding to this line, Bruno Bettelheim states that Barnes represents "the child's unconscious equation of sexual excitement, violence, and anxiety" on viewing the primal scene (from *The Uses of Enchantment*, quoted in Garber 385). Marjorie Garber revises Bettelheim's argument by suggesting that the child displays simultaneous disgust and fascination not with the "primal scene . . . of parental coitus," but with the transvestite's ambivalent gender and sexuality (386). Before she visits O'Connor, Nora does, in fact, exhibit a desire to be a female transvestite when she dreams that she is her grandmother in drag. Envisioning a symbol of her heredity, Nora first imagines her grandmother's room in her ancestral home which "was as bereft as the nest of a bird which will not return" (*Nightwood* 62). Actually, the grandmother's room, which appears both to be this woman's chamber and the "absolute opposite of any known room [she] had moved or lived in" evokes in Nora a sense of the uncanny (63). Seeking this unfamiliarity, Nora fantasizes that she can transcend the culture into which she was born. As Nora disfigures her ancestral home by rendering it uncanny, she also defaces her grandmother by transforming her into a woman in drag. This grandmother who wears "a billycock and a corked moustache, ridiculous and plump in tight trousers and a red waistcoat," wears the garb of a circus ringleader or a carny talker (63). Realizing that she is projecting herself into this transvestite grandmother who bellows "My little sweetheart!," she imagines that this entity acts upon Robin and "disfigure[s] her" (63).

Jane Marcus notes that Nora, who imagines her grandmother's "plume and . . . inkwell, wants to "appropriate [this woman's] profession of writing" (246). Yet this female fetishist, who has taken the role of *flâneur* colonizer, can only deform what she possesses erotically and recreates through language. Marcus believes that as Nora envisions herself as a ring leader, the narrator also takes on this role of "master of ceremonies" and Barnes, herself [writes] the novel" and an "eight ring circus" (246). While Barnes represents multiple spectators and spectacles in *Nightwood*, she also emphasizes that subjects fail to capture objects wholly and always impose their own forms of disfiguration on them. Commenting on her painful inability to capture Robin and her imprisonment within her own desires, Nora tells O'Connor, "I thought I loved her for her sake, and I found it was for my own" (*Nightwood* 151). With characteristic crudeness, O'Connor ridicules Nora's fantasy of possessing Robin: "I know . . . there you were sitting high and fine with a rose-bush up your arse" (151). Yet when Nora asks him how he should know this, he explains his own painful awareness with her and shows an awareness of the limits of erotic and intellectual appropriation: "I'm a lady in no need of insults . . . I know" (151). Unlike Eliot, who believes that Tiresias can possess objects of his gaze through his transcendent vision, Barnes emphasizes that this form of appropriation is unattainable. However, like Heisenberg and other modernist intellectuals, Barnes brings to light the subject's inability to remove itself from its object of perception. Thus authentic possession—either as understanding or identification—is an illusion.

For Barnes, the subject merely asserts its consciousness by disfiguring or remaking the object of the gaze through acts of perception and artistic representation. But, as De Man asserts, disfiguration is a property of all language, and even the autobiographical subject who claims to represent himself or herself is not immune to linguistic defacement. Among Barnes's characters, only Robin Vote evades this property of language by refusing to enter the symbolic. Remaining within the pre-mirror stage of development, she is a decontextualized object who tantalizes the appropriative gaze as she resists it. The narrator describes Robin Vote as a dangerous spectacle because of her associations with the unconscious and the return of the repressed as "an infected carrier of the past" (37). Felix Von Volkbein is attracted to this uncanny catalyst of repressed desire, despite an internalized anti-Semitism, that makes him "racially incapable of abandon" (38). Instead, he regards Robin as "a figurehead in a museum" which while "static" seemed oddly in motion (38). Felix associates Robin's perpetual motion with the state of malleable consciousness characteristic of American self-fashioning. When O'Connor asks whether he will ever marry, Felix responds that he would choose "the American" because "with an American anything can be done" (39). However, Felix's prime reason for wanting to marry is the opportunity to produce an heir—"a son who would feel as he felt about the 'great past'"(38). O'Connor ridicules Felix's desire for aristocracy and proclaims that The last muscle of aristocracy is madness—remember that . . . the last child born to aristocracy is sometimes an idiot, out of respect—we group—but we come down" (40). Ironically, despite Felix's wish for social respectability, he chooses the least likely marriage partner in trying to fulfill this desire. As a figure of the demimonde, himself, who must be satisfied with parodying the upper classes, Felix chooses the quintessential representation of the grotesque.

As a psychosexual freak and lesbian other, Robin Vote enters a heterosexual bond with Felix only to reject him. After her son Guido is born, she abandons both him and Felix and takes to wandering the streets, occasionally stopping in bars and cafes. Whereas the conventionally masculinized consciousness seeks diverse identities, the undifferentiated female psychosexual freak exists perpetually in an ineffable, uncanny state outside of language and beyond intersubjective connections. Robin's aimless trajectory through the streets of Paris inverts the stereotypically masculine impulse towards totalizing knowledge through observation and changing identifications by walking in a disoriented state: "If she was diverted, as was sometimes the case, by the interposition of a company of soldiers, a wedding or a funeral, then by her agitation she seemed a part of the function of the persons she stumbled against, . . ." (60).

Through her representation of the uncanny Robin, Barnes articulates a feminine and lesbian vision of knowledge and power that poses a challenge both to the dominant male heterosexual and homosexual epistemologies of modernism. However, Barnes poses this challenge not so much through a complete identification with this character's uncanniness, but through a presentation that is both sympathetic and ironic. Barnes, who identifies both with the ineffable Robin and the intellectual Nora, takes the position of the female fetishist who can occupy both masculine and feminine subject positions. Moreover, in her effort to demonstrate the limitations of the male gaze, she shows that the uncanny feminine Other stubbornly resists commodification.

Despite Robin's defiance of other's gazes, she may, as O'Connor suggests, be imprisoned within her own narcissism, like the Coney Island freak who performed before a mirror as a spectacle for himself and others:

> Robin was outside the "human type"—a wild thing caught in a woman's skin, monstrously alone, monstrously vain; like the paralysed man in Coney Island (take away a man's conformity and you take away his remedy) who had to lie on his back in a box, but the box was lined with velvet, his fingers jeweled with stones, and suspended over him where he could never take his eyes off, a sky—blue mirror; for he wanted to enjoy his own "difference" (146).

Like the paralyzed man who revels in his own reflection, Robin Vote approaches the mirror stage only to delight narcissistically in her difference. Nineteenth and early twentieth century sexologists and psychoanalysts often defined homosexuality in terms of narcissism, and Barnes seems to be drawing from this definition as she characterizes Robin's solipsism. Yet for O'Connor, "inverts" are not completely self-contained within their own narcissism because their difference seduces the prurient gaze of those who objectify them as if they are dolls:

> The doll and the immature have something right about them, the doll because it resembles but does not contain life, and the third sex because it contains life but resembles the doll (148).

Unlike the doll-like, paralyzed freak, Robin resists the very appropriative gaze that she seduces by wandering away from her *flâneur* colonizers. Her defiance of the repressive masculine gaze linked with rational knowledge is also evident when she casts down a doll that Nora had given her. Dolls represent the transformation of women into objects, and Robin violently repudiates this objectification.[27] However, by refusing to enter the symbolic order in her solipsistic wanderings, Robin resists appropriation and revels in embodying the feminine uncanny as a decontextualized object.

If Barnes links lesbian consciousness with the seductive feminine uncanny character Robin Vote, the source of Robin's uncanniness remains ambivalent. Indeed, there are conflicting hints that it may be due to both nature or self-deformation. On the one hand, the narrator essentializes Robin's difference by describing her as a "born somnambule, who lives in two worlds—meet of child and desperado" (35) and "a tall girl with the body of a boy" (46). Yet the text also makes clear that Robin's oddness is also called by alcoholism. She "curse[s] loudly" when drunk and her wanderings are often precipitated by bouts of drinking (48–49).[28] Also, O'Connor suggests that Robin's deviance may be due to self-fashioning when he tells Felix that if she finds no one to give her moral focus "she will *make* [emphasis mine] an innocence for herself; a fearful sort of primitive innocence" (118). Further emphasizing her willful deviance, he states, "One's life is peculiarly one's own when one has invented it" (118). At various points, such as these, O'Connor vacillates between essentialist and constructivist views of identity—an inconsistency that is also characteristic of Barnes throughout her career.

Regardless of whether Robin is a born or a made freak, the child that she produces displays what O'Connor describes as hereditary deviance that makes him a natural freakish aristocrat (121). A physically stunted child who represents the last line of the pseudo-aristocratic Von-Volkbein clan, Guido is "emotionally excessive" and "an addict to death" (107).[29] O'Connor tells Felix that Guido dwells in unconscious experience and that this simultaneously draws and repels spectators: "In the average person it is the peculiar that has been scuttled, and in the peculiar the ordinary has been sunk; people always fear what requires watching" (120). Despite the text's occasional ambivalence towards essentializing heredity, *Nightwood* ultimately makes a strong case for this view. While Guido's mother may to some extent choose to defy normality, Guido has no choice but to dwell in his uncanny pre-verbal state that seduces those who wish to re-experience the pre-mirror stage. *Nightwood* rigorously demonstrates that the disfigurations of rhetoric and self-fashioning fail to counteract completely the effects of heredity and cultural inheritance. Just as the freakish *flâneur* O'Connor cannot achieve womanhood through transvestism, Felix remains tied to his Jewish identity despite his attempts to escape it. However, in *Nightwood*, heredity refers not only to ancestral lineage, but to the development of mature consciousness from earlier modes of experience. For Barnes, we all carry this form of heredity, but it is more dominant in some than in others. In psychosexual freaks such as Robin and Guido, uncanniness remains resistant to the masculine gaze and challenges this voyeuristic impulse.

CHAPTER FIVE

Horror, Melodrama, and Mutable Masculine Identity in Tod Browning's Films

> Longing to discover why Hollywood attracts and rewards so many "little monsters," [Frankie Jordan is] compelled to confront how Jews feel about themselves in a town that both loves and hates its own invention—the beautiful WASP.[1]

Dori Carter's wittily titled recent novel *Beautiful WASPS Having Sex* (2000), considers the plight of Frankie Jordan (nee Francine Fingerman), a Jewish-American screenwriter who fails to gain the approval of Hollywood producers who consistently view her work as "too Jewish" and uncommercial despite (or because of) the fact that they, too, are from this ethnic background. Instead, they prefer to represent American experience in terms of an idealized and sanitized suburbia populated by blandly blond and conventionally beautiful white Anglo Saxon Protestants. Herself a Jew, Dori Carter suggests throughout her novel that Hollywood's Jewish film moguls perpetuate Jewish self-hatred by manufacturing the image of idealized WASPishness.

The dominance of Jews in the contemporary and early Hollywood film industry is a widely established fact.[2] Louis B. Mayer, the most powerful Hollywood producer, consistently reinforced an idealized but rigidly conservative vision of American culture. Characterized by an emphasis on the middle class decency and physical beauty of his characters, Mayer's conservative cinematic vision scorned overtly sexual themes and images. Nonetheless, given the exigencies of the film industry, Mayer often begrudgingly allowed the production of films he found morally problematic such as *The Temptress* (1925 and *Flesh and the Devil* (1925), vehicles for Greta Garbo where the actress portrayed brazen *femme fatales*.[3] More characteristically, Mayer prided himself on producing films that promoted lofty moral content as they celebrated an ultra white and northern

European ideal of beauty. In this sense, Mayer's tendency to equate physical perfection with moral uprightness resembled fascist aesthetics.[4] Relentless in his quest to make his actresses conform to the dominant cultural ideal, he subjected them to an intense process of beautification that often created their legendary blonde beauty. Quoting Julie Burchill, bell hooks calls into question Hollywood's tendency to exaggerate the whiteness of its female stars:

> With characteristic wit [Burchill] asserts: "What does it say about racial purity that the best blondes have all been brunettes (Harlowe, Monroe, Bardot?) I think it says that we are not as white as we think." Burchill could easily have said, "we are not as white as we want to be, . . ."[5]

Burchill and hooks expose the "best blondes" of mainstream cinema as creatures created by the film industry, rather than by genes and chromosomes. If, as hooks suggests, "we are not as white as we want to be," the glorification of white women may well be an idealized projection of Caucasian characteristics—a racist fantasy in which the signifiers of white identity are exaggerated by theatrical lighting, hair dye, and make-up.

At the same time, Mayer was obsessed with discovering and cultivating what he regarded as "natural" beauty, and was particularly unforgiving towards female performers who failed to live up to this ideal. In a legendary comment that he made to the young Judy Garland regarding her slight scoliosis or spinal curvature, he said, "How is my little hunchback this morning?"[6] In this blunt remark, which a biographer of Garland deems "affectionate" but "heartless," Mayer constructs the singer according to a freakish image. While the Hollywood star making system claimed that it could create beauties, it also drew the line between those who had *it* and those who did not. While Mayer clearly deemed Garland a lost cause in this department, he and other film moguls rigorously sought those whose facial and body types fit dominant notions of "natural" beauty.

Mayer's biographer Charles Higham refers frequently to the director's piercing gaze which had become especially penetrating by the time he reached the middle of his life (273). Mayer's gaze, which he used to appropriate and construct spectacles of female beauty and an idealized vision of America is that of the colonizing *flâneur*. Neil Gabler describes the moguls of the early film industry as the creators of "powerful images" who "colonized the American imagination" (7). In his effort to appropriate and colonize American tastes and values for his own self-aggrandizement, Mayer, in effect, behaved also like the Benjaminian *flâneur* when he aimed "to make the world his family." Mayer's intense desire to make the world his own was born of a painful awareness that he was not accepted by the Americans with the most money and power. His stultifyingly bourgeois tastes resulted from his strenuous efforts to gain the respect of the Anglo-Saxon Protestant establishment. Citing Isaiah Berlin,

Neil Gabler explains that, despite the establishment's demonization of Jewish film moguls, "the Jews in the movie industry had 'an over-intense admiration or even worship' for the majority" (Gabler 2). America in the 1920's was characterized by an important cultural divide. On the one hand, there were the white Anglo Saxon Protestant traditionalists who were clinging to their strenuous moral values of family life, hard work and economic mobility. On the other hand, European immigrants, African Americans, and other individuals outside of the cultural and economic mainstream posed a definite challenge to the dominant sanctimonious and snobbish attitudes (Gabler 43). In his effort to gain upper class respectability, Mayer mimicked the tastes and habits of the wealthy in ways that recall the fatuous excess and pathetic sycophancy of Barnes's Felix Von Volkbein. Yet despite his awareness that the WASPS judged him as a pretentious arriviste, Mayer viewed himself as "the pretender who would become the legend" (Gabler 218).

Mayer's bravado regarding his pursuit of economic and social power stood as a challenge to the establishment. In fact, his Hollywood can be viewed as a heterotopia that brought into play an immigrant's economic and social ambition with genteel Anglo-American values. However, Mayer's vision, which served mainly to reorder class expectations, did not extend to his political, social and artistic vision, which some of his employees felt did not go far enough. Tod Browning, a director of horror flicks in the 1920's and 1930's, inverted and subverted Mayer's fascination with extreme beauty and bourgeois morality. His iconoclastic films posed a roguish challenge to America's pristine white Protestant identity by glamorizing racial others, transvestites, circus freaks, and con men. Browning called into question the values of the bourgeois mainstream by using a mainstream medium. While racial difference and freakish bodies are dominant themes in Browning's best known films *Dracula* (1931) and *Freaks* (1932), deception is the overriding concern of most of his works. In his representation of confidence men with a penchant for self-transformation, Browning dramatizes a trickster impulse dominant in American culture, as well as in his own psychology. While the trickster may perform as a con artist, he cannot be reduced to a knave who dupes others only for the fun of it. Anthropologists have defined the trickster as a symbol of ambivalence who performs important cultural work by mediating opposites such as nature/culture, animal/human, and sacred/profane (*On Longing* 106). Susan Stewart explains that by inverting conventions, the trickster functions as "a spirit of creativity, a refuser of rigid systems, and thus is both credited with founding culture and accused of violating the norms of a culture" (*On Longing* 106). A dualistic figure, the trickster embraces paradox and shuns monovocal productions of meaning. Cultural anthropologists William J. Hynes and William G. Doty argue that by crossing forbidden boundaries, "the trickster seems to dwell in no single place but to be in continual transit through all realms marginal and liminal."[7] Given the trickster's malleable identity, he, like the freakish *flâneur* and the female fetishist, can identify simultaneously with subject and object, male and female, carny talker and freak.

Trickster imagery abounds in discourses about Jewish moguls of early cinema who were less class conscious than Mayer. For instance, the producer Carl Laemmle named his studio "Independent Motion Pictures Company of America," which went according to the acronym "IMP"—a distinct trickster image (Gabler 63). Producer Jack Warner, who was far less interested in assimilation and social status than Mayer, was described by one writer as a "fast talking Broadway type, who's got a flippant manner, thinks of himself as a witty man, and has pretty bad taste in the stories he tells" (Gabler 120). In fact, Warner's son referred to him as a "street Arab"—an orientalizing image than carries the implication of a fast talking charlatan or trickster. In a similar vein, Jack's older brother Sam had worked as a carny talker in the Mid-West before putting his salesmanship to task in the film industry (Gabler 125). The Jews of the early film industry used their trickster impulses and their desire for wealth and upward mobility to forge identities as *flâneur* colonizers.

※ ※ ※

In Tod Browning, the film industry encountered a different kind of trickster, one who not only challenged the preoccupation with beauty and bourgeois values characteristic of Mayer, but who aimed to mediate the seemingly antithetical cinematic genres of melodrama and horror. In fact, Browning was not the first artist who attempted to merge horror with melodrama; far from mutually exclusive, horror and melodrama frequently complement one another in eighteenth and nineteenth century novels from *Clarissa* to *Jane Eyre*. While gothicism is concerned primarily with the representation of supernatural evil that threatens a stable moral order, melodrama describes the psychic turmoil of those who either fail to fit the dominant social structure, or who fear a loss of status within it. Browning's gothic melodramas are defined by the morally ambivalent outsider who cannot decide whether to preserve dominant values or destroy them through some dark power. In his own time, few film reviewers and movie goers appreciated the ambivalences inherent in Browning's most provocative works, and most viewed him as a purveyor of prurience. John McCarty defends this longstanding view by arguing that Browning's work lacks the depth that contemporary critics attribute to it. For McCarty, Browning is "a pioneer in the craft of exploitation filmmaking, whose artistic credo rang with the call of his step-right-up carny man career."[8] While Browning the carny talker certainly enjoyed gaining the confidence of his audience, a detailed analysis of his work reveals that there is more to Browning than a simple desire to seduce and titillate these spectators with a cinematic freak show.

Contemporary critical commentary on Browning has focused almost exclusively on the gothic elements of his work. Joanne Berning Hawkins argues that

Browning's cinematic style bears a striking resemblance to films of the early European avant-garde, which challenged the bourgeois values of narrative cinema.[9] Citing Mattei Calinescu, Hawkins explains that most avant-garde artists attempt to wreck nihilistic havoc on dominant artistic conventions and that this "destructive aspect of the avant-garde links it to horror" (12). By representing evil and doomed characters who reject conventional morality, horror films encode a nihilism that threatens bourgeois pieties. While early twentieth century America was becoming increasingly dominated by a middle class sensibility that valued homogeneity and domestic comfort, the atrocities of World War I threatened this acquisitive bliss. Cultural historians have noted that surrealism developed as a response to the hideous deformities and permanent injuries that resulted from the first mass conflict (*The Monster Show* 48). Fascinated by the new cultural dichotomy characterized by danger and comfort, the surrealists began to question other boundaries between normality and deviance, and between high and low culture (*Horror Cinema and the Avant-Garde* 29). Attempting to mediate these distinct spheres, surrealist poets and directors enacted a tricksterish impulse that refused to accept cultural boundaries.

Like the literary and cinematic surrealists, Browning attempted to make sense of the dichotomy between danger and comfort that emerged in America and Europe after the First World War. Yet unlike his surrealist counterparts Breton and Bunuel, whose rejection of conventional logic and normal consciousness signaled a trenchant anti-bourgeois stance, Browning was firmly entrenched in the bourgeois genre of cinematic melodrama that both fascinated and repelled him. By the early 1930's, most films released by Hollywood studios were categorized as melodramas. In this vein, MGM defined *Dracula* as a "Horror Melodrama" and *Freaks* as a "Circus/Horror Melodrama."[10] Robert Lang defines the cinematic melodrama as a genre that "represents a struggle against, or within, the partriarchy."[11] He adds that what seeks release and definition is a repressed identity" (Lang 4). Family melodramas, in particular, dramatize problems that arise in the construction of bourgeois identity, such as a man's "failure to be masculine," and a woman's inability "to accept the subjectivity denying terms of patriarchal femininity" (Lang 8). Most of Browning's films that I discuss in this chapter inscribe Freudian dramas that materialize as family melodramas, even when conventional families are not evident. Lang notes that while melodramas encourage the male and female spectator to realize that others may feel trapped within bourgeois patriarchal culture, the genre fails to pose adequate alternatives (45). While melodramas incite a desire for liberation, they ultimately promote the conservative social vision that most early movie moguls cherished: the struggling character's conversion to the dominant culture's gender norms and class values.

In his introduction to Paul Radin's important study of the trickster, Stanley Diamond discusses this archetype in relation to ancient narratives that have strong melodramatic elements.[12] Diamond explains that in a 1927 study titled

Primitive Man as Philosopher, Radin explores the cross cultural problems of injustice and ambiguity in an ancient African myth and in the Book of Job. The former, which represents an old woman who laments her failure to achieve her desires, demonstrates "[her refusal] to accept the relationship between good and evil, and their expression in human ambiguity" (*The Trickster* xii). Similarly, the Book of Job represents a man who fails to make sense of his pointless suffering, and in so doing suggests that God is a tricksterish "principle of ambivalence" rather than the embodiment of justice (xii). However, the Book of Job fails to question the acts of an ambivalent and unjust God, and is therefore "fully in accord with the status quo" (xvi). Like the bourgeois melodrama, the Book of Job represents victims who remain trapped within conservative social structures, despite their desire for change. Lang explains that as an offshoot of tragic vision, melodrama emerged as a dominant form during the French Revolution, when the idea of God began to erode (14). As Peter Brooks makes clear, "The melodramatic imagination is profoundly moral; the melodrama does not simply stage a battle between good and evil (with good triumphing), but rather tries to establish that clear notions of good and evil prevail, that there are moral imperatives" (Lang 14). While a sense of moral ambiguity began to replace the notion of God, the patriarchal order in melodramas began to assume the role of moral arbiter. In this respect, melodrama emerges as an historically specific genre, but the melodramatic impulse, as the ancient African tale and the Book of Job suggest, predates the modern era.

As I will argue, Tod Browning conflates melodrama and horror in order to explore the trickster's potential to subvert the dominant order. However, Browning's impulse towards subversion is tempered by an understanding of conservative social forces and an ambivalent desire to preserve them. Like the classic trickster, Browning attempts to merge conflicting values. When exploring the relationship between melodrama and horror, Browning analyzes the ambivalences in the modern world, such as the co-existence of danger and bourgeois comfort, as well as the failure of the American dream. Critics have so frequently pigeonholed Browning as the "bad boy" of early cinema that any attempt to present him as a melodramatist must proceed with caution. In his early and later works, Browning never completely abandons melodramatic themes and moralizing messages; however, he poignantly devises more ingenious methods of calling them into question, without dismissing them entirely.

Tod Browning's enactment of tricksterism through his fusion of horror and melodrama was made possible by his liaison with Irving Thalberg, a young producer at MGM who displayed a genius for balancing revolutionary and conservative forces. A protégé of Louis B. Mayer, Thalberg had become the vice president and production assistant for Metro Goldwyn Mayer by the age of twenty three. As the son of German Jewish immigrants, Thalberg belonged to the dominant ethnic group that created the American film industry. Yet unlike his mentor Mayer, who rarely strayed from his bourgeois tastes and moralistic values, Thalberg occasionally lent his support to offbeat projects that presented greater financial risks. For example, despite Mayer's condemnation of *Freaks* before it went into production, Thalberg insisted that the film be made, perhaps aware that the older man's excessive caution could lead to the constant production of dull, homogeneous films (*Dark Carnival* 173). Thalberg, however, was no avant-gardist; he never abandoned catering to popular taste, and consistently produced works that conform to the conventions of bourgeois melodrama—the most marketable film genre. According to one biographer, Thalberg's films were "marred by synthetic, tacked on happy endings because he believed that Americans were by nature optimistic, . . . but in other instances, he defied public response."[13]

While Thalberg, like Mayer, colonized the American mainstream through his production of bourgeois melodramas, his association with Tod Browning's horror, crime and orientalist fantasy films also demonstrates leanings towards freakish *flâneurism*. Besides his role as one of many powerful Jewish *flâneur* colonizers, whom the WASP mainstream regarded as freaks, Thalberg was physically disabled due to a congenital heart condition. Because of his limitations, his "physique [remained] painfully undeveloped, almost stunted for life" (*Dark Carnival* 56). His biographer Roland Flamini explains that Thalberg "may have come to think of himself as something of a freak" (quoted in *Dark Carnival* 89). Thalberg's "freakishness," however, resulted not only from his physical limitations, but from his reputation as an intellectual genius and a "boy wonder." Thalberg's contemporaries in the film industry revered not only his business acumen, but what they regarded as his cultural sophistication. Yet while Thalberg enjoyed literature and associated with novelists and screen writers, he was not the arbiter of taste that others assumed him to be (Gabler 226). However, this image, which combines Jewishness, an affinity for high culture, physical disability, and a predisposition to gaze at the masses has all the attributes of the freakish *flâneur*.

In their collaborations, Browning and Thalberg present performances of racial, cultural, and bodily difference that explore the experience of social deviance, while operating within the familiar context of bourgeois melodrama. Affixing their gaze to the dominant culture, Browning and Thalberg construct mainstream American spectators as middle class subjects who expect to see their values mirrored in conventional moralizing melodramas, only to be shocked when their expectations are not fulfilled. Maintaining an identification with both mainstream and counter cultural values, Browning and Thalberg produced films that dramatize their own freakish *flâneurish* and tricksterish impulses. Through their unification of opposing roles and cultural attitudes they promote a narrative vision that, like West's and Barnes's, defies rigid, totalizing perspectives. Central to Browning and Thalberg's melodramas is a concern with failed masculinity within a popular culture that, since the mid nineteenth century, had become increasingly dominated by a domestic feminine sensibility operating within a patriarchal order.

❦ ❦ ❦

Robert Lang explains that in the melodramas of D.W. Griffith, "we are given a window on that moment in American culture where, in Ann Douglas' words, 'America lost its male dominated theological tradition without gaining a comprehensive feminism or an adequately modernized religious sensibility'" (63). In *The Feminization of American Culture*, Douglas demonstrates that during the mid-nineteenth century in America, motherhood became an important cultural ideal and the middle class mother began to gain an unprecedented amount of power in the home.[14] As masculine authority began to lose ground as the guiding superego of the American family, a feminized morality became a dominant force not only in the domestic sphere, but in the political realm.[15] Paradoxically, patriarchy constructed and ordained this politicized cult of motherhood, pretending to surrender moral and cultural power.[16]

Before Louis B. Mayer condemned *Freaks* and eventually disowned this project, Tod Browning had directed earlier horror films that dramatize failed masculinity and mutable masculine identity. In *The Unholy Three* (1925), he satirizes the new moral dominance of women in America by presenting a felonious male character who masquerades as a benign old woman named Mrs. O'Grady.[17] But while the tricksterish thieves in *The Unholy Three* seem to subvert the values of feminized melodrama, the film's structure ultimately supports these values. Exploring the theme of a considerably weakened masculinity, Browning tests the boundaries of a tricksterish impulse, which he ultimately relegates to the culture of lower class performers. In this film, he uses the overlapping genres of horror, mystery and melodrama to explore their significance and to question their boundaries. Lon Chaney, a frequent collaborator with Browning and Thalberg, portrays Echo, a ventriloquist capable of assuming different identities either to entertain or to dupe others. Known as "the man of a thousand faces," Chaney's cinematic experimentation with different identities "touched millions more who struggled with their own sense of identity in a decade of bewildering and rapid social change" (*Dark Carnival* 89). Browning's version of *The Unholy Three* presents the view that while malleable identity provides the pleasures of transgressive knowledge, moralizing forces ultimately contain it. The film opens by presenting a side show and its denizens which include a grossly overweight woman, a sword swallower, and fake or "gaffed" Siamese twins. We are introduced to "Hercules—the mighty, marvelous . . . mastedonic model of muscular masculinity"—a strong man who eventually joins the crime syndicate and proves to be the least cunning of the group. Browning's presentation of Hercules suggests that physical strength and an idealized masculine physique are no longer enough to produce a man. In fact, as a glamorized spectacle of maleness, Hercules is akin to a doll or a puppet that lacks subjectivity. The central male consciousness in *The Unholy Three* is Echo, a ventriloquist whose name denotes both his profession, and his ability to take on the mutable characteristics of language itself. An expert mimic and imposter, Echo lacks a stable identity, and is reduced to his voice. Appropriately, his ventriloquist's dummy is named "Nemo," the Latin term for "no one." Engaging in light banter with Nemo, Echo ends his performance with the truism, "That's all there is to life, friends. A little laughter . . . a little tear." This approach to life is too dull and simplistic for Echo who is too much of a manipulator to take things as they come. At the end of his spiel, Echo presents ten cent pamphlets of his jokes to the spectators. While he exploits his mutable identity for profit, he is also distressed by his psychic discontinuity. Thus, he tries to define and stabilize his existence through rhetoric in his pamphlets.[18] On Christmas day, when Echo discovers that his cohorts decided to "turn the trick alone" by committing a double murder, Echo intones "You—filth! Don't you realize that you've murdered a man? That's why I said we'd never carry a gun." Arguably, Echo's occasional displays of morality reflect the part of Browning that embraces bourgeois culture and plays by the rules of moralizing melodrama. However, Browning's oeuvre, like Echo's career, is fraught with tension between these moralizing impulses, and a desire to transgress conventional moral boundaries through various modes of deception and forms of freakery. While Echo tries to identify with the moral and benign Mrs. O'Grady, he ultimately embraces the ventriloquist's penchant for mutable identity—a subject position that defies the goals of conventional melodrama. From the perspective of mainstream melodrama, the film's ending is sad, because Echo ends up loveless and insane, identifying only with Nemo, a nonentity. When a crowd assembles around Echo, he performs his usual spiel and says, "That's all there is to life, friends . . . a little laughter . . . a little tear." The film ends as he passes his ten cent pamphlets to the audience, still attempting to define himself through language. From the standpoint of conventional melodrama, Echo fails to resolve the problem of unstable identity, and it is uncertain whether he will ever again put his penchant for self-transformation to lawless use. Nevertheless, as a modern representation of changeable identity, Echo's capacity for mutability gives him access to a more complex subject position that the narrative simultaneously affirms and resists.

Echo's hysterical vacillation between ego states has interesting gender implications, especially since clinical and historical narratives before Freud have frequently categorized hysteria as a female disorder. Psychoanalytic discourses have defined hysteria as a malady characterized by psychosomatic complaints, catatonic body positions, and paralyzing phobias. The earliest etiologies of hysteria that date from classical Greece and Rome to the Renaissance, attribute it to a uterus that dries up and wanders through the body.[19] Janet Beizer explains that this image of feminine mutability or wandering served to reify fears that woman would "dislocate ostensibly fixed social boundaries and values" if she moves outside the circumscribed woman's sphere (*Ventriloquized Bodies* 48). Medical discourses also attributed the image of mobility and instability to male hysterics, most of whom tended to be from the working and destitute classes. Lynne Kirby explains that "If mobility of mind is one of the chief characteristics of female hysteria (the rapid ease with which the hysteric passes from tears to laughter, for example), mobility of social place is the male hysterical equivalent."[20] Citing the work of Michel Oeurd, Kirby explains that the social instability of the nineteenth century working class in France resembled "the migratory uterus of traditional hysteria" (78). As a member of a traveling circus, and as one who takes on numerous identities, Browning's Echo belongs to the unstable, migratory marginal class from which came many male hysterics in Europe and the United States. His hysterical nature is made evident not only by his class position and his ease at impersonating women, but by his tendency towards mutable identity.

Janet Beizer suggests that the nineteenth century female hysteric became ventriloquized by male medical discourses that aimed to interpret and control her symptoms (9). While Browning's Echo can use his tricksterish voice to provide commentary and ventriloquizing deception, he also allows himself to be ventriloquized by the dominant discourses. In this case, the dominant ideology is feminized morality, which causes Echo to engage in self-castration by impersonating an old woman. Psychoanalytic discourses have traditionally associated castration with the castrated female other. However, some nineteenth century psychoanalysts deemed that male hysterics could "carry" or take on the role of the castrated woman (Beizer 51). The male hysteric was frequently characterized as weak, effeminate, and doomed to bad heredity (Beizer 36). However, in *The Unholy Three*, Browning represents a mutable male psyche that becomes subordinated to the ostensibly stabilizing forces of feminine morality. Browning's oeuvre encodes tension between the feminized superego that imposes bourgeois morality, and the hysteric's more complex subject position that vacillates between the roles of subject and object. Arguably, female reformers during the early twentieth century tried (usually with male support) to appropriate the stereotypically masculine superego. In this attempt to take possession of the phallus in order to gain a political voice, women waged a war against seductive cultural forces, particularly those that made spectacles of both male and female bodies.

During the 1920's and 1930's in America, moral reform movements, usually led by politically active Protestant women, posed the greatest threat to subversive tricksterish forces.[21] As Alison Parker explains in *Purifying America*, these reformers were steadfastly against both "high" and "low" cultural practices that failed to conform to their standards of decency and wholesomeness (7). For those who led organizations such as the Women's Christian Temperance Movement, "nude sculptures, the ballet, and Theodore Dreiser's realism" were as suspect as movies, boxing, "crime story papers," and Sunday comics (Parker 7). In their effort to forge a middlebrow American culture that celebrated the bourgeois family, these reformers rejected anything that was too foreign, too risqué, and therefore too threatening to a narrowly middle class American sensibility. Parker emphasizes that contemporary intellectuals often unfairly characterize the leaders and followers of such movements as unsophisticated prudes who promoted sexual repression as a moral and cultural ideal (Parker 69–70). Paradoxically, these movements enabled women to gain a voice in the political realm by stressing their traditional dominance in the moral and domestic spheres (Parker 5). Ann Douglas suggests that women who actively advocated censorship may have internalized the false authority that patriarchy bestowed on them:

> Naturally desirous of seeing others in a state of ideal susceptibility to their "influence," they were inevitably conflicted about, sometimes hostile to, whatever diminished that receptivity: atheism, "demon rum," or any kind of scientific, intellectual, and artistic achievement from which they had themselves been painfully isolated (76).

Just as a dominant patriarchal voice ventriloquizes female hysterics, it manipulates female reformers into internalizing and performing masculine authority. Throughout his oeuvre, Browning aims to transgress the feminine sphere of influence that imposes rigid conformity and unified subjectivity based on stifling bourgeois pieties. Seemingly unaware that feminized morality is patriarchally ordained, Browning's work consistently rebels against women who impose the superego.

By focusing on the male hysteric's more complex and transgressive role as subject/object, Browning calls into question the dominant ideology that demonizes seduction and spectacles of desire. But perhaps motivated by his own superego, part of Browning refuses to relinquish a moralizing impulse, which he codes as specifically feminine in *The Unholy Three*. Nonetheless, in many of his works, Browning centers on the male hysteric's simultaneous pleasure and disgust in performing the feminized role. As trickster/seducer, Browning lures his middle class audience into confronting the relative fragility of male identity, particularly when faced with the dominance of the feminized superego.

Browning's *The Unknown* (1927) represents a transgressive male figure who initially feigns castration, paradoxically in order to avoid and transcend the state of castration.[22] Set within the orientalized context of a Spanish circus, the main character in *The Unknown* is "Alonzo the Armless, "a sharpshooter and sword swallower who is also a murderer at large. Played by Lon Chaney, Alonzo binds his arms in a corset-like contraption in order to hide his identity and preserve himself from the castrating force of the law. While he performs as a gaffed freak, he is also a real freak, whose double thumb on one hand is his distinguishing feature, already known to the police. Skal and Savada note that Browning, who was acquainted with popular Freudian theory, was well aware that anatomical doubling is a means of avoiding castration: "The double thumb seems yet more evidence of the possible influence of Freud's 'The Uncanny'; doubling is viewed by Freud as an imaginative defense against the feared loss of the self, or a part of the self" (111). In fact, *The Unknown* represents another form of doubling in which Alonzo's "real" and "feigned" identities begin to blur into each other. Like Echo, who eventually views himself as one with Nemo, Alonzo comes to identify completely with his role as the armless, castrated, freakish Other. Maintaining his force as a desiring subject, Alonzo, in a symbolic act of self-castration, eventually goes as far as to amputate his arms in order to win the woman he loves. Paradoxically, in order to possess her, he must negate the means towards possession.

As Lewis Hyde notes in his recent study of trickster tales, the trickster figure usually ends in one of three ways. In the first, the trickster refuses to conform to society's rules and remains a mischief maker; in the second, he becomes "domesticated" into the dominant culture; but in the third, the trickster becomes "exiled," "destroyed," or "bound."[23] Conforming to the standards of moralizing melodrama, *The Unknown* kills off Alonzo, a character prone to theft, to murder, and perhaps to homosexual desire. The film also pathologizes Alonzo's hysterical tendency towards mutable identity, which corresponds with the trickster's more creative impulse towards self-transformation and a mediation of opposites. Ultimately, the conventional oedipal and moral focus of *The Unknown* suggests that one who is prone to such mutability is better off dead. However, the film's ostensibly conventional ideological focus is balanced by its uncompromisingly repugnant subject matter, as well as its main character's amorality. Unlike Echo, Alonzo has no impulses towards conventional morality, and his criminality and self-mutilation challenge middle class values. The film's melodramatic aspects tease conventional bourgeois viewers to identify with the criminal Alonzo; when they see his capacity for feeling—even if it is a self-destructive desire—they realize that he is more human than he appears to be. Skal and Savada note that *The Unknown* "was the first Browning-Chaney film to be frankly and aggressively attacked in the press for its melodramatic morbidity" (114). In Skal and Savada's terms, the melodramatic and the morbid are conflated to serve the ideological agenda of melodrama, which was the dominant cinematic discourse. However, film reviewers did not fail to notice Browning's counter discourse (evident in his stylistic vision), and apparent sympathy towards a criminal character. According to a critic from *the New York Herald Tribune*, "Mr. Browning's methods of picture making; his avoidance of exteriors and sunlit scenes in favor of black, cavernous interiors, with hideous shadows gaping menacingly; his preoccupations with sideshow freaks; his love for the Grand Guignol manner in story telling, have long been recognized, but never before have these traits been so strongly emphasized."[24] Thus, despite

Horror, Melodrama, and Mutable Masculine Identity | 93

Browning's destruction of the tricksterish Alonzo, he nonetheless infuses the film with a surrealistic and morally provocative trickster impulse.

In his early films *The Unholy Three* and *The Unknown*, Tod Browning establishes that physically and mentally deviant Others are pained by desires that they will never satisfy. The central conflicts of these films occur when freakish characters are caught within the popular narrative framework of melodrama, which reproduces conventional solutions for excessive or misdirected desire. Browning never disavows the melodrama, as this was the dominant narrative structure of early cinema, and continues to be one of the most marketable forms in the contemporary film industry. However, Browning's freakish tricksters often call into question the narrative logic of melodrama, and his works therefore often produce subversive commentary on the genre by questioning Freudian definitions of male authority. Browning's later works *Dracula* (1931) and *Freaks* (1932), present more focused attempts to question and disassemble the melodrama's thematic and cultural goals.

Tod Browning and the screenwriter Garret Fort derived their 1932 screen adaptation of *Dracula* from a popular theatrical version of Bram Stoker's novel. Gregory A. Waller emphasizes that Browning borrowed dialogue verbatim from the earlier production, titled *Dracula, the Vampire Play*, by Hamilton Deane and John L. Balderston. Despite Browning's reliance on the older script, his use of bold visual effects enlarges the play's scope by "[providing] us with additional information about the principle characters and about the values involved when the living confront the undead."[25] While Browning gives the madman Renfield the exact language of the play, he places a far greater emphasis on this character than any other version, including Stoker's novel (Waller 388). Through his representation of the ostensibly insane Renfield, who is controlled and ventriloquized by his "master" Dracula, Browning continues to develop his fascination with male hysteria evident in his earlier, silent films. Building upon Stoker's version, Browning makes male hysteria his fundamental concern. Browning's appropriations and transformations of Stoker's work provide not only textual background, but also a basis for cultural and historical commentary on the problem of male hysteria.

Published at the turn-of-the-century, Stoker's *Dracula* (1897) combines gothic and melodramatic elements to produce a dramatic response to Victorian British xenophobia, gynophobia, and homophobia. A theme common in gothic melodramas is the contamination of a "pure" woman by a seductive macabre power. Stoker's novel certainly confronts this issue by representing Dracula's ravishment of the principal women characters, Lucy and Mina. The vampire transforms the sexually aggressive Lucy into an abomination by making her into one of his own kind, but the more conventionally feminine Mina remains throughout the narrative in an ontological nether region between the undead and the living. In Stoker's work and in Browning's adaptation, the medical doctors Seward and Von Helsing are the main guardians of patriarchal normality who aim to kill Dracula and thus eliminate the threat to the moral order.

Stoker's and Browning's gothic melodramas differ from the bourgeois cinematic melodramas in some fundamental ways. While middle class melodramas typically represent an outsider's failure to conform to the demands of patriarchy, *Dracula* represents an Other who threatens to usurp the power of the patriarchy itself. Therefore, in *Dracula*, the patriarchs fear that the vampire will relegate them to the role of outsiders within their own society. As active subjects who feel compelled to defend their masculine prerogatives, Stoker's Seward, Van Helsing, and Harker paradoxically occupy roles analogous to those of male outsiders in bourgeois melodrama. When experiencing the self-doubt that rigorous self-analysis engenders, these men, like male hysterics, experience their subjectivity as inherently malleable. Unlike certain romantic and modernist characters who view unstable identity as a means towards gaining greater self-knowledge, these professional men in *Dracula* find the idea of mutable masculine consciousness profoundly threatening. As mentioned in chapter one, the burgeoning pseudo-sciences of eugenics and physiognomy developed complex methods of locating deviance in physical type. In predicting mental instability on the basis of racial and ethnic origin, theorists such as Cesare Lombroso sought to solidify and stabilize a "superior" white, Western European male identity.[26]

Seward, Van Helsing, and Harker embody the white, Western European ideal, but Stoker's *Dracula* presents the Romanian count in terms of racist stereotypes of Eastern Europeans and Jews. Lucy reports that a cockney zookeeper describes Dracula as "a tall, thin chap, with a 'ook nose and a pointed beard, . . . He had a ard, cold look and red eyes, and I took a sort of mislike to him, . . ." (126). In her analysis of anti-Semitic discourses in *Dracula*, Judith Halbertstam demonstrates that Stoker based his presentation of *Dracula* on theories of degenerate physiognomy proposed by Cesare Lombroso and Max Nordau.[27]

In her journal, Mina describes the "beaky [nosed] Dracula as a man with "hard . . . cruel" and "sensual" features who stares voyeuristically at a "pretty girl" (155). As noted in Chapter One, a common anti-Semitic stereotype presented Jewish men as urban sexual predators who direct their keen gaze at gentile women. Unlike Murnau's hideously deformed *Nosferatu* (1922), Browning's Dracula is at once grotesque and alluring. Joyce Carol Oates explains that Bella Lugosi's pale skin, slicked dark hair, and slanted eyes convey a seductive "ethnic exoticism" alien to mainstream American audiences. In fact, this Dracula's foreignness reminds Oates of both her Hungarian immigrant step grandfather and the theatricalized gestures of a Catholic priest.[28] Early in his film version of

Dracula, Tod Browning presents this frightening and seductive vampire in a *flâneurish* guise as he walks in a black suit and top hat through London, trying to pass for human. Posing as a consummate social climber, this Dracula mesmerizes a woman usher into leading him to Dr. Seward's balcony so that he can introduce himself. Feigning obsequiousness, Dracula tells Seward, "I could not help overhearing your name. Might I inquire if you are the Dr. Seward whose sanitarium is at Whitby?" Playing the seductive Other to a hilt, Dracula tries to charm Mina and Lucy by comparing his new estate, Carfax Abbey, to "the broken battlements" of his more decadent and romantic castle in Transylvania.

As a seductive *flâneur* and a self-aggrandizing climber, Browning's Dracula, while freakish, displays the power and social authority of a colonizing *flâneur* early in the film. But the colonizing tendencies of Browning's and Stoker's *Dracula* go beyond mere social climbing. Stephen D. Arata makes a case for Dracula as a "reverse colonizer"—an outsider who imposes his social and political ideologies as well as his sexuality on members of the dominant culture. As Arata argues, Dracula forces a new racial identity onto his victims: "Having yielded to his assault, one literally 'goes native' by becoming a vampire oneself."[29] As a manipulative force who imposes his will and identity on others, Dracula also functions as a seducer, in Freudian terms. Freud's early model for hysteria proposed that this neurosis results from early childhood traumas where a seductive (usually) masculine force imposes his will and sexuality on a sexually ambivalent (female) child. Freud later revised this theory to suggest that the neurotic's trauma was imagined rather than real, thus making the theory of seduction and the etiology of hysteria more complex.[30] Through his representation of Dracula, Browning enacts a seductive, tricksterish force that tantalizes the bourgeois audience to question the stability of these Western dichotomies.

As a seductive racial Other who figuratively rapes his victims, both Stoker's and Browning's version of *Dracula* embodies everything that bourgeois moralists feared, loathed, and aimed to control. George Mitchell Jr., a "silent era reader for Universal," viewed *Dracula* as a sensationalistic spectacle geared only towards titillating the audience's gaze. Moreover, he found the film too outré for most people to figure out its meanings: "[*Dracula*] passes beyond the point of what the average person can stand or cares to stand . . . It would take a thousand titles to tell the people what it was about . . . and then they wouldn't know" (Skal and Savada 137). Mitchell's prudery prevents him from seeing that Browning's mainstream audience was far from unaware that the subject of *Dracula* was American culture's xenophobic and sexual fears. Noting the relative mediocrity of Browning's staging, John McCarty suggests that the film's prurient elements led to its success: "Browning was not stupid. He knew that *Dracula* was about eroticism and sex—elements that always spelled big box office" (*The Fearmakers* 7).

Browning represents deviant eroticism forcefully in Renfield, Dracula'a only male victim. Both Stoker's and Browning's versions represent Renfield as an hysterical and feminized Other who cannot resist "reverse colonization." At the same time, while Renfield has been ravished and transformed by Dracula's seductive powers, he also functions as a seductive spectacle for the physicians Seward and Van Helsing. Contemporary psychoanalytic feminists have argued that the patient as well as the psychoanalyst can exert seductive powers, particularly during transference.[31] Martha Noel Evans explains that for contemporary French psychoanalysts, questions regarding the quality of the hysteric's subjectivity have stirred much debate. For many French theorists, the hysteric's subjectivity as a seducer rests in her role as an *allumeuse* or a tease . ("Hysteria and the Seduction of Theory" in *Seduction and Theory* 78). From this perspective, the feminized hysteric ritually entices her male observer but then withdraws from him without symbolically consummating the encounter by validating his approach to knowledge.[32] In a similar vein, as a seductive trickster/director, Browing engages his audience in an epistemological game where we must confront our own desire to see and understand deviance. When presenting prurient material, Browning entices his audience to realize that we desire to know more than we think we do. Despite George Mitchell's suggestion that good bourgeois people could never want to know such things, Browning realized his viewers' capacity to gain forbidden knowledge. In his cinematic explorations of characters with mutable identities, Browning invites his viewers to question their own sense of stable subjectivity and conventional desire.

By representing the hysteric Renfield's vacillation between subject and object in a game of seduction, Browning rebels not only against moralizing forces, but against the unified male subjectivity that society's more repressive elements hold so dear. Browning tapped into America's cultural fear of moral ambiguity by creating characters and works who embodied moral conflict. Browning consistently represents hysterical male subjects who feel ambivalent towards both the moralizing forces, and their own rebellious impulses. Never resolving this dichotomy, Browning's subjects make their inner conflict into an hysterical spectacle that simultaneously affirms and rejects bourgeois morality. In this film, Renfield embodies a tendency to vacillate between the desire for a stable, moral self and an impulse towards embodying a more transgressive identity. As *Dracula* dramatizes the unresolved conflicts between science vs. the supernatural, it also presents Browning's exploration of tension between rigid morality and moral ambiguity.

Both Browning and Stoker's versions of *Dracula* function, to a limited extent, as moralizing melodramas, by ending with the death of Dracula, the evil, seductive trickster. As a male hysteric torn between moral and immoral forces, Renfield also embodies this trickster impulse as he puts himself on display before the medical community. In fact, because of his moral ambivalence, Renfield can be considered the work's central trickster figure, since this vacillation corresponds with Browning's own. In Browning's version of *Dracula*, moralizing melodrama ostensibly wins because the subversive tricksters—the count and Renfield—who embody mutable masculine identity, die. However, as Joyce Carol Oates observes, the ending of Browning's *Dracula* seems rushed, and the film has an "air of incompletion" (Oates 503). Oates observes that the film's conventional structure and predictable ending fail to explore the theme that Dracula "is not really immortal or supernatural, but trapped in flesh, condemned to forever feed upon the warm blood of living creatures" (Oates 507). Browning's rushed conclusion, which seems to parody conventional melodramatic endings, leaves open the possibility that Dracula's evil may not have truly dissipated. More fascinated with Dracula's seductive, tricksterish powers, Browning makes the ending seem more like an afterthought. In his more controversial *Freaks* (1932), Browning refuses to kill off his seductive tricksters, and thus presents a greater challenge to the convention of moralizing melodrama.

> The ghastly part of it is that the horrible thing may become a swell box office success. With public taste lower than it has been in generations, not only will it attract the inframen of Main Street, who like snakes, two-headed calves, Chambers of Horrors and Halls of Anatomy, but the morbidly curious and psychically sick whose libidos are stimulated by contemplating the sex-life of abnormalities and monsters.[33]

Only a year after *Dracula* achieved box office success and critical acclaim, Tod Browning directed the more morally ambivalent and aesthetically provocative *Freaks*. *Freaks* pushes to the limit the public's tolerance for grotesque spectacles, and functions as the culmination of Browning's tricksterish attempt not merely to link horror and melodrama, but to test the hybrid genre's moral parameters. I will argue that in the spirit of tricksterism, Browning ultimately demonstrates that the two parts of this cinematic dichotomy are mutually dependent: while horror and melodrama may function as impediments to one another, they may also complement each other within a larger moral and aesthetic framework. As in his earlier films, Browning's central concern in *Freaks* is not so much the presentation of freakish bodies, but the representation of malleable masculine identity. *The Unholy Three*, *The Unknown*, and *Dracula* represent unstable masculinity most poignantly as male hysteria. *Freaks* frequently uses physical disability to represent a similarly unstable male identity, but the film's disjunctive reliance on multiple male points of view, creates an inherently hysterical structure. By undercutting the development of a central male consciousness, Browning creates a structured vacillation between horror and melodrama that mirrors the hysteric's wavering identity. The disunity inherent in the visual organization of *Freaks* can be termed "structural hysteria."

Ostensibly, the central male character in *Freaks* is Hans, the childlike midget who pines for the evil and narcissistic trapeze artist, Cleopatra. As a desiring subject who is incapable of fulfilling his needs in a hostile world, and as a man whose masculinity is in question, Hans is a conventional subject of melodrama. However, the other male freaks in the film who become murderous and revengeful when threatened, function primarily as agents of horror. Like Hans, they need to prove their masculinity, yet they do so within the confines of a different genre. Besides Hans and the vindictive freaks, other male characters display questionable masculinity. For example, Phroso the clown tells Venus, the bareback rider, that she should have "caught" him before his "operation"—a veiled reference to sexual dysfunction. Some biographical commentary on Browning has attributed his preoccupation with emasculation to injuries that he suffered in a 1915 car accident. Driving drunk from a party with a group of D.W. Griffith's actors, Browning sped from a railroad intersection into a train. The impact killed the actor Elmer Booth, and caused Browning's "upper body [to be] pinned and crushed, with unspecified internal injuries" (*Dark Carnival* 48). Skal and Savada believe that Browning, who wore dentures from a supposedly early age, may have lost all of his teeth during this trauma: "In any event, it is more than likely that Browning carried a painful oral reminder of the night of June 16, 1915, for the rest of his life . . . Dentofacial injuries tend to have significant psychological ramifications, and for a man, teeth have a primal symbolic resonance with hardness, aggression, and maleness—the loss of teeth can be experienced as a kind of emasculation" (Skal and Savada 49).[34] Horror film critic John McCarty states that some insiders in the film industry believe that Browning's accident "resulted in the loss of his genitals, a trauma that turned him to alcoholism and an excessive preoccupation with themes of sexual frustration, castration, and other forms of mutilation (*The Fear Makers: The Screen's Directorial Masters of Suspense and Terror* 4). While rather implausible, this explanation nonetheless demonstrates the extent to which Browning has consistently been identified with problems regarding masculine identity.

In *Freaks*, as in his earlier films, Browning calls into question the moral feminization of American culture, primarily through his melodramatic plot. However, rather than creating a hysterical male character who transvestizes the dominant feminine morality, as he had in *The Unholy Three*, Browning presents a female character who is herself morally ambiguous. Madame Tetralini, the owner of the freak show, exerts moral force by trying to protect her physically small and often feebleminded performers from those who taunt and exploit them. When two insensitive men comment that the dwarves and pinheads appear to be subhuman, Madame Tetralini responds that her freaks are children:

> These are children from my circus . . . when I get the chance I like to take them into the sunshine and let them play like—children. That is what most of them are—children (quoted in "Horror Cinema and the Avant Garde" 142).

In her analysis of the freaks' moral ambivalence, Joanne Hawkins suggests that Madame Tetralini incorrectly assumes that the freaks are innocent and vulnerable because they appear childlike ("Horror Cinema and the Avant Garde"144). While Madame Tetralini's melodramatic view of the freaks fails to take into account the complexity of their nature, her role as their owner and commodifier also makes her morally ambiguous. Paradoxically, Madame Tetralini tries to protect her freaks from the very forces of the morbid curiosity that she exploits in presenting them to the public. Although she projects an idealized unified subjectivity onto her charges, she is yet another of the film's agents of moral duality.

As we have seen, Browning's film abounds in dualisms, and Skal and Savada note that the film maker was aware of the Freudian theme of doubling as a means of avoiding castration (111). Freud advances this theory in his essay on the uncanny, where he traces the origin of the double to artifacts by pre-literate and ancient people which represent the replication and preservation of the self.[35] Browning's frequent use of doubles may represent his means of avoiding and evading castrating forces that impose unified masculine subjectivity. Within a Freudian context, the male child achieves a unified sense of masculine identity only when he accepts the threat of castration, and therefore of inherent sexual difference. Mikita Brottman locates the hysteria of divided consciousness in the frequent forms of linguistic doubling in *Freaks*, such as puns, "jokes, tricks, [and] clowns' gags."[36] For Brottman, the clown Roscoe's "puns, stutters, and verbal redundancies are emblematic of the film's obsession with otherness and duality in the form of mutilation, amputation, doubling and renunciation" (Brottman 30). Brottman further notes that these examples of linguistic doubling "are all symptoms of the unconscious fear and anxiety provoked by any manifestation of the human body distorted, twisted, truncated, *out of control*, and thereby made abject and exliminal" (54). From a more positive perspective, these hysterical doublings may be interpreted as Browning's celebration of mutable identity. Given the lack of detailed biographical material regarding Browning's reading habits, one can only speculate about the degree to which his knowledge of popular Freudianism enriched his perspective on hysteria and doubling. One thing is clear: in *Freaks*, Browning reinforces male sexual hysteria through a multiplication of points of view; rather than employing one central consciousness, he provides structural and linguistic devices that double the viewer's perspective.

Ronald V. Borst has suggested that *Freaks* is the conjured story of the carny talker who opens the film by promising to present "living, breathing monstrosities": "[i]t is entirely possible to view the entire story the barker relates to his customers—from the flashback to the carnival up until the freaks' revenge—as a purely fictional account dreamed up by the showman to dupe the crowd at the film's off-set."[37] From this perspective, the carny talker can be viewed as a *flâneur* colonizer who sets out to terrify, dupe, and extract money from the voyeurs he attracts. Yet arguably, this *flâneur* colonizer, who resembles Browning as conjurer/ presenter, also projects the narrative of *Freaks* as his deviant imaginative fantasy.³⁸ In this scene, the talker functions not so much as a colonizing *flâneur*, but as a freakish *flâneur* who performs his own psychological deviance through the narrative, as he casts a critical eye on the spectators. In his opening spiel, the talker urges the audience to stay, daring them to see just how much they can take:

> We didn't lie to you, folks. We told you we had living, breathing monstrosities. You laughed at them, shuddered at them; and yet, but for the accident of birth, *you* might be even as they are. They did not ask to be brought into the world, but into the world they came. Their code is a law unto themselves. Offend one and you offend them all. And now, folks, if you'll just step this way. You are about to witness the *most* amazing, the *most* astounding living monstrosity of all time. Friends, she was once a beautiful woman (quoted in "Horror Cinema and the Avant-Garde" 137).

In this pitch, the talker contradicts his initial assertion that most freaks are born. While he first states that freakishness results from an "accident of birth," he makes known that the most horrific spectacle, who was born physically normal and even beautiful, became the most grotesque human horror of all time. Perhaps another example of hysterical doubling, this contradiction introduces the film's central horror, which is the freaks' transformation of Cleopatra into "one of them." On the one hand, Cleopatra, played by the Russian actress Olga Baclanova, is a statuesque blonde—the physical type cherished by Mayer. Yet as Joanne Hawkins notes, Cleo's great height and physical strength "[establish] her as an androgynous creature" ("Horror Cinema and the Avant Garde" 158). Also, Cleo's exhibitionistic tendencies place her outside bourgeois notions of feminine modesty, a mode of behavior that Mayer held in high esteem.

Despite the talker's titillating and sadistic tone, the film's preamble seems to frame *Freaks* as an "uplifting" moral message—one that is in sync with Mayer's moralizing, melodramatic vision:

> Before proceeding with the showing of this HIGHLY UNUSUAL ATTRACTION, a few words should be said about the amazing subject matter. BELIEVE IT OR NOT . . . STRANGE AS IT SEEMS . . . In ancient times anything that deviated from the normal was considered an omen of ill luck or representative of evil . . . The majority of freaks themselves are endowed with normal thoughts and emotions. Their lot is a truly heart breaking one . . . with humility for the many injustices done (they have no power to control their lot) we present the most startling horror story of the ABNORMAL and the UNWANTED (quoted in *Dark Carnival* 223).

Browning, in fact, had nothing to do with this opening statement, which functions more as an ironic disclaimer for the film's more lurid aspects. By the late 1940's, Dwain Esper, an exhibitor of exploitation films, had added the written preamble after buying the distribution rights for *Freaks*. This statement, which is set to maudlin, and somewhat orientalized music, promotes the film as a moralizing melodrama. It asks that we pity and even identify with these poor creatures "endowed with normal thoughts and emotions" but encased in deviant bodies that often prevent them from fulfilling their desires.[39] Given Esper's flair for satirizing the middle class viewer, the preamble creates a deliberately ambivalent effect. Esper became notorious for distributing films that ostensibly promote moralizing messages, even as they brutally satirize bourgeois values. The most notable of these productions is *Reefer Madness* (1938), a cult film that seems to condemn marijuana, while actually ridiculing those who demonize this drug. Whatever Esper's intentions for adding the opening statement, its role as a pitch for the melodramatic elements of *Freaks* stands in contrast to the talker's more lurid spiel that immediately follows. Curiously, this prologue enforces Browning's own ambivalent perspective, for the film consistently attempts to present two contradictory but often complementary genres. It is therefore appropriate that the work we see begins with two different pitches, one stressing horror, and the other invoking melodrama.

Even in his later films, Browning never completely abandons the melodramatic themes and moralizing messages that both repel and fascinate him in his early work. Instead, he progressively devises more ingenious methods of calling them into question, while never dismissing them entirely. Given the lurid subject matter of *Freaks*, it is a wonder that the film was made during its time. Before production began, Louis B. Mayer regarded the project as an embarrassment, and tried to use as much influence as possible to halt its production (*Dark Carnival* 173). In fact, the film's near celebration of physical ugliness and sexual deviance inverts Mayer's moral and aesthetic values to the point where it seems odd that MGM initially financed the film. However, Irving Thalberg provided Browning with the financial support and artistic freedom to make this risky film (*Dark Carnival* 163–164). Exerting freakish *flâneurish* tendencies and a tricksterish force, Browning and Thalberg worked as partners in crime, striving to join the spheres of horror and melodrama, two genres that often dramatize problems of gender identity.

The most obvious example of gender ambivalence in *Freaks* is Josephine/Joseph, the hermaphrodite who frequently casts his gaze on Hercules, the hypermasculine strong man whose strength and extreme masculinity also render him freakish When the half-man, half-woman slowly walks by Hercules and Roscoe the clown, the latter quips, "Shh . . . Sh . . . sh . . . he likes you, but he . . . he don't." As Roscoe removes the drag accouterments of a "Roman lady," he perceives that the masculine side of Josephine Joseph resents Hercules' exaggerated manliness, while his feminine side is drawn to him. In another scene,

Josephine/Joseph casts a voyeuristic gaze on Hercules and Cleopatra as they engage in sex play. The strong man shouts, "Here's one for your eye," as he brutally punches the hermaphrodite in the face. From Hercules' phallocentric perspective, the sexually ambivalent freak has no right to exert or derive visual pleasure by objectifying him. Since Browning revels in representing freakish subjectivity throughout the film, he intends for us to identify more with the gazing hermaphrodite, than with the indignant strongman. However, Browning frequently represents the transgressive nature of the freak's gaze by linking it with violence and subversive power. When Josephine/Joseph functions as a voyeur, s/he becomes the victim of Hercules' sadism, thus showing the difficulty that deviants encounter when trying to appropriate the gaze. Yet before the freaks subject Cleopatra to violent retaliation, they empower themselves by frightening her with their constant stares.

In his attempt to render the freaks as real human beings, Browning often endows them with piercing subjectivity. In fact, Browning even provides the pinhead Schlitze, another sexually ambivalent and physically grotesque character, with a brief opportunity to exert what appears to be resistance to "her" perpetual role as spectacle. As Phroso the Clown playfully flatters Schlitze's "beautiful" dress and promises to buy "her" a hat from Paris, Schlitze playfully protests the clown's attentions. While Schlitze's speech is incomprehensible, s/he appears to reject Phroso's mischievous advances, as s/he feigns hitting the clown in the shoulder. That Schlitze, a retardate with a mental age of three was also a forty year old man when *Freaks* was filmed merely reinforces Browning's assault on binary approaches to gender. While sideshow proprietors had consistently presented Schlitze as female, he seems to reject Phroso's feminization of him. Joanne Berning Hawkins notes that "Phroso is so flirtatious and seductive in this scene that his motive and relation to the freaks becomes difficult to read" ("Horror Cinema and the Avant-Garde" 143). As a deviant male who is feminized and eroticized within the sideshow context, Schlitze is, in fact, a seductive object. Phroso's playfully ironic teasing of Schlitze brings this to light, and, in so doing, presents one of the film's central conflicts. The deviant male performer who becomes a seductive, theatrical spectacle, acquires the power of female performers who rely primarily on their beauty. Just as beautiful women become the phallus that signifies male desire when they perform to titillate male viewers, freakish men who have been deprived of phallic powers in the economic, political, and sexual spheres, gain power mainly as phallicized spectacles. However, *Freaks* frequently problematizes the male performer's acquired power by questioning whether this is a real form of masculinity. In this regard, Phroso relates to Venus, his love interest, a telling dream, in which he makes known his private anxiety about being a sideshow performer. Phroso dreamed that when he visited Paris, he discovered to his amazement and embarrassment that he was wearing his clown make-up and costume when sightseeing—accouterments that hide his masculine identity and make him look silly. Playing the fool to a hilt, he asks Venus to hit him over the head with a rubber hatchet, an obvious enactment of the castration that he both desires and fears. When she begrudgingly hits him, and refuses to laugh, Phroso, who is frustrated with having to entertain people constantly says, "It's sad, isn't it?" The structure of this sentence resembles a question that Venus had angrily posed to Phroso in an earlier scene, after she broke her liaison with Hercules: "Women are funny, ain' t they? They're tramps, ain't they? Except when you can get money from them." The structure "it's _____, isn't it?," represents the speaker's ironic and confrontational attempt to make the auditor question a conventional attitude. Venus vents her anger on Phroso when he begins to remove his clown make-up: she automatically assumes that because he's a clown, he's bound to ridicule everyone. Phroso quickly defends himself by saying, "You dames are all alike . . . and how you squeal when you get what's coming to you." Taken out of context, this statement has definite misogynistic force; yet Phroso seems to be criticizing women who fall for the most conventionally masculine men.[40] After Venus berates herself for "[falling for Hercules] that big hunk of beef," she praises Phroso for his concern.

Later in the scene, Phroso recounts to Venus the second part of his dream, where he asserts his desire to engage in heterosexual spectatorship. Here, Phroso dreams that he admiringly watches Venus as she wears a bathing suit and poses, standing on a rock. As Phroso expresses his desire to remove his clown mask, and thus become a spectator rather than a spectacle, the legless Johnny Eck enters, walking on his hands and seemingly upstages Phroso with his spectacle of deformity. Perhaps with a twist of black humor, Browning suggests that Phroso's desire for conventional male spectatorship pales in comparison to the kind of transgressive power exerted by spectacles of deviant masculinity. Phroso and Venus treat Eck in as normal a manner as possible by bantering with him, but Eck's deformity and disability are impossible for them to ignore. In fact, Venus casts a fleeting look of pity on him as he enters the room. According to a farfetched rumor, Eck was born without a penis, and compensated by immersing himself in art, music, and philosophy in order to forget his numerous disabilities.[41] Despite these achievements, he can never rise above the state of freakish object. Recognizing this objectification, Browning dubbed Eck "Mr. Johnny,"—a slang word for "penis" (*Dark Carnival* 172). Thus, in Browning's crude terms, the dephallicized spectacle becomes the phallus in the eyes of the normates.

In his most controversial film, Browing raises the question of whether freaks can ever remove their performative masks. For example, after Phroso and Venus jest with Johnny Eck, they visit the bearded lady, who has just engaged in the normal act of giving birth. Browning frequently presents the physically deviant and disabled players engaged in normal activities such as the armless woman who gracefully holds a spoon with her feet in order to eat, and the armless and legless man who lights a cigarette using his mouth. Ronald Borst argues that Browning's moralizing efforts to reassure us that the freaks are more "normal" than they appear, compromise the film's grotesque aspects: "The result is that in trying to present too much of a portrayal of circus life and its performers, the director has partially failed to sustain a mood of horror. He only initiates this atmosphere during the latter portion of the film, and even then there are occasional unneeded cuts to comic relief" ("Re-Evaluating a Screen Classic" 31). Browning's purposes are actually more complex; for he often emphasizes the freaks' relative normality in order to demonstrate that, at least among themselves, they may cease to act like performers. Yet whether or not the freaks may really drop their "masks" before Browning's audience of normates is questionable, and depends on the extent to which normal people are willing to accept the freaks as "one of them."

Challenging Borst's reading, Jean-Marie Leger holds that the scenes presenting the "living torso" and the armless woman engaged in lighting a cigarette and eating, respectively, pander to a voyeuristic audience rather than contributing to the narrative's development (quoted in Brottman 26). Rather than titillating his spectators, Browning is, I believe, challenging us to question whether freaks must always remain grotesque and seductive spectacles. Towards this end, Borst believes that Browning could have balanced the scenes that emphasize the freaks' normality by presenting them performing before spectators more frequently:

> [Browning] could have aroused the shame of his viewers (and painted a more complete picture of circus life as well) had he presented the freaks performing in their actual acts along with the abundance of behind-the-scenes events . . . Would not scenes of massed audiences . . . gaping . . . peering . . . hooting . . . at the freaks, have served as well in arousing the audiences' respect and understanding for the carnival people as well as illustrating all the more clearly which group is actually the more monstrous (33).

Unlike Borst, I don't believe that Browning wants to present a balanced portrayal of circus life, nor does he really want to elicit the audience's shame for their fascination with deformed bodies. Instead, Browning teases the audience's perception of freaks, invoking both our voyeuristic fascination and our pity, by asking us to consider whether or not freaks always remain spectacles of deviance and difference. Like a seductive hysteric, Browning's narrative performs as an *alleumeuse* before its cinematic spectators, alternately inviting and preventing us from viewing the freaks as either normal people or as seductive spectacles. Along with Browning's attempt to merge horror and melodrama, this tonal vacillation is linked to the structural hysteria evident in *Freaks*.

Browning's use of structural hysteria and tonal variation to challenge the implied audience's perception of freaks as mere objects marks a change in his career. In earlier films he presents scenes that demonstrate spectators' reactions to freakish performers, but such scenes are largely absent in *Freaks*. In *The Unholy Three*, Browning shows Tweedledeedee's bitter and violent rebellion against his audience and his role as a spectacle, but in *Freaks*, he discovers a far more subtle means whereby freaks might empower themselves through their difference. During the wedding feast scene, the freaks ritualistically celebrate their difference by performing as spectacles for themselves and for the ostensible normate Cleopatra, whom they ironically invite to become "one of them." The freaks chant, "We drink to one of us . . . we accept her . . . gooble gabble," as the dwarf Angelino passes a loving cup to all his guests. As Mikita Brottman explains, the nonsense term "gooble gabble" is one of the film's many references to chickens "who function as the totemic fetish of the freaks"—a representation of deviance and deformity with which they identify and celebrate (28). Cleopatra's grotesque transformation into a chicken at the end of *Freaks* is the film's most striking and lurid example of this fetish. As the transformed Cleopatra performs before a normate audience, a woman screams, perhaps imagining that this could happen to her. Earlier, during the wedding scene, we see Cuckoo the bird girl dancing on the table with frenzied glee—the film's only other representation of a freak engaged in an actual theatrical performance. As this other chicken fetish dances, Roscoe tells her to stop grabbing the spotlight in order to "give someone else a chance." In a revoltingly crude gesture, Cuckoo responds to this request by farting loudly. In this case, the freakish fetish who enjoys performing her difference, also displays childish egotism The set of *Freaks*, in fact, was beset with numerous prima donnas. Browning, himself, observed that each of the freakish cast members had been the "star" of a sideshow, and "their professional jealousy was amazing. Not one of them had a good word for the other" (*Dark Carnival* 169). Through competitive displays, their performative masks became a means of empowerment within their own circle. In *Freaks*, however, Browning considers a much larger question: the extent to which the physically deformed performers may, in fact, empower themselves through their difference from society at large. Throughout the film, Browning suggests that while the freaks may attempt to lead "normal" lives, they can never fully escape the theatrical and potentially transgressive implications of their freakish difference. Therefore, they are bound within their own world, based on hierarchies which arise from petty rivalries of their own making. However, from Browning's perspective, abusive normates pose the most formidable threat to freaks, and provide them with opportunities to defend their identity. Thus freakish subjectivity becomes more viable when faced with degradation.

Within the sideshow, the biggest threat to the freaks is Cleopatra, who relies on conventional modes of seduction such as beauty and elegance to captivate her audience. When Cleopatra refuses to become "one of them," she refuses to acknowledge the freaks as theatrical competitors. Ironically, however, both the freaks and the bitch queen are performers who become the phallus when they put themselves before desiring male eyes. In the face of rejection, the freaks fear that Cleopatra really possesses power within the social and sexual order, and therefore attempt to cut her down to size. As Joanne Hawkins notes, "[e]ven Cleopatra, the 'Queen of the trapeze' and the 'most beautiful big woman' Hans has ever seen, appears here as somewhat too large."[42] In this case, the phallic woman, who should placate male sexual anxieties as the ultimate fetish, proves more of a castration threat than a means to disavowal.

After the wedding feast scene, Browning's narrative is geared towards castrating the supposedly phallic woman, and endowing freakish men with phallic power. After discovering that Cleopatra has attempted to poison and murder Hans in order to inherit his fortune, the male freaks will spare her nothing. Exerting their keen gaze, they constantly keep watch over her not only from windows, but from under doorsteps and from half open doors. Here, Browning associates the power to look with the power to castrate. The same freaks who stare relentlessly at Cleopatra, threaten to maul her with phallic weapons in order to force her to hand them the bottle of poison. In this scene, Johnny Eck points a gun at her, while a dwarf wields a switchblade. In the film's most lurid scene, the male freaks hold such weapons as they slither and glide through a rainstorm, chasing Cleopatra. Much critical commentary has focused on the film's deviation from the story's original ending, which requires the castration of Hercules as well as the mutilation of Cleopatra. Joanne Hawkins argues that "[a]s (Cleo's body symbolically becomes the sight for Hercules' punishment as well as her own, [she] becomes the figure onto which the male experience of castration may be quite literally displaced ("One of Us" 202).

Cleo's transformation into a chicken woman makes this displacement obvious in a manner that is simultaneously horrifying, humorous, and campy. Once again, the talker presents the "living, breathing monstrosity" who was once "a beautiful woman." But this time the camera presents Cleopatra as this pathetic creature with amputated limbs and a gouged out eye, who quacks in what looks like a baby's playpen. Borst suggests that this ending represents a culmination of the talker's fantasy, but is one which, I believe, enacts his quest for greater masculine power. At first glance, the talker, who functions as a *flâneur* colonizer, looks like the film's trickster, for he achieves his aims through deception. Yet Browning infuses the narrative with a far more subtle trickster impulse. As in his earlier films, Browning is himself the primary trickster in *Freaks*, and he exercises this impulse by calling into question the cinematic union of horror and melodrama that he had helped to establish. The film concludes ambivalently with what may be regarded as two separate endings that emphasize Browning's "failure" to resolve the dichotomy that he poses constantly in his work. On the one hand, Browning presents us with the mutilated Cleo, thus reinforcing the horror plot which stresses the freaks' penchant for revenge. Yet in the scene that follows, Phroso, Venus, and Frieda, his former love, visit a dejected and guilt ridden Hans, who has retired from the sideshow, and retreated into his estate. At the end, Frieda tries to reassure the sobbing

Hans that he is not responsible for the horrific transformation of Cleo. Joanne Hawkins observes that the crying Hans "seems to be completely feminized in this scene; in fact, this scene can be viewed as a culmination of Cleo's campaign of sexual humiliation against [him]" ("One of Us" 271). Hans cries not merely at Cleo's transformation, but because he has discovered her true intentions, and thus his inability to win the love of a normal-sized woman (271). As in melodrama, he finds his efforts to overcome his marginal status and gain social acceptance have failed.

In this melodramatic ending, the tiny Frieda is a maternal figure to an "infantalized" and desexualized Hans ("Horror Cinema and the Avant-Garde" 156). That Browning identifies both as castrators demonstrates his misogynistic fear of female power in general. Like the two spiels that open this film, both endings correspond respectively to the genres of horror and melodrama. In the former, the freaks function as castrators, while in the latter, a freaksish man must come to accept his own castration and relinquish his unlawful erotic desires. As noted earlier, cinematic melodramas usually represent characters who must learn to make the best of their disempowerment within the dominant social order. For Hans, this means that he must accept his role as a midget who will appeal mainly to women of his own childlike size. Gary Morris interprets *Freaks* as a satirical inversion of MGM's values, and as Hans, in particular, as a caricature of Louis B. Mayer, himself:

> The midget Hans, a "good" but fallible character, is Mayer's distorted double, a specific satire of the short, gauche, Old World European impresario of humble origins, with the film even reproducing physical affectations in Hans, like Mayer's cigar smoking. Like Mayer, Hans has access to enormous wealth (he is coming into a large inheritance); hence he must be cultivated, appreciated, honored, indulged, and loved by the more glamorous but considerably less wealthy "normals" who surround him.[43]

Viewed through the lens of Morris's reading, Browning cruelly tapped into Mayer's status anxiety by rendering the newly powerful, nouveau riche Hans as dejected, childlike, and subject to the force of others. Browning's exploration of the problem of mutable masculine identity that was endemic in American culture may also have had particular resonance for the immigrant mogul who desperately wanted to be a fully assimilated, wealthy American. Yet Browning also satirizes Mayer's extreme desire for acceptance by the mainstream—a tendency that often led to the production of aesthetically conventional films that promoted simplistic morality.

The "incoherent" and unconventional structure of *Freaks* that vacillates between horror and melodrama represents wavering male identity that vacillates between aggression, and acceptance of castration. Through the dual plot and dual ending, Browning brings into play unresolved tensions between horror and melodrama, as he dramatizes the unstable identity that forms the basis of male hysteria. To a lesser degree, Browning's earlier films which simultaneously juxtapose and question the co-existence of horror and melodrama, also demonstrate structural hysteria. Yet the glaring (and perhaps intentional) disunity of tone and perspective in *Freaks* suggests that Browning never resolved the problem of male hysteria, and never stopped questioning the two genres preoccupied with this hysteria: horror and melodrama. Whatever Browning's intentions, his moral, melodramatic ending did not prevent reformers from trying to censor *Freaks*. While *Freaks* was released for circulation in movie theaters in early February, 1932, pressure from various American censors caused MGM to halt the distribution of the film by July of that year. Censors in Great Britain banned *Freaks* for thirty years.

At the end of Browning's career, the film industry's rigid enforcement of melodramatic storylines may have won over his transgressive, tricksterish will. By the late 1930's, Browning retired from film making and lived as a recluse in Malibu for the rest of his life. However, while American moralists shunned his work for the next thirty years, some French intellectuals during the 1950's regarded him as a twentieth century Poe (*Horror Cinema and the Avant Garde* 134). Just as the French admired Browning, the director often demonstrated an affinity for French settings; both *Freaks* and *The Devil Doll* (1936) take place in France. By the 1970's, some French critics regarded Browning's use of France and foreign characters in *Freaks* as an "unsophisticated device for attempting to reassure his public that *Freaks* was not necessarily a reflection of American ideology" (Brottman 26). Yet given Browning's complicated transgression of mainstream American values, it is unlikely that he would want to reassure an American audience of anything. More plausibly, Browning set *Freaks* within a less censorious culture more likely to consciously embrace tricksterish forces. In this vein, it is not accidental that Barnes, McCullers, and West lived and worked in Paris, where they absorbed the influences of a less prudish and more aesthetically sophisticated culture. It was not until after his death in 1962 that Browning received acclaim from critics and film makers in America. By the late 1960's, when the American counterculture embraced transgressive desire and sundry forms of freakery, Browning's hysterical tricksterism became an important cultural spectacle. Yet, much of the American criticism of *Freaks* still focused on the representation of a "human" drama, thus emphasizing its melodramatic elements. While these assessments are not completely inaccurate, they fail to take into account Browning's exploration of his own culture's ambivalences.

CHAPTER SIX

"This Thing I Long For I Know Not What"
Carson McCullers and the Melodrama of the Domesticated Freak

In most of her works, Carson McCullers produces freakish *flâneurs* who remain bound within small southern towns. Rather than limiting their capacity to develop an expansive, subversive vision within these communities, she creates an alternative to the cosmopolitan modernist *flâneur* who explores modern heterotopic cities. Her provincial observers provide a poignant critique of mainstream America from within. While the cosmopolitan Baudelarian and Benjaminian *flâneurs* observe the sundry folk of large cities, McCullers's improbable *flâneurs* include deaf mutes, hunchbacks, working class misfits, and pre-adolescent girls who revel both in watching others and in evaluating their own perceptions. McCullers's *flâneurs* usually display freakish tendencies, but they also function as transgressive tricksters who initially resist domestication within claustrophobic towns and restrictive families. While uncontrollable circumstances eventually force these figures to accept domestication, their secret point-of-resistance forms the basis of these melodramas. In her short fiction and in her novels, *The Heart is a Lonely Hunter* (1940) and *The Member of the Wedding* (1946), McCullers explores the extent to which eccentric others can develop their identities outside the American mainstream. That many of these outsiders are Jewish, homosexual, or aspiring artists is essential here, since stereotypical Jewish intelligence, homosexual difference, and artistic originality have often raised the hackles of those who cherish petty bourgeois conformity. In this same vein, McCullers often represents African Americans who cannot use their intellectual and artistic gifts in the racist South. For McCullers, marginalized creative others figure prominently as symbols and models of constructive defiance.

From the 1950's through the 1970's, numerous critics consigned McCullers work to the middlebrow bin, deeming her a gothic melodramatist with a skewered sense of human psychology. The most detailed attempt to pigeon hole McCullers comes from Leslie Fiedler, who describes McCullers as a cheap version of Faulkner. He complains that her prose is both laden with sentiment and decidedly apolitical.[1] Most tellingly, Fiedler damns McCullers as a fashionable writer who appeals mainly to "rich American women with cultural aspirations" and (male) homosexuals who display similar pretensions ("Adolescence and Maturity in the American Novel" 201). Fiedler disdains both McCullers and her gay male counterpart Truman Capote as the exemplars of "a new sort of sensibility, defined by a taste for haute couture, classical ballet, baroque opera, the rites and vestments of Catholicism—and above all for a kind of literature at once elegantly delicate and bitterly grotesque" ("Adolescence and Maturity in the American Novel" 201). Curiously, what Fiedler objects to most are the magazines in which McCullers published her fiction. McCullers's work was often serialized in *Harpers Bazaar,* a fashion magazine ostensibly geared towards women, but whose gay male editors, writers, and photographers infused the publication with urbane homosexual tastes. Fiedler assumes that a publication so distanced from mainstream American masculinity could never provide serious cultural commentary. In fact, he goes as far as to suggest that the inclusion of literary fiction in such a publication is a mere pretension, since a short story "tucked away between the picture of a determinedly unbeautiful model and an ad for a brassiere" would most likely remain unread" ("Adolescence and Maturity in the American Novel" 201). Put more bluntly, Fiedler believes that a fashion magazine found on the "table of a beauty parlor waiting room" cannot contain any fiction worth reading, since it is consumed mainly by what he regards as frivolous women ("Adolescence and Maturity in the American Novel" 201).

Fiedler's transparent contempt for women and gay men forms the basis of his argument that a feminized and homosexualized sensibility produces debased art forms. For Fiedler, the literary exemplars of American masculinity are Faulkner, Melville, and James—writers who display a constant struggle for heterosexual male definition and resistance to their homosexual demons. While these novelists demonstrate what Fiedler terms "overall moral maturity," they also are characterized by "a weakness in dealing with women" which often results in a failed sense of heterosexuality and a flight into male communities" ("Adolescence and Maturity in the American Novel" 199). According to Fiedler, the best mid-twentieth century American writers working within this tradition reproduce the "psychological, symbolic [and] gothic" aspects that Faulkner, Melville and James developed:

> The strengths of contemporary writing correspond to the strengths of this tradition, boldness of imagery, subtlety of insight, and especially the willingness

to plunge deep below the lintel of consciousness, and the weaknesses to its weakness, a tendency to involution and hysteria, to a rhetoric that becomes pseudo-poetry at its weakest ("Adolescence and Maturity in the American Novel" 199).

While championing this tradition, Fiedler believes that American fiction must move beyond the representation of masculine identity conflicts in order to signal a new moral and aesthetic maturity, a progression he finds in writers who fuse political radicalism with artistic experimentation. He cites Saul Bellow as the exemplar of a more mature American masculinity, one that, in this case, is nurtured largely by the Jewish American experience. In this vein, Fiedler argues that the work of Jewish writers such as Bellow, Delmore Schwartz, and Lionel Trilling convey an ironic sensibility that prevents them from sinking into the immature, bathetic depths of "nostalgia and self-pity"—elements that he finds characteristic of Carson McCullers's fiction" ("Adolescence and Maturity in the American Novel" 207).

In assessing McCullers's work, Fiedler characterizes *The Heart is a Lonely Hunter* as a "heartbreakingly wonderful" melodrama where "scene and symbol [fuse] into a single poetry without strain" (203). Acknowledging that McCullers works within a distinguished American novelistic tradition where self-definition often occurs through gender conflict, Fiedler notes that her main characters often are sexually ambivalent girls: "(Frankie and Mick: the names make the point)" (203). Despite his awareness of the importance of gender in McCullers's work, he trivializes this point by stressing what he regards as its immaturity. Similarly, he dismisses Truman Capote's writing style as the literary embodiment of a homosexual queen:

> One can take [Truman Capote] as almost a caricature of the type: the "queen" as American author, possessing a kind of beauty, both in person and as an artist, which belongs to childhood and early adolescence, and which withers before it can ripen ("Adolescence and Maturity in the American Novel" 202).

Fiedler celebrates what he regards as a tradition of authentic American experience, one that only heterosexual men can truly understand—particularly if they are Jewish. The "queenishness" that Fiedler condemns in Capote's writing is also evident in McCullers's work, which often explores female gender conflicts from the position of the male homosexual.

Contemporary critical discourse about McCullers frequently cites the indeterminacy of her sexual orientation.[2] As a teenager, McCullers's aggressively unfashionable boyish clothes once provoked some female schoolmates to stone her, and the androgynous adult McCullers seduced the camera eye of photographers such as Louise Dahl-Wolfe and Richard Avedon. Some of McCullers's contemporaries were convinced that she used her relatively "masculine" appearance to project a lesbian identity.[3] After reading *The Heart is a Lonely Hunter*, English professor Albert Erskine reportedly declared to his wife, Katherine Ann Porter: "Katherine Anne, that woman is a lesbian . . . I can tell from the author's mind in that novel and by what she makes her characters say and do" (quoted in Carr 155). Unfortunately, the anecdote fails to explain what Erskine meant by a lesbian sensibility. Perhaps he meant that only a non-heterosexual writer, whether male or female, could so convincingly present the experience of a homosexual deaf mute and a teenage girl who defies norms of heterosexual femininity. Notions of "queerness" and "gayness" saturate most of McCullers's novels.[4] However, one cannot assume that a woman writer who projects a "queer" sensibility necessarily does so from the subject position of a lesbian. Similarly, a queer male sensibility need not signal a male homosexual writer. McCullers once announced to a friend that she "was born a man," but it is uncertain whether she claimed inherent maleness because she had loved women or because she coveted the prerogatives of male subjectivity. McCullers's sexual experience, in fact, most closely fits patterns of bisexuality. While involved in a long, troubled marriage to Reeves McCullers, an aspiring writer, she carried on relationships with women, most notably Annemarie Clarac-Schwarzenbach, a brilliant but unstable Swiss historian. Throughout her life, McCullers also maintained close friendships with male homosexual artists, particularly Tennessee Williams, whom she seems to have regarded as a soul mate.

Williams's and McCullers's intense but platonic friendship was based on a shared sensibility that privileged a deeply emotional view of life. The playwright felt compelled to meet the author of *The Member of the Wedding* after his initial reading of the novel moved him to tears. According to Virginia Spencer Carr, Williams was so consumed with imaginary illnesses and the notion of dying young, that he placed meeting McCullers high on his list of priorities. After spending time with McCullers on Nantucket island in 1947, Williams claimed that he was so moved by her warmth that he became miraculously cured of his hysterical symptoms and his romantic obsession with death. Williams's companion Pancho Rodriguez viewed McCullers as a luminously feminine woman who cooked skillfully and "magically transformed every room in the house through her warm, womanly touch" (Carr 273–274). As male homosexuals, both Williams and Rodriguez regarded McCullers as an ideal embodiment of female empathy, taste, and gentility.

Finding their relationship uncomplicated by sexual desire, Williams's idealization of McCullers extended to her work, and he encouraged her to try her hand as a playwright. Just as Williams recognized in McCullers traces of his own feminine identity, she saw in him aspects of herself that went beyond mainstream gender roles. McCullers particularly sees her image in the male homosexual artist like Williams, whose sensitive and imaginative qualities go against the grain of conventional American masculinity. Rather than identifying completely with the prerogatives of the father, McCullers recognizes herself more in the male homosexual who embraces maleness (and a male subject position) as he identifies with the feminine. She explores this subject position most thoroughly in *The Heart is a Lonely Hunter*, where a closeted homosexual deaf mute becomes the icon onto which small town denizens project their unconscious desires. In other novels, the male homosexual's subject position emerges less directly through the perspective of women who love them. *The Ballad of the Sad Cafe* (1951), her novel about a doomed menage a trois, demonstrates an eccentric women's tragic love for an effeminate hunchback. In these novels and in many of her short stories, McCullers projects empathy, passion and creative genius onto the body and psyche of the male homosexual.

McCullers responds similarly to the Jewish intellectual or artist, whose subjectivity she admires for reasons very different from Fiedler's. In many of her works, McCullers displays a fascination and identification with the mental abilities of the stereotypical "smart Jew."[5] As she identifies with the "Jewish gaze" and its *flâneurish* tendencies, she also fills both her short and long fiction with generalizations about the intellectual abilities of Jews. Sander Gilman explains that late nineteenth century eugenicists and physiognomists began to associate the piercing Jewish gaze not only with craftiness in the commercial sphere, but with high mental aptitudes: "It is in the Jews' gaze that the pathology of their soul, the true meaning of their superior intelligence can be found" (*Smart Jews* 37). This stereotype, which twentieth century racists have repackaged in various insidious forms, coexists with the notion that Jews also display remarkable aesthetic taste and artistic talent.[6] Gilman demonstrates that in nineteenth century Germany, the notion of superior Jewish creative ability generated controversy and jealousy. Wagner, for instance, dismissed Jews as mere mimics, while Nietzsche proclaimed them the creators of "the noblest human being (Christ), the purest sage (Spinoza), the mightiest book and the most efficacious moral code in the world" (From *Human All Too Human*, quoted in *Smart Jews* 45). The image of Jewish creativity persists in many contemporary discourses that construct the Jew as artistically gifted. The older version of this stereotype is linked inextricably to the notion that Jewish creativity is based on a tendency towards "nervousness," particularly in men. This pathological image of the Jew represents him as an effeminate man with a theatrical predisposition towards mimicry (*Smart Jews* 48). For McCullers, the smart or effeminate Jew and the male homosexual are both figures of transgressive creativity through which she challenges mainstream American values. In *The Heart is a Lonely Hunter*, McCullers conflates the Jew and the homosexual in Singer, whose sexuality is closeted and whose Jewishness is only reputed. Through her entwined exploration of Jewishness and homosexuality, McCullers produces domesticated freaks who simultaneously defy and accept oppressive cultural values of small town America.

Twentieth century American cultural history is filled with accounts of the persecution of gays, Jews, and artists in small towns and provincial cities.[7] Despite middle America's resistance to outsiders, some individuals born into the dominant culture still define themselves as avowedly non-mainstream because of their sexual preferences or artistic interests. Many late twentieth century popular biographies present artistic women as rebels trapped within stifling backgrounds who often descend to alcoholism or mental illness.[8] Carson McCullers differs in some important ways from these casualties of middle American indifference and hostility. Most significantly, she came from a family that supported her artistic goals and promoted her childhood promise as a musical prodigy. Her mother, in particular, encouraged her sense of creative entitlement, which often provoked the resentment and ridicule of other children (Carr 30). Despite McCullers's eventual success as a writer, her biography still reads as a familiar account of a woman artist doomed to hysteria and alcoholism. Like many of her less successful contemporaries, she identifies strongly with the unfulfilled, transgressive longing that characterizes so many twentieth century writers, from Kafka to Nabokov. In *The Heart is a Lonely Hunter*, McCullers poignantly represents this longing in the young Mick Kelly, a twelve year old girl obsessed with music, who composes a song called "This Thing I Long For, I Know Not What" (*The Heart is a Lonely Hunter* 205). As in her earlier short fiction, McCullers presents a desire not only for an escape from lower bourgeois mediocrity, but for the kind of creative power that would foster such an escape.

In "Wunderkind," (1936) and "Poldi" (1941), McCullers's exemplars of would-be liberating talent are young Jewish musicians. When McCullers wrote and published "Wunderkind" in 1936 at the age of nineteen, she had already abandoned her ambition to become a concert pianist, and instead professed a commitment to becoming a writer. In "Wunderkind," Frances, a fifteen year old aspiring pianist, comes to understand the unpleasant reality that she is simply not good enough to achieve her goal. McCullers herself began to question her potential for a career in music at the age of fifteen and gave up her desire to study at Julliard a year and a half later after her piano teacher, Mary Tucker, moved to California (Carr 28–36). Critics have noted that in "Wunderkind," McCullers works through her feelings of abandonment by Tucker by having the teenaged Frances turn her back on both music and her music teacher. However, "Wunderkind" also suggests that Frances's early promise is blighted by her burgeoning female sexuality—a conventional observation on the incompatibility of femininity with artistic goals. When Frances fails to play a Bach fugue with passion, her instructor, Mister Lafkowitz comments that since Bach had twenty children, "He could not have been so cold—then."[9] As "Wunderkind" ratifies the longstanding view that high creativity is a male domain, it also suggests that male geniuses are particularly formidable if they are Jewish. Frances's Jewish piano teacher, Mister Lafkowitz, tells her that only Jews have the emotional depth to interpret complex pieces of music. While Frances tried to play Bloch, critics "had said she lacked the temperament for that kind of music" and "called her playing thin and lacking in feeling" ("Wunderkind" 64). Mister Lafkowitz tries to placate Frances by telling her to avoid working with "that oie oie stuff" (64): "Not for you, Bienchen. Leave all that to the Heimies and vitses and skys" ("Wunderkind" 64).

Frances's young rival, Heime Isralesky, is everything that she is not: as a Jewish male, he is a fine, passionate interpreter of Bloch. Consumed with jealousy, Frances often wonders, "Why was it Heime had done so much better at the concert than she? It wasn't just the Bloch and her not being Jewish—not entirely. It wasn't that Heime didn't have to go to school and had begun training so early, either. It was—?" ("Wunderkind" 64). The latter half of the narrative suggests that the missing detail may be Frances's femininity—her difference from heterosexual masculinity that blights her interpretative abilities. Although Lafkowitz and Heime Israelsky are heterosexual males ostensibly capable of stereotypical masculine energy, they are also Jews who are constructed as far more passionate and emotional than mainstream American men. While this passion is a common feature of fictional Jews, it is not always a sign of masculine power.

McCullers also considers the stereotype of Jewish men as effeminate and hypersensitive in *The Ballad of the Sad Cafe* (1936), where the narrator compares the hunchbacked dwarf Cousin Lymon to an overemotional Jewish man:

> Morris Finestein was a person who had lived in the town years before. He was only a quick, skipping little Jew who cried if you called him Christkiller . . . A calamity had come over him and he had moved away to Society City. But since then if a man were prissy in any way, or if a man wept, he was known as a Morris Finestein.[10]

Shortly after the serialization of *Ballad,* an anonymous reader wrote an angry letter to McCullers, complaining that the above passage is anti-Semitic. Deeply troubled by this accusation, she wrote an "open letter to *Harper's Bazaar,* defending herself against this charge" (Carr 236–237). Virginia Spencer Carr demonstrates that in the unpublished letter, McCullers emphasizes that her intention was not to denigrate Jews, but to use poignant irony in order to indict "the society which allowed such degradations to occur" (Carr 238). In his biography of McCullers, Oliver Evans mentions that Cousin Lymon is based on a hunchback McCullers often saw in a Brooklyn bar:

> For some reason she could not put him out of her mind—just as, years before, she had been haunted by the portrait of the Jew who provided her with the visual image of her first protagonist.[11]

With humanistic, rather than with racist or anti-Semitic intentions, McCullers draws upon conventional Western images that conflate Jewishness with effeminacy, homosexuality, and deformity. Although she does not develop the "Jewish" aspect of Cousin Lymon, she makes it implicit earlier with Mister Lafkowitz and Heime Israelsky, and later with Singer.

Mainstream American culture has traditionally held that real men not only do not display emotion, but they also do not become artists. In McCullers's revision of this stereotype, Heime Israelsky, the archetypal Jewish male artist, combines masculine force with more conventionally feminine passion to produce an androgynous ideal of creativity. This figure had, of course, emerged as a modernist stereotype before McCullers began to write. Women artists such as Virginia Woolf and Djuna Barnes both celebrated and questioned the creative androgyne, and this ideal persists even in modernist and postmodern culture. In "Wunderkind," McCullers's protagonist accepts this model of androgynous creativity as a male prerogative and acts accordingly. Conceiving of herself as a conventional female, Frances decides to accept the culturally ordained fate of her sex—intellectual and artistic mediocrity.

However, in "Poldi" (1941), another of McCullers's early short stories, the artist who embodies stereotypical Jewish warmth and artistic talent is a woman. The narrative describes how Hans, Poldi's love-struck admirer, strives without success to gain her affection. Ironically, the unattainable Poldi is characterized by passion and unabashed sensuality, rather than elusive coolness: "Warm, she always was. And if he held her it would be so that he would want to bite his tongue in two."[12] This image of self-castration suggests that Hans would only maim himself if he gained access to Poldi's warmth. This representation of castration differs from the classic Freudian model where the male subject fears castration at the hands of the father for secretly desiring the mother. Hans's reversal, or inversion of this pattern suggests more of an identification with Poldi than sexual desire for her. He symbolically castrates himself *after* he has attained his object of desire and exhibits no need to fetishize a replacement by imagining her as a phallic mother. Instead, he desires in the female a double whose castrated state resembles his own. In this sense, Hans bears a striking resemblance to the male homosexual who identifies with the mother's "warmth . . . receptivity . . . and narcissism" (Silverman 355). That Poldi is "warm," "maternal," "receptive," and "narcissistic" figures prominently here. Her narcissism is evident both in her preoccupation with her musical ability and in her tendency to put her femininity on display. In discussing the effects of her love life on her progress as a musician, Poldi offers the following cliche: "I believe my playing has deepened much in the last month . . . It's only after you've suffered that you can play" ("Poldi" 22).

Poldi's "suffering" at the hands of numerous suitors pales in comparison to the angst that she inadvertently inflicts on Hans. The narrator's representation of his suffering produces a pathos that is characteristic of McCullers:

"Tell me, Hans, he loves—don't you think so? You really think he loves me but is only waiting until he feels it's best to reply—you think so?"

A thin haze seemed to cover everything in the room. "Yes," he said slowly. Her expression changed. "Hans!"

"He leaned forward, trembling."

"You—you look so queer. Your nose is wiggling and your lips shake like you are ready to cry. What—"

Poldi—

A sudden laugh broke into her question. "You look like a peculiar cat my Papa used to have" ("Poldi" 25).

McCullers emphasizes Hans's sense of estrangement in the face of frustrated longing. Poldi's observation that Hans looks "so queer" is one of McCullers's coded references to homosexuality. While Hans does not display homosexual desire for a man, his "queer" orientation is evident rather in his identification with Poldi, and his thwarted desire to become her. Ironically, Poldi is unaware that Hans feels lovelorn because of her indifference to him, and his "queerness" only heightens the melodrama of blighted love. Richard Gray argues that McCullers's penchant for representing pathos is both her strength and her downfall. On the one hand, Gray describes her tendency to produce this "specific emotional effect" as an "impressive" and even "subtle" achievement that "helps to establish an intimate, usually searching relationship between tale and reader."[13] On the other hand, he suggests that McCullers's intense focus on pathos prevents her from exploring the social and political dimensions of her characters' problems (Gray 80–83). While the political implications of this shortcoming figure prominently in McCullers's longer works, her emphasis on pathos also has a performative function: through the exaggeration of pathos, her narratives emphasize the plight of deviant others who become domesticated within a conservative American milieu. In the process, McCullers encodes a parodic "gay sensibility" into her representation of pathos. Her many instances of pathetic melodrama project the tensions that result from unrequited love and blighted expectations—a familiar theme in homosexual literature from Proust to pulp novels.

In many of her works, McCullers filters her evocation of pathos through the keen vision of observer figures. While characters in her short fiction often provide a central observational stance, McCullers offers a more diffuse and subtle, but nonetheless powerful observational perspective in her major works, by presenting overlapping multiple viewpoints. She began to experiment with this more complex point of view in "Court in the West Eighties" (1935 or 1936), a short story that explores the vision of a voyeuristic young woman who lives alone in an apartment while attending college in New York City. The young observer in the story enjoys staying by her window, watching several neighbors in her tenement building. The narrative emphasizes the difference and distance between the perceiving subject, and the often unpleasant lives of those on display. Especially fascinated by a young couple who go hungry before her eyes, the narrator/observer comments on both the tragedy of their situation and her inability to help them:

> It is hard to tell how you feel when you watch someone go hungry. You see their room was not more than a few yards from mine and I couldn't quit thinking about them. At first I wouldn't believe what I saw.[14]

The narrator suggests that as much as she would like to help the indigent couple, this is impossible since she has no real connection with them. When trying to make sense of what she sees, she idealizes and tries to enter the observational sensibility of a red-haired man who lives across from her. Viewed by some critics as a prototype for Singer, the homosexual Jewish deaf mute whom others idealize in *The Heart is a Lonely Hunter*, this man is characterized as an omniscient being.[15] Sensing that "he understood more than most people," the narrator feels that he would have the most enlightened response to tragic scenes of poverty and violence. She could not "explain . . . this faith [she] had in him," but she would look to his heavy lidded eyes for answers ("Court in the West Eighties" 16).

McCullers's idealized observational stance in this story is only peripherally engaged with social and political reality. While the narrator is aware that others' lives have been tragically affected by the Great Depression, she realizes that there is little she can do about this. Instead, she aspires to be like the red-haired man, a *flâneurish* figure whom Robert Philips describes as an "unfeeling demiurge" ("Freaking Out" 175). This godlike observational consciousness that the narrator tries to emulate in some ways resembles the gaze of the Baudelarian and Benjaminian *flâneur*, who briefly revels in identifying with scenes and people from whom he remains personally detached. However, a prime difference between this earlier model and McCullers's is her use of the observer to evoke pathetic spectacles of suffering. The Baudelarian and Benjaminian *flâneur* is so narcissistically wrapped up in his own perceptions that he fails to feel for anything beyond his own self. However, McCullers's narrator presents a comparable, though not identical, form of narcissism, when she alludes to political reality without representing possibilities for social change.

McCullers more successfully historicizes the observer's position in "The Aliens" (1935 or 1936), a short story which represents a Jewish immigrant's painful perceptions as he rides a bus from New York City to the South. The traveler, who is only known as "The Jew," is "an observant person" who "had scanned each fellow passenger" early during the ride.[16] The proverbial wandering Jew, he does not know what to answer when a man asks "Where is your home, sir" ("The Aliens" 74). As an immigrant from Munich rather than a native New Yorker, he feels no identification with the American landscape and perceives himself as incontrovertibly alien. When a young Southern passenger stares perplexedly at him and says, "You *are* a foreign man?," the Jew becomes self-conscious about his difference. To divert attention from himself, he points to a deformed black woman whose poverty is evident in her torn clothing and "the roving, hungry, vacant look" on her face ("The Aliens" 76). When he comments, with genuine concern, that there is obviously something wrong with this woman, the Southern man responds, "Why there's nothing the matter with her . . . Not that I can see" ("The Aliens" 76). In a culture that enfreaks blackness, the woman's race becomes indistinguishable from her deformity. When confronted with a "deaf old man in overalls," the Jew feels overwhelmed with emotion at this pathetic spectacle, and begins to grieve over his lost daughter, Karen. McCullers identifies the Jew's capacity for empathy with his ethnicity and his marginalized role as a cultural outsider.

The Jew in "Aliens" never performs his own difference in the bitterly ironic manner of the freakish *flâneur*. However, McCullers explores this perspective more fully in "The Jockey" (193?), a short story in which the title character makes a spectacle of his disgust for the unscrupulous men who run a racetrack. When "a trainer, a bookie, and a rich man" show no sympathy for a young Irish jockey who broke his leg and hip when racing, the diminutive jockey admonishes them for their callousness. When they continue to condescend to him, the jockey spits "a pulpy mouthful" of French fries and scoffs "Libertines."[17] At this, the jockey's bosses merely shrug—a sign of their indifference and their power over him. As we will see, most of McCullers's freakish *flâneurs*—homosexuals, Jews, and the disabled alike—aspire to the jockey's level of defiance, but end up "domesticated" by the dominant social conventions.

Some critics have maintained that McCullers kitschifies her observer figures by associating their penchant for looking with a pathos and nostalgia that readers often find appealing. This "kitschiness" has been noted by *The New York Times* book reviewer Michiko Kakutani, who associates the writer primarily with high school English courses: "[McCullers's short stories are] well-crafted parables, easy to decipher, easy to comprehend.[18] Part of their accessibility, she argues, lies in McCullers's outdated use of an omniscient "authorial voice" (168). However, this reliable narrative voice, which puts pathos on display, also creates ironic melodramas that represent the symbiotic relationship between rigidly conventional cultures and eccentric outsiders. Commenting on the seemingly unbridgeable difference between tough philistines and sensitive oddballs, McCullers sophisticated narrators use a *flâneurish* gaze to demonstrate the extent to which the eccentric Other depends on the mainstream for self-definition and vice versa. In most cases, these incisive *flâneurs* identify with the freakish characters by affirming their differences and by calling into question the values of communities that eventually domesticate them. In this sense, the dominant narrative stance in most of McCullers's works is that of the freakish *flâneur*.

In *The Heart is a Lonely Hunter,* McCullers presents the perspectives of numerous observers, whose gazes are framed by the omniscient narrator's overarching vision. The first of these small town characters to display *flâneurish* tendencies is Biff Brannon, the owner of the New York Café. The part-Jewish Biff exhibits the stereotypical Jewish gaze with heavy lidded eyes that are "cold and staring."[19] Proud of his penchant for observation, he berates his wife Alice for her lack of curiosity: "You don't ever see or notice anything important that goes on. You never watch and think and try to figure anything out. Maybe that's the biggest difference between you and me after all . . . The enjoyment of a spectacle is something you have never known" (12). When Alice Brannon complains that Jake Blount, an obstreperous drunk refuses to pay for his meals, Biff replies nonchalantly, "I like freaks" (11). The narrator's observational stance melds with Biff's gaze when the latter tries to make sense of Jake Blount's freakish difference:

> Blount was not a freak, although when you first saw him he gave you that impression. It was like something was deformed about him—but when you looked at him closely each part of him was normal and as it ought to be. Therefore if this difference was not in the body it was probably in the mind . . . He was like a person who had been somewhere that other people are not likely to go or had done something that others are not apt to (17).

The narrator's simple yet highly evocative language shares vicariously in Biff's perception of Blount's psychological difference. In fact, the narrative perspective, in interpreting Biff's gaze, puts the restaurant owner's fetishistic tendencies on display. As the narrator explains and affirms Biff's fetishism, he/she also reinforces *The Heart is A Lonely Hunter* as a text that fetishizes deviance. As we will see, McCullers's many observer figures display a fascination with deviance and difference which the narrator presents as an unconventional but potentially illuminating stance towards life.

A consummate fetishist, Biff displays a prurient interest in stigmas. Showing this fascination, the narrator explains that Biff "had a special feeling for sick people and cripples. Whenever somebody with a harelip or T.B. came into the place he would set him up to beer. Or if the customer were a hunchback or a bad cripple, then it would be whiskey on the house" (18). The form of psychological deviance that Biff finds intriguing in Blount is his tendency towards mutable identity. In a drunken stupor, Blount exclaims, "I'm part nigger and wop and bohunk and chink. All of those . . . And I'm Dutch and Turkish and Japanese and American. . . . I'm one who knows. I'm a stranger in a strange land" (18–19). The narrator explains that Biff, troubled by this effusion, regards it as Blount's need to express something "personal" that was festering within (27). Unlike Alice, who preaches the Christian dictum "All men seek for thee," the atheistic Biff believes that people must look within in order to discover essential truths about themselves:

> In some men it is in them—the text is "All men seek for thee." Maybe that was why—maybe—He was a Chinaman, the fellow had said. And a nigger and a wop and a Jew. And if he believed it hard enough maybe it was so. Every person and everything he said was—(27).

Blount's self-perception as one who embodies multiple identities recalls nineteenth and early twentieth century etiologies of male hysteria, which associated this malady with the social instability and excessive mobility of working class men ("Male Hysteria and Early Cinema" 78). In a similar vein, Biff's *flâneurish* penchant for observing others and attempting to figure out their minds demonstrates his aim to go beyond the boundaries of the fixed self. The Baudelarian and Benjaminian *flâneur's* desire to fathom everyone's consciousness resembles the male hysteric's inability—or refusal—to conform to monolithic notions of identity. Both Biff and Blount demonstrate these hysterical leanings. While Blount's hysteria is more overtly dramatized, Biff displays hysterical mutability in his heightened sensitivity and androgynous nature. Despite his identity as a half-Jew with androgynous personality traits, Biff's *flâneurism* is more in the Baudelarian than in the freakish mold because he does not exaggerate and perform his difference for others.

Biff's androgyny becomes evident when he displays both a desire for and an identification with his mother. He muses that when he was a child, he "had loved" to gaze at her spectacle of femininity when he "enjoyed watch[ing] her comb and knot her long black hair" (192). At the same time that he sexualizes his mother, he identifies with the feminine role of a girl who plays with dolls: "He had thought that hairpins were curved as they were to copy the shape of a lady and he would sometimes play with them like dolls" (192). Biff's identification with femininity later becomes obvious to others who note his maternal tendencies. For example, his sister Lucille comments: "Bartholomew, you'd make a mighty good mother" (196). As Biff exhibits an androgynous consciousness, he tolerates these tendencies in others. As Biff notes Mick's boyish appearance, the narrator observes that all people are inherently androgynous and heterosexuality is not an end for everyone: "And on that subject why was it that the smartest people mostly missed that point? By nature all people are of both sexes. So that marriage and the bed is not all by any means" (112). Critics are divided regarding the authority of Biff's consciousness in *The Heart is a Lonely Hunter*. Lawrence Graver argues that although the narrator presents Biff as an incisive, objective consciousness, Biff's observations are often "banal."[20] As a case in point, Graver cites Biff's comment on androgyny, and finds more troublesome the lack of closure evident in many of Biff's reflections (Graver 55). On the other hand, Barbara A. White views Biff as "one of the strongest and most self-sufficient characters in McCullers's fiction "because of his insight and androgyny."[21] Perhaps by simultaneously evoking strength and uncertainty in Biff, McCullers demonstrates that his vision, while powerful, cannot fathom everyone. Thus despite Biff's *flâneurish* tendencies, the narrative demonstrates that a single character's observational stance is inadequate, even when it attempts to incorporate other perspectives within it.

Other *flâneurs* provide balance to Biff's perspective in the novel, particularly Mick and Singer, outsiders whose visible differences also make them function as freakish spectacles. A teenaged androgyne who defies conventional femininity, Mick also delights in observing others. When sitting in Biff's restaurant, "She took in the drunk in one long gaze, and then she turned her eyes to the middle of the room, where the mute sat at his table alone" (15). Mick exerts her voyeuristic tendencies more powerfully when she walks alone at night through the wealthier parts of her town and listens to music coming from various houses. Mick's *flâneurism,* which is considerably more selective than the Baudelarian and Benjaminian models, represents her desire to acquire upper middle class status and cultural capital:

> ... When she walked out in the rich parts of town every house had a radio. All the windows were open and she could hear the music very marvelous. ... There was one special house that got all the good orchestras. And at night she would go to this house and sneak into the dark yard to listen. There was beautiful shrubbery around the house, and she would sit under a bush near the window (86).

The Baudelarian and Benjaminian *flâneur,* by contrast, roams through parts of the city, oblivious to class distinctions. He, who "[wants] to make the whole world his family" aims to go beyond the boundaries of his elite background (Benjamin 9). On the one hand, Mick perceives and rebels against cultural restrictions imposed on women who aspire to develop their talents. When walking through an abandoned house in her neighborhood, she performs a small act of vandalism by writing on the walls the names of noted men: "EDISON, DICK TRACY, MUSSOLINI" (132). Attempting to view herself as one of them, she first "writes her initials—MK" and in a seemingly obnoxious gesture "crossed over to the opposite wall and wrote a very bad word—PUSSY," and beneath that she put her initials, too" (31). Throughout the novel, Mick frequently makes a distinction between "the inside room" of her consciousness that desires artistic achievement, and the "outside room" of the masculine sphere, which is indifferent to her desires. When writing the epithet "pussy," Mick satirizes the patriarchal relegation of women to sex objects who cannot exert power within the male dominated world where she desires admittance.

Gayatri Spivak, however, demonstrates that class boundaries hinder Mick far more than gender limitations.[22] Spivak suggests that, although the narrative does not state explicitly the relations among the words on the wall and expects the reader to make the connections, this "inside room" is the way to the real outside—the man's world, where the only viable female commodity is sex" (Spivak 132). Spivak notes, however, that despite obstacles posed by sexism, Mick faces greater losses when she must leave school to take a menial job to support her family during the Depression. Thus, the desire for class mobility that Mick expresses through her *flâneurism* becomes blighted less through gender than through poverty.

By virtue of his class position, the Baudelarian and Benjaminian *flâneur* can achieve unlimited satisfaction of his desires—he can possess what he merely observes. Through Mick, however, McCullers represents the pain that results from an impoverished *flâneur's* unfulfilled desires. The characteristic pathos of McCullers's prose accentuates this pain and rarely provides a means for transcending it. As noted earlier, this constant identification of pain and pathos annoys critics such as Leslie Fiedler, who prefers the "mature" acceptance of blighted desire. Unlike McCullers, Faulkner, Melville and James provide moral critiques of those who refuse to accept the inherent limitations of what they can attain. In *Moby Dick,* Melville presents Ahab dying in megalomaniacal pursuit of the white whale, that embodiment of feminine difference and undefinable deviance he has sought obsessively. By contrast, Henry James poignantly explores deliberate unfulfilled desire in *The Ambassadors* where the *flâneurish* Strether shares his creator's moral maturity by recognizing life's limitations. Faulkner's Southern fiction also provides a realistic perspective on blighted desire by representing, in Fiedler's words, "the eternal war between the dream of mobility and order and the fact of disorder and failure and sorrow" ("Adolescence and Maturity in the American Novel" 199).

In spite of his "maturity," Singer, the seemingly detached and godlike deaf mute in *The Heart is a Lonely Hunter,* appears to have gone beyond desire—a point that Fiedler overlooks in his reading of the novel. Simultaneously a spectator and a spectacle, Singer has an awe inspiring ability to draw others to him while appearing self-sufficient:

> The mute never smiled until several seconds after the funny remark had been made; then when the talk was gloomy the smile still hung on his face a little too long. The fellow was downright uncanny. People felt themselves watching him even before they knew there was anything different about him. His eyes made a person think he heard things nobody else had ever heard, that he knew things no one had ever guessed before. He did not seem quite human (21).

Though not immediately perceptible, Singer's deafness causes him to display odd, socially inappropriate responses. Unlike his friend, the retarded mute Antonapoulos, Singer is far from physically grotesque. Nonetheless, others display a fascination for his silence and his gaze, which are the outward manifestations of his difference. Singer's uncanny muteness resembles the Freudian uncanny in its ability to evoke simultaneous feelings of familiarity and strangeness in others. While his muteness makes him odd and "other," his placidity gives him a godlike cast that prompts spectators to project upon him their desire for comfort. For example, when Mick "thought of God she [imagined] Mister Singer with a long, white sheet around him. God was silent—maybe that was why she was reminded" (102). Singer inadvertently affirms his spectators' values by appearing to be anything they want him to be. He is a "white sheet" for their projected desires. When thinking about Blount's and Mick's fascination with Singer, Biff notes that the mute's silence enables others "to give him all the qualities they wanted him to have" (198). Singer's inherent strangeness is heightened by the spectators, whose manifold projections seem to free him from the bond of fixed identity. As McCullers makes clear, her characters' unstable identities result, in part, from their restless desire for self-transformation.

Another of Singer's admirers is Doctor Copeland, an African American physician who aims to effect Marxist revolutionary change for racial equality. Convinced that Singer is Jewish, Copeland describes the historical parallels between Blacks and Jews, as he projects a Jewish identity onto Singer. Copeland argues that he is "positive" that Singer is Jewish: "The name, Singer. I recognized his race the first time I saw him. From his eyes. Besides, he told me so" (257). Despite Singer's penetrating, ostensibly Semitic gaze, his Jewishness may well be a projection of Copeland's imagination. Highly literate and intellectual, Copeland, himself, fits cultural patterns that are stereotypically "Jewish."[23] The bane of Copeland's existence is his children's lack of interest in education and the attendant cultural advancement (68). Copeland's identification with stereotypical Jewishness is evident in his desire to see Singer as Jewish. When Copeland's daughter Portia affirms his belief that the newcomer Singer looked "not like someone from this town—more like a Northerner or maybe a Jew," Copeland takes on a look of "eagerness" (72).

McCullers also represents reactions to a stereotypical "smart Jew" in her final novel *Clock Without Hands* (1961), when J. T. Malone, a pharmacist dying of leukemia, displays resentment towards stereotypical Jewish intelligence. Malone, who had hoped to become a physician, claimed he had flunked out of Columbia University's School of Medicine because "Jew grinds . . . ran up the grade average so that an ordinary average student had no fair chance."[24] Malone also envies the Jewish Dr. Hayden, his friend and the physician who diagnoses his disease. As Malone ponders his own failed career goals, Hayden's Jewishness gains significance:

> The realization that Dr. Hayden was a Jew seemed of such importance that Malone wondered how he could have ignored it for so long. . . . Why had he

failed to notice? Maybe the doctor's given name had tricked him—Kenneth Hale. Malone said to himself that he had no prejudice, but when Jews used the good old Anglo-Saxon, Southern names like that, he felt it was somehow wrong (7).

More influenced by racist ideology than he is willing to admit, Malone prefers that people stay within given hereditary categories. He feels reassured when he remembers "that the Hayden children had hooked noses" and that he once saw the Hayden family by a synagogue (7).

Singer's ethnicity is more ambiguous, as Jake Blount scoffs at Copeland's notion that the mute has Semitic origins and insists that he must be Anglo-Saxon (257). While Blount shares Copeland's vision of radical social change, his unstable personality links him with madness and prurient spectacles. As a machinist, he works at numerous odd jobs at a carnival known as the Sunny Dixie, where on Saturdays he takes the most trying task of managing the crowds (130). When handling unruly groups of people he displays "savage energy" coupled with a weak gaze:

> Only his eyes did not share the violence of the rest of him. Wide gazing beneath his massive scowling forehead, they had a withdrawn and distracted appearance (130).

Displaying only an inward gaze, the solipsistic Blount is even less capable of expansive *flâneurism* than McCullers's other characters. Despite his hysterical inclination towards mutable identities, he cannot escape his own deviance, which is based on alcoholism. When he tries to break up a melee between black and white men, Blount loses his sense of self as he merges with the scene: "But he was caught. And without knowing when it happened he piled into the fight himself . . . senseless words were in his mind and he was laughing. He did not see who he hit and did not know who hit him" (289). Blount's loss of control resembles Tod Hackett's final transformation into an unruly member of the crowd in *The Day of the Locust*. In both instances, men who aspire to be all-knowing *flâneurs* end up consumed by the urban landscape that fascinates them.

Ostensibly, Singer displays a more expansive gaze than the other characters, one that successfully crosses racial and class boundaries. Unlike Mick, whose most significant *flâneurism* consists of glimpsing the homes of the wealthy, Singer ventures through the working class black and white sections, as well as "the neighborhoods of the rich" (169). During these walks, "Singer's gray eyes seemed to take in everything around him "and those whom he encounters project various identities onto him (170). Projection, the tendency to ascribe one's own emotions and desires on to others is inherently narcissistic, while a *flâneur*'s identification, which is based on the appropriation of others' roles and values, requires the subject to look beyond his or her self. The would-be *flâneur* who merely projects desires without any strong sense of identification with the object of his gaze comes to no end except narcissism. While he seems less narcissistic than the novel's other characters, Singer's *flâneurism* is not a satisfying or enlightening end in itself: "For after all he was only walking and going nowhere" (170). Singer's trajectory without an end suggests the mute's feelings of aimless solipsism without his companion Antonapoulos.

Charlie Parker, the cousin of the clownish, gluttonous, and childish retardate, committed Antonopoulous to a mental institution for exhibiting bizarre behavior in public. One of the novel's central mysteries centers on why Singer, who had proven from childhood to have high intelligence, loves the unselfconsciously buffoonish Antonapoulos. In a revealing dream, Singer sees the Greek mute as a naked godlike entity before whom many people kneel. That Antonoupolos holds an unspecified medal shows the vagueness of his religious significance and, perhaps, Singer's understanding that divinity is a human projection, rather than a universal truth. Tellingly, after the dream, Singer buys Antonapoulos a home movie projector, a symbol of his awareness that projection figures prominently both in their relationship and in their social roles. Ultimately, this understanding of the dynamics of narcissistic projection does not save Singer from this habit. He shows Antonapoulos two animated Disney films, one of Popeye and the other of Mickey Mouse. Viewing Antonoupolos as essentially childlike, Singer decides to project images that are linked mainly with children's entertainment—but he does so for his own visual pleasure. As Singer gazes lovingly at his friend, the latter stares transfixed at Mickey Mouse (189). However, Antonapoulos's difference is beyond the banal and comfortable realm of Mickey Mouse; he functions mainly as Singer's self-projection as a deviant Other with religious powers. As a retardate who indulges in sensual pleasures, Antonapoulos serves as Singer's naive, sexually alluring ego ideal.

Singer's projection of Mickey Mouse has broader significance in the text. Noting the fascistic nature of ubiquitous icons, Richard Burt states that, the Nazis were fascinated with Disney's ability to generate mass images. In this vein, Benjamin and Adorno could not decide whether Mickey Mouse was an insidious element of mass culture or a means towards creative self-expression.[25] As the site of others' projections, Singer has more in common with Mickey Mouse than Antonapoulos, for when he takes his *flâneurish* walks, he becomes a magnet for others' desires. Shortly after the publication of *The Heart is a Lonely Hunter*, McCullers described the book as "an ironic parable of fascism . . . presenting the spiritual rather than the political side of the phenomenon" (quoted in Evans 43). Critics have debated the significance of this claim. McCullers's friend and biographer Oliver Evans, for example, believes that, while this interpretation fails to capture the novel's breadth, it makes sense if we view the two mutes "as leaders, blindly invested by others with attributes in which they are only too conspicuously . . . lacking . . . ; in this absurdly grim game of follow-the-leader, the power beyond the power is a lunatic" (Evans 42). Just as blighted people project their fantasies of transcendence onto Singer, the placid, Godlike mute projects his own desire for divine perfection onto the "onanistic and exhibitionistic" Antonapoulos (Evans 42). This tendency to invest human beings with iconic power may be at the heart of the fascist cult of personality. However, the analogy may still be too narrow and limiting to fit the narrative's patterns. Questioning McCullers's claims for the novel, Laurence Graver asks, "In what sense does Singer actively tyrannize anyone; who is being regimented, and to what degree? Can Christ and Hitler live comfortably within the confines of the same myth?" (58). McCullers suggests that they can coexist within the psychodynamics of projection—the mechanism through which subjects may express and signify their desires for an all powerful version of themselves.

Far from the serene, godlike entity that others imagine him to be, Singer is not beyond the desire and self-doubt that gives rise to projection. Singer's God, a most unlikely deity in a Judeo-Christian context, is freakish, sensual and self-dramatizing. Noting Antonapoulos's penchant for masturbation and other bizarre exhibitionistic displays, Oliver Evans suggests that the mad mute resembles both "a pagan idol of some kind" and "a phallus" (42). As a freakish, phallicized spectacle, Antonapoulos is the embodiment both of Singer's sexual desires and his own deviance and difference raised to the level of divine beauty. Singer commits suicide after the death of Antonapoulos because of the loss of his stimulus to narcissistic self-projection. While Singer approximates a freakish *flâneur* who performs his difference as he gazes at those who make a spectacle of him, he can only love one who embodies his own freakish difference. Evans believes that "the ironic source of Singer's "selfless love may be sexual after all, and the meaning of the dream may be that the spirit must ultimately kneel before the altar of the flesh—a meaning which does not fit easily into the pattern of the novel" (42). While Evans focuses on McCullers's ostensible preoccupation with spiritual desire, he fails to comment on the centrality of deviant desire, which is linked with homosexuality throughout the novel. Thus, the ideological pattern in *The Heart is a Lonely Hunter* links the spirit and the flesh in ways that may be more obvious to contemporary readers.

Deviant desire, however, is also evident in Mick's aspirations for class mobility and creative androgyny within a small Southern town. Trapped in their social roles, she and other characters remain suspended within their difference and desires. For McCullers, attempted *flâneurism* leads to no end, since desire and projection produce an endless process of narcissism rather than identification and understanding. McCullers exaggerates the plight of the eccentric other by creating imprisoning melodramas from which there is no escape but death. The distance and the difference between McCullers's paralyzed characters and her own literary success raises questions. One may ask why her works dwell so much on small town tragedies, in view of her own apparently successful escape to New York and her meteoric rise as a young writer. In an article attacking McCullers's work and personality, Delma Eugene Presley trenchantly suggests that the writer was primarily out for fame.[26] According to some commentators from Columbus, Georgia, McCullers flaunted her bohemian ways and astonishing success before her neighbors. Presley considers this an immature, and self-serving performance that brings to light McCullers's lust for attention:

> Of course she was baiting the provincials—a temptation she could not resist, at least until she had made her point. Eventually her emotional war with Columbus ended, and she did feel very much the victor (25).

Despite the seemingly adolescent nature of McCullers's attitude towards her home town, her performance was also an enacted cultural commentary about provincial Southern towns. In playing this role, McCullers adopts the pose of the trickster who remains on the threshold of a household he or she aims to disrupt. According to Lewis Hyde, "[f]rom the trickster's point of view, [the one who stays on the threshold] must be an ideal type; it gives us the plot that never resolves itself . . ." (220). Like this trickster, McCullers gained a sense of power over those who have marginalized her by symbolically lingering in their "doorway," and making inappropriate gestures. Neither a complete insider nor outsider to Columbus, Georgia, McCullers proved a disruptive, tricksterish force by making small town Southern culture seem philistine and unyielding to difference. However, despite her "victorious" escape, McCullers remained troubled throughout her life by forms of paralysis, some of which may have had a psychosomatic basis.[27] Some would argue that McCullers maintained a constant battle with those from her hometown who snubbed and ridiculed her during her childhood. In *The Heart is a Lonely Hunter,* the only overtly hysterical character is Blount, whose penchant for mutable identities is based on psychological distress caused by self-contempt. While not himself an hysteric, Singer brings out others' potential for this malady by causing them to project onto him their transgressive desires. A kind of trickster, Singer functions as a mediator of antithetical values who affirms others's attempts to question the status quo, without altering it completely. Yet Singer is eventually destroyed, and this destruction emphasizes the futility of transgression in small Southern towns.

In her fourth novel, *The Member of the Wedding* (1946), McCullers returns to the study of a precocious pre-teenaged girl confined within a culture that tries to suppress her gifts and ambitions. Frankie Adams, like her predecessor Mick Kelly, wants to violate constraints of conventional femininity in order to gain expansive vision and the freedom to engage in self-fashioning. While Mick is limited primarily by socioeconomic barriers, Frankie is more clearly hindered by gender roles, thus revealing McCullers's growing preoccupation with the construction of gender in mid-twentieth century America. Displaying a strong tendency towards *flâneurism* Frankie seeks to go beyond the boundaries of the self by identifying with members of the working class and black communities. In this sense, she differs from Mick, who identifies mainly with wealthy whites who display cultural capital.

Thirteen year old Frankie's greatest fear is that by the age of eighteen, she will become freakishly tall enough to become a sideshow performer. When Frankie encounters freaks at a local visiting carnival, she fears them precisely because she identifies with them: "She was afraid of all the Freaks, for it seemed to her that they had looked at her in a secret way and tried to connect their eyes with hers, as though to say: we know you. She was afraid of their long Freak eyes."[28] Fascinated and repelled by the pin head, the hermaphrodite, and the racist spectacle known as the "Wild Nigger," Frankie fears that, like them, she will be categorized as an "unjoined" person fated never to marry (257, 272). Even as she fears defying gender norms, she also desires the prerogatives of those unconfined by the bonds of feminine expectations. For example, she envies men who fought in World War II, and associates the military draft with exotic travel and the opportunity to show bravery (275). Thus, from the outset, Frankie demonstrates an inner struggle based on cultural vs. personal approaches to gender.

As one who embodies and enacts differing values, Frankie functions as a trickster who tries to bridge antithetical ideas about men and women in order to destabilize rigid gender hierarchies. In his 1962 essay, Irving Malin suggests that, until the end of the novel, Frankie is a liminal figure who stays at the threshold of doorways closed to her—an image associated with the trickster (*Wunderkind* 121). Occasionally, when Frankie goes on her *flâneurish* adventures through the town, she enjoys putting on false identities in order to trick people:

> Me no speak English—Adios Buenos Noches—abla pokie peekie poo, she had jabbed in mock Mexican. Sometimes a little crowd of children gathered and the old Frankie would swell with pride and trickery—but when the game was over, and she was home, there would come over her a cheated discontent (306).

During these forays, Frankie tries to convince herself, as well as others, that she is capable of stepping outside the boundaries of her given identity to enjoy exotic re-constructed selves. At the same time, Frankie desires a more coherent self-concept aligned with conventional notions of sexual and social identity. Although she tries, she never successfully combines the potential for malleable identity with a stable core.

Throughout the novel, Frankie is plagued by a fear of going insane, which Berenice, the black housekeeper frequently reinforces. When Frankie declares that she will attach herself to her brother's wedding as the third member of the marital relationship, Berenice declares, "You going crazy. That's where you going" (286). In some instances, Berenice's function as a feminized superego who fosters Frankie's domestication contrasts her freakish image as a black woman with a prosthetic blue eye. The narrator emphasizes the strangeness of her appearance by stating, "why she had wanted a blue eye nobody human would ever know" (259). At other times, when she unknowingly facilitates Frankie's psychosexual difference, Berenice's social role corresponds more clearly to her freakish appearance McCullers uses sexually charged language to describe Berenice's attempt to subdue Frankie after an emotional outburst:

> . . . the two of them were close together as one body, and Berenice's stiffened hands were clasped around F. Jasmine's chest. . . . It was Berenice who finally sighed and started the conclusion of the last queer conversation (357).

Leslie Fiedler describes this scene as an example of what he views as a strain of "biracial homosexuality" evident throughout nineteenth and twentieth century American literature (*Wunderkind* 6). In a scene that blurs the distinction between motherly and lesbian love, McCullers subtly creates a space for subversive desire within a small Southern context. While everyone, as Berenice explains, may be "caught" within the boundaries of identity, McCullers suggests that there is room for "queer" transgressions even within the most repressive circumstances. From this perspective, Berenice's freakishness is evident in her role as an agent of ambivalent values.

Frankie engages in her most notable hysterical performance when she pleads with her brother and sister-in-law to take her with them on their honeymoon (376). Still determined to make her desire for boundary-crossing go beyond hysterical spectacles, Frankie makes a failed attempt to leave town, as her father sends a police officer to stop her. When Frankie is finally subdued by "The Law," she replaces her *flâneurish* desire for mutable identity with a keen perception of her conditioned role within the eyes of male authority: "At last she was staring at the Law and finally he looked into her eyes. He looked at her with eyes as china as a dolls, and in them there was only the reflection of her own lost face" (388). At the end of *The Member of the Wedding*, the narrator's detached, neutral tone reflects the normalizing force of the dominant culture that inflicts domestication on Frankie. Unable to alter the way things are, Frankie puts away her childish things and attempts to take on a adult identity. After her androgynous and artistic cousin John Henry dies of meningitis, Frankie displays more conventionally feminine interests in cooking and entertaining, even befriending Mary Littlejohn, a girl her own age. Both share interests in poetry and visual arts, and before Berenice Frankie declares, "I am just mad about Michelangelo" (389).

In gushing about the titanic male artist, Frankie unknowingly echoes Prufrock's ladies. Robbed of her ability to make daring and creative choices,

Frankie seems to dwell in a banal bourgeois world where sexually and intellectually frustrated women make trite comments. Having successfully confined her freakishness to pseudo-intellectual musings, Frankie now knows her place. Instead she now aspires to write poetry and travel to Europe with Mary Littlejohn—goals that while unconventional, are ostensibly more acceptable for women. While Frankie may have accepted a more mature identity, her new goals suggest an underlying desire to be an expatriate artist—a role far from acceptable to mainstream middle class America, especially during the 1950's. The potential for transgression remains, for Frankie's closeness to Mary has lesbian implications that are also evident in Berenice's strange disapproval of this friend. Even Mary last name, "Littlejohn," suggests a masculine woman. Berenice's rejection of Mary's "lumpy," "marshmallow white" appearance and her Catholic background, seem at once the grievances of a disapproving mother and a jealous lover. Unknown to her family—and even to herself—Frankie transfers her initial lesbian desire for Berenice to Mary Littlejohn, initiating a friendship that simultaneously fosters social acceptance and gender transgression.

CONCLUSION

Deviance, Defiance, and the Problem of "Weirdness"

"He can't be a real intellectual or artist; he's only being weird just to be weird." As a college student during the Reagan era, I often heard this refrain used both by conservative proto-yuppies and moderately left, would- be-intellectuals to disdain blue haired punks, hippie wannabes, anti-nuclear activists, and frisbee fanatics. The dominant conservative youth culture of the 1980's viewed the adaptation and performance of such forms of difference as inherently shallow and inauthentic. A "real" artist, intellectual, (or mentally balanced person), by contrast, would not have to behave in such an attention-starved manner. Not surprisingly, from the mid-1980's through the early 1990's, performance art, a radical theatrical form that highlights deviance, defiance, and the social construction of difference became a more visible counter discourse to the prevalent conservative ideologies, particularly in urban intellectual cultures.[1] Some critics viewed performance art as yet another symptom of 1980's narcissism, and of mindless prurience based on a pointless, juvenile impulse to embody weirdness.[2] The Dadaistic impulse to make fun of the bourgeoisie remains alive and well in late twentieth and early twenty first century America.

A precursor to many of the artists currently demonized by conservative critics of the National Endowment for the Arts is the photographer Diane Arbus, whose representations of transvestites, dwarves, retardates, and other deviants during the 1960's provoked sharply polarized reactions during her time. While some viewers were so disgusted by her work that they spat on it, others found her oddly compassionate towards those who embody difference.[3] In her analysis of Arbus's work, Susan Sontag praises the photographer for her empathy, yet questions her political engagement with her subjects.[4] For Sontag, photography itself tends to "colonize new experiences," and Arbus often lapses into fetishizing deviant others for mere shock effect (42). When investigating artists notorious for their fascination with oddity, one must always ask whether their primary aim in appropriating difference is to titillate and amuse an audience for profit, as *flâneur* colonizers. While critics accused West, Barnes, Browning, and McCullers of this form of exploitation, all of these artists used their engagement with oddity to foster a social criticism that explored issues of class, ethnicity, and gender. Although many recent representations of freakishness lack the depth with which these artists invest this subject, we must resist the conventional bourgeois impulse to dismiss all of them as gratuitously weird and consider the possibility that they constitute a socio-political critique.

At the height of the Reagan era in 1984, Patricia Bosworth wrote the only existing biography of Arbus, one filled with many tantalizing details about her private life, many of which speculate on her reasons for identifying with freaks. During the summer of 1984, before my senior year in college, I read Bosworth's highly descriptive and perhaps excessively anecdotal book, which presents Arbus as an artist who uses her remarkable freakish sensibility to question bourgeois norms. During the late 1960's and early 1970's, Arbus posed a poignant alternative to the ethos of money, class, conspicuous consumption, and social conformity which would become a national obsession in 1980's America. In 1991, art critic Catherine Lord published a scathing critique of Bosworth's book, one that targets the biographer as a gossip monger who merely accuses Arbus of having a morbid fascination with strangeness and alienation. Mimicking Bosworth's perspective, Lord writes, "In sum, Diane Arbus was weird. She may have started out a nice Jewish girl, but it obviously takes more than family."[5] Lord particularly takes Bosworth to task for presenting Arbus in terms of the cliché that artists must experience estrangement in order to gain creative insight. In fact, she finds Bosworth's reliance on this stereotype a fault with far more serious consequences than her annoying lack of citations and habitual use of unnamed sources.[6] The fact remains, however, that Arbus had once told an interviewer that as a child of privilege, she had never experienced adversity and found the *bourgeois* normality of her life alienating and "unreal."[7] Instead, Arbus envied social deviants, whom she likened to aristocrats:

> Most people go through life dreading they'll have a traumatic experience. Freaks are born with their trauma. They've already passed their test in life. They're aristocrats (*Diane Arbus* 5).

According to Lord, Bosworth's premise that Arbus identified with deviance is wrong headed because it is based on the cliché that the artist must suffer in order to produce intelligent and emotionally complex works. I argue that this notion remains a cliché only if it is repeated without adequate support, and is rendered mainly for its sensationalistic force. As Lord suggests, Bosworth advances this idea primarily to make the pulpy statement that Arbus suffered consequences that resulted from her transformation from a nice upper middle class daughter to a transgressive and self-destructive artist. In light of my argument in *Freaks and Desire*, I maintain that more than enough evidence suggests that late modernist artists were drawn to spectacles of deviance. However, this premise must be properly historicized and theorized to raise it from the level of cliché and sensationalism.

Lord states that Bosworth reverses Arbus's oft quoted comment that freaks are born with their trauma: "the really interesting freaks, Arbus's famous pronouncement to the contrary, aren't born with their trauma—they *create* it" (7). From this perspective, the made freak who wants to identify with deviance looks for trouble, since by taking the role of the alienated artist, she may find herself in situations and in psychic terrain that she is unable to handle. As *Freaks and Desire* has demonstrated, deviance, itself, is largely a social construct, and artists who create their own trauma by identifying with freaks, attempt to discover the ways that cultures construct difference. Had Bosworth understood the modernist and feminist context that frames Arbus's fascination with deviance, she could have produced a much stronger work. Like other artists of her class, ethnicity, and time, Arbus was fascinated by complex performances of deviance and difference where individuals are capable of functioning as both subjects and objects. Susan Sontag notes that Arbus, like Nathanel West, rebelled against a "verbally skilled, compulsively health-minded, indignation-prone, well-to-do Jewish family, for whom minority sexual tastes lived way below the threshold of awareness (*On Photography* 43). A Jewish freakish *flâneur* of the 1960's, Arbus produced a number of photographs that put on display and perform Jewish difference, while simultaneously calling into question the larger cultural enfreakment of Jews. More broadly, Arbus's sensibility is similar to that of all of the artists in this study in that it represents a freakish *flâneur's* modern, heterotopic mode of consciousness. Her photographs of New York's lurid underworld recall Barnes's interviews of showmen and freakish performers. Fascinated by Browning's *Freaks*, Arbus viewed the film numerous times when it was available at an art cinema on the Upper West Side of Manhattan.

In an interview during the mid 1970's, art critic A.C. Coleman suggested that Arbus's fascination with freaks stemmed from internalized anti-Semitism and sexism:

> I think that Arbus had a lot of self-loathing. I think that's what her pictures are about. If she were not Jewish, she would probably be accused of being anti-Semitic. Her characters of Jews are really obvious and come out of what psychologists call masochism, self hate. . . . And her pictures of women are uniformly hostile, unless they are in some way freaks—freaky women.[9]

However, cultural historian C. Zoe Smith believes that she disproves this accusation by showing that Jewish women subjects claimed to be not at all offended by Arbus's representation of Jews. In fact, they found these photographs to be parodic commentaries on Jewish women vaudevillians, Jewish mothers, and Jewish women who dye their hair blonde in an effort to affect idealized WASPishness (Smith 18).

Arbus did have an incisive parodic perspective, which she used to exaggerate and explore the enfreakment of Jews, and the performance of Jewish difference in one of her most provocative photographs titled "A Jewish Giant at Home With His Parents in the Bronx," NY 1970 (*Diane Arbus* 120). This photograph represents a victim of excessive growth standing in his family's living room, facing his two progenitors, both of whom are Jewish. The difference between the parents' relative diminutive size and the son's abnormal height is shocking. By posing three related individuals together, Arbus suggests that two normal points-of-origin produced an anomalous result, one that does not seem to have been derived from them. Bosworth notes that, for Arbus, Eddie Carmel's gargantuan body evokes the sense of disproportion that Alice perceived in Wonderland: "He's really very moving, when he lies down, because he looks in a way like Alice. I mean there's something extraordinary about the way he fills a couch. I don't know—like a mountain range" (194). While Arbus objectifies Carmel as a fascinating embodiment of difference, it is unclear whether he viewed himself as such a marvelous creature. An insurance salesman who harbored fantasies of becoming a "great actor," he could only get roles playing monsters on television shows. Despite his gradual deterioration from a bone disease, he also dreamed of joining a carnival (Bosworth 194). Instead of regarding himself as a victim, Carmel seems to have viewed himself as a born performer, one who would take any opportunity to play roles, including those that made a spectacle of his own difference.

For Arbus, Eddie Carmel is the Jew who both literally and figuratively does not fit his own context; he has outgrown his bourgeois surroundings to the point that he is anomalous and grotesque. As an artist who consistently aimed to shock the bourgeoisie which she "outgrew" both culturally and psychologically, Arbus also regarded herself as a freak within her own family, which valued material success and the conventional accouterments of power. Her fascination with the giant, as well as her tendency to ridicule and challenge middle class mores, demonstrates her powerful identification with the freak. When discussing this photograph, Arbus facetiously remarked, "You know how every mother has nightmares when she's pregnant that her baby will be born a monster? I think I got that in the mother's face as she glares up at Eddie thinking, "Oh MY GOD NO!" (Bosworth, 149). While identifying with Eddie's oddity, Arbus, a mother of two children, may have also identified with this maternal point of view. In her numerous renderings of deviants, we see multiple identification and the odd combination of compassion and fetishism that recalls Browning's tricksterish sensibility.

Deviance, Defiance, and the Problem of "Weirdness" | 137

Affixing her camera's eye on spectacles of difference, Diane Arbus was a freakish *flâneur* of the 1960's—the decade in which explorations of freakishness re-emerged as dominant themes in high and popular culture. In fact, by the late 1960's and early 1970's, various manifestations of freakishness became so ubiquitous that they risked losing both their shock value and their potential to foster incisive social criticism. Nonetheless, freakish *flâneurism* has survived until the end of the century as a counter discourse to bourgeois capitalism's equation of conventionality with virtue. This is not to say that deviance and difference are synonymous with virtue, but that in a culture economically driven towards a mainstream sensibility, freakish *flâneurs* present the enlightened engagement with weirdness as a valid alternative to the acceptance of stifling norms. The freakish *flâneur* does not merely fetishize the oddity of others, but aims to explore his or her own deviance as means towards enlightened defiance.

Notes

 INTRODUCTION

1. Andreas Huyssen, *After the Great Divide: Modernism, Mass Culture, Postmodernism* (Bloomington: Indiana UP, 1986), 16.

2. Mark Haller, *Eugenics: Hereditarian Attitudes in American Thought* (New Brunswick: Rutgers UP, 1963), 51.

3. For a fuller discussion of Sartje Baartman, see Rosemarie Garland Thomson, *Extraordinary Bodies: Figuring Physical Disability in American Culture and Literature* (New York: Columbia UP, 1997), 70–78. Also, Robert Bogdan goes into detail about Hiram and Barney Davis, the two brothers presented as "the Wild Men of Borneo," in *Freak Show: Presenting Human Oddities For Amusement and Profit* (Chicago: U of Chicago P, 1988), 121–127.

4. Donald K. Pickens, *Eugenics and Progressives.* (Nashville: Vanderbilt UP, 1968), 214.

5. Sander Gilman, *Difference and Pathology: Stereotypes of Sexuality, Race, and Madness* (Ithaca: Cornell UP, 1985), xiii.

6. Fredric Jameson, *Postmodernism: The Cultural Logic of Late Capitalism* (Durham: Duke UP, 1991), xi.

7. Robert Bogdan, "The Social Construction of Freaks," in *Freakery: Cultural Spectacles of the Extraordinary Body*, ed. Rosemarie Garland Thomson (New York: New York UP, 1996), 35.

8. Rosemarie Garland Thomson states that the freak show's main purpose was to "[construct] . . . the self-governed, iterable subject of American democracy—the American cultural self. . . . A freak show's cultural work is to make the physical particularity of the freak into a hypervisible instrument of the autonomous will, suitable to the uniform abstract citizenry democracy institutes." See Rosemarie Garland Thomson, introduction to *Freakery*, 11.

9. David A. Gerber, "The Careers of People Exhibited," in *Freakery*, 35.

10. Susan Stewart, *On Longing: Narratives of the Miniature, the Gigantic, the Souvenir, the Collection* (Baltimore: Johns Hopkins UP, 1984), 109.

11. Robin Blyn, "From Stage to Page: Franz Kafka, Djuna Barnes, and Modernism's Freak Fictions," *Narrative* 8:2 (May 2000), 138. Blyn cites the following important Marxist critiques of the spectacle: Guy Debord, *The Society of Spectacle*. 1968. Trans. By Donald Nicholson Smith. (New York: Zone Books, 1995); Walter Benjamin, "The Work of Art in the Age of Mechanical Reproduction," in *Illuminations*, edited by Hannah Arendt and translated by Harry Zohn, 217–51. (New York; Shocken Books, 1969). One of the most influential psychoanalytic critiques of the spectacle is Laura Mulvey's "Visual Pleasure and Narrative Cinema," in *Art After Modernism: Rethinking Representation*, ed. Brian Wallis, 361–374 (New York: New York Museum of Contemporary Art, 1984).

12. Kevin Hetherington, *The Badlands of Modernity: Heterotopia and Social Ordering* (New York: Routledge, 1997), 31. Gary Saul Morson and Caryl Emerson present a detailed critique of the Bakhtinian carnival as utopia in *Mikhail Bakhtin: Creation of Prosaics* (Stanford: Stanford UP, 1990) 86–96. Michael Gardiner counters some of their views in "Bakhtin's Carnival: Utopia as Critique," in *Critical Essays on Bakhtin*, ed. Caryl Emerson (New York: G.K. Hall,1999), 252–276. Michael Andre Bernstein challenges conventional approaches to the carnivalesque in *Bitter Carnival: Ressentiment and the Abject Hero* (Princeton: Princeton UP, 1992). Also see Stacy Burton, "Paradoxical Relations: Bakhtin and Modernism," *Modern Language Quarterly: A Journal of Literary History* 61:3 (September 2000), 519–543.

13. Robert Bogdan, *Freak Show: Presenting Human Oddities For Amusement and Profit* (Chicago: University of Chicago Press, 1990), 234–235.

14. For Foucault, heterotopia can be narrative and textual as well as spatial and geographic: " . . . heterotopias . . . dessicate speech, stop words in their tracks, contest the very possibility of grammar at its source; they dissolve our myths and sterilize the lyricism of our sentences." See Michel Foucault, *The Order of Things: The Archeology of Human Sciences* (New York: Vintage Books, 1973), xviii.

Chapter One

1. Rosemarie Garland Thomson uses the term "enfreakment" to define the social construction of the deviant body (Introduction to *Freakery* 10). This term has been adopted by cultural critics in the field of disability studies.

2. Max Nordau, *Degeneration*, (New York: D. Appleton, 1895; Lincoln: University of Nebraska Press, 1993), 9.

3. Nordau observes, "Next to the stiff monumental trim of Catharine de Medicis, and the high ruff of Mary, Queen of the Scots, goes the flowing white raiment of the angel in the Annunciation in Memling's pictures, and by the way of antithesis, that caricature of masculine array, the fitting cloth coat, with widely opened lapels, waistcoat, stiffened shirt-front, small stand-up collar, and necktie" (*Degeneration* 8).

4. See Judith Butler, *Gender Trouble: Feminism and the Subversion of Identity* (New York: Routledge, 1990).

5. See Jonas Barish, *The Antitheatrical Prejudice* (Berkeley: University of California Press, 1981).

6. George L. Mosse, inroduction to *Degeneration*, by Max Nordau, xvi.

7. Jay Geller, "The Aromatics of Jewish Difference; or Benjamin's Allegory of Aura," in *Jews and Other Differences: The New Jewish Cultural Studies*, ed. Jonathan Boyarin and Daniel Boyarin (Minneapolis: U of Minnesota Press, 1997), 239.

8. For a detailed analysis of such discourses, see Sander Gilman, *The Jew's Body* (New York: Routledge, Chapman and Hall., Inc., 1986).

9. Johanna Keller, "They Called Him Ugly, and the Pain is in His Music," *New York Times* (9 June 2002): sec. AR, p. 30.

10. Christoph Zuschlag, "A 'Educational Exhibition': The Precursors of *Entartete Kunst* and its Individual Venues," in *"Degenerate Art": The Fate of the Avant-Garde in Nazi Germany*, ed by Stephanie Barron (New York: Harry N. Abrams Inc., 1991), 87.

11. George L. Mosse, "Beauty Without Sensuality: The Exhibition *Entartete Kunst*," in *Degenerate Art*, 26.

12. Mario-Andreas Von Luttichau, "*Entartete Kunst*, Munich 1937: A Reconstruction," in *Degenerate Art*, 46.

13. Stephanie Barron, "1937: Modern Art and Politics in Prewar Germany," in *Degenerate Art*, 13.

14. "Facsimile of the *Entartete Kunst* Exhibition," in *Entartete Kunst*, 376.

15. Mosse explains, "The ideal of beauty played a dominant role as a symbol of morality, extending far beyond the realm of art: beauty helped to maintain control over the passions" (27).

16. Richard Burt, "Degenerate 'Art': Public Aesthetics and the Simulation of Censorship in Postliberal Los Angeles and Berlin," in *The Administration of Aesthetics: Censorship, Political Criticism, and the Public Sphere*, ed. Richard Burt (Minneapolis: U of Minnesota P, 1994), 231.

17. Clement Greenberg, "Avant Garde and Kitsch," 1939, in *Clement Greenberg: The Collected Essays and Criticism: Volume I, Perceptions and Judgements, 1939–1944*, ed. John O' Brian (Chicago: U of Chicago P, 1988), 7.

18. Clement Greenberg, "Surrealist Painting," 1944, in *Clement Greenberg, The Collected Essays and Criticism: Volume I*, 225.

19. Clement Greenberg, "Under Forty," 1944, in *The Collected Essays and Criticism: Volume I*, 177.

20. Clement Greenberg, "Abstract, Representational and So Forth," 1954, in *Art and Culture* (New York: Beacon Press), 135.

21. Florence Rubenfeld, *Clement Greenberg: A Life* (New York: Scribner, 1997), 57.

22. Darby Bannard, "The Unconditional Aesthete," http://www.sharecom.ca/greenberg/bannard.html.

23. Neil Jumonville, *Critical Crossings: The New York Intellectuals in Postwar America*. (Berkeley: U of California P, 1991), 160.

24. Alexander Bloom, *Prodigal Sons: The New York Intellectuals and Their World* (New York: Oxford UP), 86.

25. Florence Rubenfield states that T.S. Eliot was Greenberg's primary role model, despite Eliot's anti-Semitism (133). Like Eliot, Greenberg preferred art that appealed to the senses (135).

26. T.S. Eliot, "Sweeney Among the Nightengales," lines 23–24.

27. T.S. Eliot, "Gerontion," line 8.

28. T. S. Eliot, "Burbank with a Baedeker: Bleistein with a Cigar," 13–32.

29. Anthony Julius, *T.S. Eliot, Anti-Semitism, and Literary Form* (New York: Cambridge UP, 1996), 33.

30. Virginia Woolf, "Street Haunting,"1927, in *The Virginia Woolf Reader*, ed. Mitchell A. Leaska (New York: Harcourt, Brace, Jovanovich, 1984), 249.

31. Bryan Cheyette, ed., *Between Race and Culture: Representations of "the Jew" in English and American Literature* (Stanford: Stanford UP, 1996), 3.

32. See "A Nightmare of History: Ireland's Jew and Joyce's *Ulysses*" by Marilyn Reizbaum in *Between Race and Culture*, 102–113. Also see Stephen Connor's, "'I . . . AM. A.': Addressing the Jewish Question in Joyce's *Ulysses*," in *The Jew in the Text*, ed. by Linda Nochlin and Tamar Garb (New York: Thames and Hudson, 1995), 219–237.

33. Richard Ellman, *James Joyce* (New York: Oxford UP, 1959), 477. Also, see Otto Weininger, *Sex and Character*.1906. Translation of the 6th German edition. London: Heinemann. New York: Putnam.

34. James Joyce, *A Portrait of the Artist as a Young Man* (1916; repr. New York: Penguin Books, 1993), 226.

35. Par Lagerkvist, *The Dwarf*, trans. Alexandra Dick (New York: L.B. Fischer, 1945), 151.

36. Par Lagerkvist, *The Death of Ahasuerus*, trans. Naomi Walford (New York: Random House, 1962), 109–110.

37. Franz Kafka, "The Metamorphosis," in *The Penal Colony: Stories and Short Pieces*, trans. Willa and Edwin Muir (New York: Schocken Books, 1977).

38. Sander Gilman, *Franz Kafka: The Jewish Patient* (New York: Routledge, 1995), 13.

39. Mark M. Anderson, *Kafka's Clothes: Ornament and Aestheticization in the Habsburg Fin-de-Siecle* (New York: Oxford UP, 1994), 135.

40. "Josephine the Singer, or the Mouse Folk," in *The Penal Colony: Stories and Short Pieces*, 268.

41. See the chapter titled "Jewish Music" in *Kafka's Clothes: Ornament and Aestheticism in Habsburg Fin de Siecle*, 194–206.

42. Based on the *Torah*, the *halacha* validates the need for modes of order in everyday life that mirror the order of religious rituals. See Clement Greenberg's "Kafka's Jewishness,"1956, in *Art and Culture*, 268.

43. "On Paul Klee," in *Clement Greenberg: The Collected Essays and Criticism: Volume I*, 69.

44. "Review of Exhibitions," in *Clement Greenberg: The Collected Essays and Criticism: Volume I*, 64.

45. Benjamin states, "In the case of the art object, a most sensitive nucleus—namely its authenticity—is interfered with whereas no natural object is vulnerable on that score" ("The Work of Art in the Age of Mechanical Reproduction" 221). He defines this "sensitive nucleus" or "that which withers in the age of mechanical reproduction" as the "aura" ("The Work of Art in the Age of Mechanical Reproduction" 221).

46. Walter Benjamin, "The Significance of Beautiful Semblance" in *Walter Benjamin: Selected Writings, 1935–1938, Volume 3*. (Cambridge: The Belknap Press of Harvard UP, 2002), 137.

47. Greenberg states, "The nonrepresentational or 'abstract,' if it is to have any aesthetic validity, cannot be arbitrary and accidental, but must stem from some worthy constraint or original. This constraint, once the world of common, extraverted experience

has ben renounced, can only be found in the very process or disciplines by which art and literature have already imitated the former. These themselves have become the subject matter of art and literature" ("Avant Garde and Kitsch" 6).

48. Geller states, "The stereotyping of the Jews in terms of the Jewish stench coincided in the nineteenth century with a more general olfactory heuristic. Smell figures all that is opposed to the bourgeois public persona. For the European bourgeoisie smell is the 'sign of the lower social strata, lesser races, base animals' and of sexuality: the *odor di femina* and the *aura seminalis*" ("The Aromatics of Jewish Difference; or, Benjamin's Allegory of Aura" 223).

49. Walter Benjamin, "Surrealism," in *Reflections: Essays, Aphorisms, Autobiographical Writings*, trans. Edmund Jephcott (New York: Schocken Books, 1986), 181.

CHAPTER TWO

1. Emerson describes this American drive towards visionary experience especially in his oft-quoted dictum from *Nature:* "I become a transparent eyeball. I am nothing. I see all. The currents of the universal being circulate through me; I am part and particle of God." See Ralph Waldo Emerson, *Nature*. 1836, edited by Jaroslav Pelikan. (Boston: Beacon, 1985), 13. See Sacvan Bercovitch, *The Puritan Origins of the American Self* (New Haven: Yale UP, 1975). Also see Joyce Rowe, *Equivocal Endings in Classic American Novels: The Scarlet Letter; Adventures of Huckleberry Finn; The Ambassadors; The Great Gatsby*. (Cambridge: Cambridge UP, 1988). Rowe suggests that Melville and Hawthorne were skeptical of the Emersonian ideal of expansive vision and cultural renewal (6).

2. See George Anderson Kumler *The Legend of the Wandering Jew* (UP of New England, 1991).

3. See Walter Benjamin, *Charles Baudelaire: A Lyric Poet in the Era of High Capitalism* (London: NLB, 1973), 9. Benjamin's version of the *flâneur* is based on Baudelaire's characterization of this observer figure in "The Painter of Modern Life":

The crowd is his element, as the air is that of birds and the water of fishes. His passion and profession are to be one flesh with the crowd [. . .] To be away from home; to see the world, and to be at the centre of the world, yet remain hidden from the world— such are a few of the slight pleas which the tongue can but clumsily define [. . .] [We might liken the spectator] to a mirror as vast as the crowd itself; or to a kaleidescope gifted with consciousness, responding to each one of its movements and reproducing the multiplicity of life and the flickering grace of all elements of life.

4. Jay Martin, *Nathanael West: The Art of His Life* (New York: Farrar, Straus, & Giroux, 1972), 37.

5. According to West's biographer, Jay Martin, "[West] found no absolute standards of value in the beliefs of his parents or family. They wanted nothing but to be Americanized as rapidly as possible. Nor did he find sources of value in the rituals and traditions of Judaism" (50).

6. Stanley Edgar Hyman. *Nathanael West* (Minneapolis: U of Minnesota P, 1962), 12.

7. C.M. Doughty, *Travels in Arabia Deserta*. (New York: Heritage, 1953), 8.

8. Stephen Ely Tabachnick, *Charles Doughty*. (Boston: Twayne, 1981), 198.

9. Nathanael West, *The Dream Life of Balso Snell*. 1931. *The Complete Works of Nathanael West* (New York: Farrar, Straus, and Giroux, 1957), 7.

10. Victor Commerchero, *Nathanael West: The Ironic Prophet* (Syracuse: Syracuse UP, 1964), 17.

11. Contemporary psychoanalytic and cultural criticism, however, have called into question the Freudian view that fetishization is predominantly masculine. See Elizabeth Grosz, "Lesbian Fetishism?," in *Fetishism as Cultural Discourse*, ed. Emily Apter and William Pietz, 101–115. (Ithaca: Cornell UP. 1993).

12. Some critics maintain that surrealism constitutes one of the many branches of modernism. Jacqueline Chenieux-Gendron makes this case in her history of surrealism, which sees connections between this movement and other modernist and proto-modernist trends such as symbolism, non-Western "naif" forms, cubism, collage, psychoanalysis, black humor, the recreation of myth, and responses to World War I. See Jacqueline Chenieux-Gendron, "The Painter of Modern Life," in *Surrealism* (New York: Columbia UP, 1994) 29–110.

Also see Robert Shattuck, *The Banquet Years: the Arts in France, 1855–1918*. (New York: Anchor, 1961) 305–14. Shattuck makes a similar case when tracing the career of Guillaume Apollinaire, a dadaist poet influenced by cubism, the quintessentially modern parodic humor of Alfred Jarry and poetic experiments with fragmented language.

13. Sander Gilman, *The Jew's Body* (New York: Routledge, 1986), 39.

14. In late nineteenth century Britain, the reputation of Jews for intellectual achievement and cultural sophistication irked gentiles who regarded themselves as gatekeepers of the life of the mind. See Kathleen Adler, "John Singer Sargent's Portraits of the Wertheimer Family," in *The Jew in the Text*, ed. Linda Nochlin and Tamar Garb, 83–96 (London: Thames and Hudson, 1995). For example, a reviewer of John Singer Sargeant's "Portrait of Mrs. Carl Meyer and Her Children" stated that the painter's "skill had not succeeded in making attractive these overcivilized Orientals" (quoted in Adler 86). The phrase "overcivlized Orientals is telling. As Adler explains, English and French discourses often associated Jews with "the otherness of 'the orient' and this racist construction served to present "assimilated English Jews. . . . as bearing the marks of civilization to excess [. . .] and secondly as other to the point of being fantasy objects from the harem" (87).

15. Laura Mulvey has consistently reinforced the Lacanian notion that the spectacle is inherently feminine. Other discourses describe the enfreaked male body as lacking essential masculine qualities. Joan Hawkins explains that in the movie *Freaks*, "physical difference can also be read as an obsession with gender difference" ("One of Us," 272). That is, the film constructs the deformed and disabled men as unmanly, and strong women as excessively "butch." This emasculation of the enfreaked male is also evident in anti-Semitic discourses that present Jewish men as castrated, deformed, and effeminate (*The Jew's Body*, 133–37).

16. Daniel J. Keveles, *In the Name of Eugenics*. (Cambridge: Harvard UP, 1995), 47.

17. Daniel Walden, "Nathanael West: A Jewish Satirist in Spite of Himself," in *Critical Essays on Nathanael West*. Ed. Ben Siegel. (New York: MacMillan, 1994), 222.

18. Irving Goffman, *Stigma: Notes on the Management of Spoiled Identity* (New York: Simon and Schuster, 1963), i.

19. David Allen, *The Fear of Looking: Scopophilic and Exhibitionistic Conflicts*. (Charlottesville: U of Virginia P, 1974), 118.

20. Eve Sedgwick argues that high modernist self-referentiality and intertextuality are closeted homosexual discourses, See Eve Sedgwick, *The Epistemology of the Closet* (Berkeley: U of California P, 1990) 164:

> [T]his rhetoric of male modernism serves a purpose of universalizing, naturalizing, and thus substantively voiding, depriving of content—elements of a specifically and historically male homosexual rhetoric. But just as the gay male rhetoric is itself already marked and structured and indeed necessitated and propelled by the historical shapes of homophobia, for instance by the contingencies and geographies of the highly permeable closet, so it is true that the homophobic male modernism bears the structuring fossil-marks of and in fact spreads and reproduces the specificity of desire that it exists to deny.

21. David Madden, "The Shrike Voice Dominates *Miss. Lonelyhearts*," in *Critical Essays on Nathanael West*, ed. Ben Siegel, (New York: MacMillan, 1994), 203.

22. West's biographer Jay Martin reveals that Perelman viewed West's satiric sensibility in terms of a rancorous dwarf:

> "There are really two Wests, Perelman intimates . [. . .] [H]e hinted that West's personality was divided between self-deluding fantasy and scorn for illusions. . . . But the West who wrote the novel [*Miss.Lonelyhearts*], Perelman continues, only apparently joking, was only eighteen inches high. "He is very sensitive and somewhat savage. He is a kind of eternal figure of revolt—having been seen at Austerlitz and Jena—savage, close to madnness, a man out of the world of dreams, the creative dwarf, the inner man. This, Perelman says, is the true Nathanael West (Martin 202).

23. Eve Sedgwick explains that sentimental kitsch during the nineteenth century was undoubtedly "feminocentric," yet by the twentieth century it developed a "complex and distinctive relation to the male body" (*Epistemology of the Closet* 150). With reference to Sedgwick, Andrew Hewitt argues that the reactionary "Kitsch representationalism" of Nazi and communist art encodes undisguised homoeroticism in its depiction of "cute boys in black uniforms." This "kitsch representationalism [. . .] marks the meeting point of homosexuality and fascism for the contemporary cultural imagination." See Andrew Hewitt, *Political Inversions: Homosexuality, Fascism, and the Modern Imaginary* (Stanford: Stanford UP, 1996), 206. After publishing *Miss. Lonelyhearts* in 1933, West had planned to write a satiric sketch about fascism in which the title character must contend with fascists and capitalists (Martin 218). While *Miss. Lonelyhearts* does not satirize the fascist elements of representational homosexualized kitsch, it demonstrates the extent to which a self-consciously kitsch figure with a messianic complex and an uncertain sense of his masculinity can develop fascistic tendencies.

24. Robert Emmet Long describes *A Cool Million* as West's "fable of the coming to power of American fascism" (99).

25. Nathanael West, *A Cool Million*. 1934. *The Complete Works of Nathanael West* (New York: Farrar, Straus, and Giroux, 1957), 142.

26. In describing Wu Fong's whorehouse as a "parodic museum" of American cultural forms, Rita Barnard argues that this collection illustrates West's disgust with the American impulse to commodify and fetishize objects and people. See Rita Barnard, *The Great Depression and the Culture of Abundance: Kenneth Fearing, Nathanael West, and Mass Culture in the 1930's.* (New York: Cambridge UP, 1995), 147.

27. Long notes that an "odd feature of *A Cool Million* is that many of its male characters have been given Hebraics or Old Testament first names" (101). According to Long, West suggests an "analogy with the tribes of Israel, a people whose lofty covenant with God has been breached, their high heritage despoiled, just as the American dream has been despoiled in the Depression" (101). Similarly, this fantasy of American aggrandizement poses a threat to the idealized observer perspective that West has stereotypically associated with Jews—a perspective that West tries to maintain with his freakish *flâneurish* stance.

28. Nathanael West, *The Day of the Locust*. 1939. *The Complete Works of Nathanael West* (New York: Farrar, Straus, and Giroux, 1957), .

29. Gerald Locklin, "The Day of the Painter, the Death of the Cock: Nathanael West's Hollywood Novel," in *Los Angeles in Fiction: A Collection of Essays From James McCann to Walter Mosley*, ed. David Fine, 69 (Albuquerque: U of New Mexico P, 1985).

30. Susan Sontag, "Notes on Camp," in *A Susan Sontag Reader* (New York: Vintage Books, 1983), 17.

31. Daniel Walden believes that West satirically identifies both the bird and Abe Kusich with Jews who have had the will to survive tragedies:

> [West's] Southern California is where people come to die. They find that here one means of survival is role playing, a discovery made by Jews centuries back. West suggested this knowledge through a series of minor characters and symbols. [. . .] Most significant and obvious is the cock named Juju (Jew Jew) that gaffs the cock Hermano in the brain. These elements alone suggest that West was trying hard to be a parodist, a heretic and a moralist (220).

32. Deborah Sue Wilson, "Lost Boundaries: Kenneth Burke, Nathanael West, Djuna Barnes and the Disorder of Things." Ph.D. diss., University of California, Irvine, 1987), 80.

33. See Richard Keller Simon, "Between Capra and Adorno: West's *Day of the Locust* and the Movies of the 1930's," *Modern Language Quarterly* 54), 515. In his analysis of the relationship between *The Day of the Locust* and the movies of the 1930's, Keller Simon argues that West's defense of "high" aesthetic standards resembles attitudes held by members of the Frankfurt school:

> Indeed, much of the argument in Adorno's 1938 essay on popular music is remarkably similar to the analysis of mass culture in West's novel, as are some elements of Walter Benjamin's essay, "The Work of Art in the Age of Mechanical Reproductions."

34. See Lori Merish, "Cuteness and Commodity Aesthetics: Tom Thumb and Shirley Temple," in *Freakery*, 185–203.

35. One critical line associates a tendency to view narratives in terms of performance and rhetoric with postmodern consciousness. Responding to Jean Francois Lyotard, Bill Readings and Bennett Schaber define the "postmodern moment" as an event or an instance that provokes questions about the value and significance of cultural narratives that have shaped history. See Bill Readings and Bennet Schaber, *Postmodernism Across the Ages* (Syracuse: Syracuse UP, 1993), 11. They argue that the "postmodern moment" could happen in any cultural context, and is based not on a critical, polemical stance towards metanarratives as constituted by rhetorical figures [of narrative] for which they are unable to account for" (12).

Chapter Three

1. Nancy Levine and Marian Urquilla. "Introduction." *The Review of Contemporary Fiction*. 13:3 (1993): 7–15.

2. With reference to Celine's *Les Beaux Draps* (1941), Kristeva exposes the anti-Semite's grotesque representation of Jews as a rejection of contamination and femininity—elements that he recognizes within his own psyche:

> The Jew becomes the feminine exalted to the point of master, the impaired master, the ambivalent, the border where exact limits between same and other, subject and object, and even beyond these, between inside and outside, and disappearing—hence, an object of fear and fascination—*Abjection itself*. He is abject, dirty, rotten. And I who identify with him, who desire to share with him a brotherly, mortal embrace in which I lose my own limits, I find myself reduced to the same abjection, a fecalized, feminized, passivated rot. . . . (Julia Kristeva, *Powers of Horror*. [New York: Columbia UP] 185).

While Levine and Urquilla describe Barnes's fascination with difference in terms of Kristeva's definition of the abject, I view it more in relation to the Freudian uncanny. For Kristeva, nothing is recognizable in the realm of the abject, yet the uncanny represents a return to a familiar, albeit more primordial state within the unconscious. As I will demonstrate, Barnes represents her explorations of deviance and difference more in terms of a return to the uncanny, which exists outside of the realm of the symbolic.

3. Since the fetishized woman represents the lack on which castration is based, "the woman as icon, displayed for the gaze and enjoyment of men, the active controller of the look, always threatens to evoke the anxiety it originally signified" (Laura Mulvey. "Visual Pleasure and Narrative Cinema." *Screen*. 16.3, Autumn 1975: 13).

4. Shari Benstock. *Women of the Left Bank: Paris 1900–1940* (Austin: University of Texas Press, 1986), 367.

5. For a detailed analysis of the female fetishist, see Elizabeth Berg, "The Third Woman." *Diacritics: A Review of Contemporary Criticism*. 12:2 (1982): 74–87. Berg explains that Jacques Derrida and Sarah Kofman have argued that the woman who refuses the Freudian imperative that she is castrated functions as "the woman who affirms, in spite of everything produced to the contrary, and the penis is both there and not there, and the question is undecidable, that she may be both active and passive, both masculine and feminine" (13). This "third woman, as Derrida and Kofman conceive her, can function in the rational masculine realm of the symbolic, and the negative, uncanny, preverbal realm of the feminine (13). Berg emphasizes that this "affirmative" woman is by no means a hybrid of the masculine and the feminine; instead, she vacillates between masculine and feminine subject positions, and, like the male fetishist, has an innate tolerance for ambiguity and paradox that fosters intellectual flexibility (19).

6. As Doane notes, quoting Michelle Montrelay, a woman's performance of feminine seductiveness usually has associations with evil women:

> This type of masquerade, an excess of femininity, is aligned with the *femme fatale* and, as Montrelay explains, it is necessarily regarded by men as evil incarnate: "It is this evil which scandalizes whenever woman plays out her sex in order to evade the word and the law. Each time she subverts a law or

word which relies on a predominately masculine structure of the look. By destablilizing the image, the masquerade confounds the masculine structure of the look." (Mary Ann Doane. "Film and Masquerade: Theorising the Female Spectator." *Screen* 23. 3.4 [1982]: 74–87).

7. In her classic essay, "Womanliness as a Masquerade," Joan Riviere argues that women who desire power associated with masculinity often behave in an exaggeratedly feminine manner in order to "avert anxiety and the retribution feared from men." (Joan Riviere, "Womanliness as a Masquerade," in *Formations of Fantasy*, ed. Victor Burgin, James Donald and Cora Kaplan [New York: Methuen, 1986]), 36.

8. Djuna Barnes. "Flo Ziegfeld is Tired of Buying Hosiery." 1914. Reprint, in *Interviews*, ed. Alyce Barry. (Los Angeles: Sun and Moon, 1989), 71.

9. Philip Herring. *Djuna: The Life and Work of Djuna Barnes*. (New York: Penguin Books, 1995), 91.

10. Djuna Barnes, "Interviewing Arthur Voegtlin is Something Like Having a Nightmare." Reprint in *Interviews*, 77.

11. Several critics have observed that Barnes never talks down to her mass audience. Nancy J. Levine notices that despite Barnes's penchant for representing sensationalistic topics, "her goal was to make the reader aware of the strange and contradictory nature of the quotidian world." (Nancy J. Levine, "'Bringing Milkshakes to Bulldogs': the Early Journalism of Djuna Barnes." *Silence and Power*. Ed. Mary Lynn Broe. [Carbondale: Southern Illinois UP, 1991],28).

12. There are contradictory accounts as to whether Florenz Ziegfeld was Jewish. While several biographies state that his background was German and Lutheran, Neal Gabler suggests that Ziegfeld, along with "other Jewish showmen," such as Marcus Loew and Lewis Selznick formed "a collaboration of outsiders" who relied on financier Attilio Giannini to provide loans. (Neil Gabler. *An Empire of Their Own: How the Jews Invented Hollywood.* [New York: Routledge, 1988], 134).

13. (Harley Erdman. *Staging the Jew: the Performance of an American Identity, 1860–1920.* [New Brunswick: Rutgers UP, 1998], 94). Harley Erdman suggests that many Jewish theatrical producers at the turn-of-the-century "came from assimilated families that had immigrated before 1881" and "were all ready to shunt aside the cultural politics of the Yiddish world." (Erdman 11).

14. Djuna Barnes. "David Belasco Dreams." 1916. Reprint, in *Interviews*, 192.

15. Djuna Barnes. *Nightwood*, ed. T.S. Eliot (Reprint, New York: New Directions, 1961), xvi.

16. Susan Buck-Morss suggests that the Benjaminian *flâneur* functions as a spectacle when he performs as a "cultural producer" who "profits by peddling the ideological fashion" (Susan Buck-Morss, *The Dialectics of Seeing: Walter Benjamin and the Arcades Project.* (Cambridge: MIT Press: 1997), 307. An extreme example of this is a dangerous, anti-Semitic journalist whom Benjamin regarded as a "salaried *flâneur*" (307). The *flâneur* as writer also becomes a spectacle or "cafe attraction" when is sits and writes in public places (306).

17. Priscilla Parkhurst Fergusson, "The *Flâneur* On and Off the Streets of Paris." *The Flaneur*, ed. Keith Tester (New York: Routledge, 1994), 27.

18. Marjorie Garber argues persuasively that by exaggerating the "artifactuality of women's bodies," male transvestites bring to light "another . . . concern about the

artifactuality and detachability of maleness" (Marjorie Garber, *Vested Interests: Cross Dressing and Cultural Anxiety* [New York: Routledge, 1992], 125.

19. Sigmund Freud. "The Uncanny." *The Standard Edition of the Complete Psychological Works of Sigmund Freud*. Trans. James Strachey. (London: The Hogarth Press, 1955), 219–251.

20. See chapter six of *Downcast Eyes*, where Martin Jay discusses Freudian and Lacanian arguments for the primacy of language over the visual. In light of what he terms the "anti-occularcentrism of many modern Western discourses, Jay ultimately argues that the realm of the verbal cannot "be shorn entirely of its sensual metaphoricality" related to the visual (Jay, Martin. *Downcast Eyes: the Denigration of Vision in Twentieth-Century Thought*. [Berkeley: University of California Press, 1994], 589–590).

21. Margaret Cohen presents a contrasting notion to the uncanny as a site of power and knowledge in *Profane Illumination*, where she elaborates on the Lacanian concept of *tuch*—an encounter with the real that provides an experience beyond the symbolic:

> . . . For Lacan the factors of material overdetermination become the symbolic order that Lacan's *tuché* situates the subject at the meeting between psychic drives and the symbolic order . . . (Cohen, Margaret. *Profane Illumination: Walter Benjamin and the Paris of Surrealist Revolution*. [Berkeley: University of California Press, 1993], 153.

22. Djuna Barnes. "Alfred Stieglitz on Life and Pictures: One Must Bleed His Own Blood." 1917, Reprint, in *Interviews*, 217.

23. Barbara Buhler Lynes. *O'Keefe, Stieglitz and the Critics, 1916–1929*. (Ann Arbor: UMI Research Press, 1989), 17.

24. Lynes explains that "Stieglitz's commitment to the idea that the expression of children and of what he regarded as primitive peoples was relevant to the concerns of modern artists is a reflection of the value he assigned the unconscious" (10). Stieglitz and his coterie of artists and theorists presented "a direct challenge to the idea that the intellect was the most distinguishing feature of the human species and the source of its creative accomplishments" (12).

25. Benita Eisler explains that Stieglitz was as much an entrepreneur as he was an artist:
> Stieglitz represented a unique mix of qualities: the artist who exuded the combative, commanding style of the new breed of entrepreneur. In many ways, he had more in common with Henry Ford—born the same year as Alfred—than with the romantic archetype of the reclusive artist Albert Pinkham Ryder, living out his solitary last years a few blocks from the future 291 [Stiegltiz's studio] (Eisler, Benita. *O'Keefe and Stiegltiz: An American Romance*. [New York: Penguin Books: 1991], 95).

26. Interestingly, Barnes, a female fetishist who displays a fascination with Jewish *flâneurs*, was named after a character in Eugene Sue's *The Wandering Jew* (1844–45). Philip Herring explains that Barnes claimed to be named after Djalma, an Indain prince in this novel (32). Jane Marcus demonstrates that this character, who "is tattooed by a 'thug' in Java in his sleep," and who kills a panther, has associations with animality and cultural marginality. (Jane Marcus, "Laughing at Leviticus: *Nightwood* as Woman's Circus Epic." *Silence and Power*, 229).

27. Djuna Barnes. "The Wild Aguglia and Her Monkeys." 1913. Reprint, in *Interviews*, 23.

28. Djuna Barnes. "The Head of Babylon." *Smoke and Other Early Stories*. Ed. Douglas Messerli. (Los Angeles: Sun and Moon Press, 1993). For a detailed analysis of the image of Salome in late nineteenth century art and literature see Bram Dijkstra's *Idols of Perversity: Fantasies of Feminine Evil in Fin-de-Siecle Culture*. (New York: Knopf, 1996), 352–401.

29. Between 1905 and 1914, British suffragists who went on hunger strikes in order to protest their government's refusal to allow women to vote were often subjected to force feedings by political authorities. Barbara Green explains that "forcible feeding, as event lent itself to a variety of representations of femininity—those produced by the Artist's Suffrage League imagined forcible feeding as a rape of the womanly woman, those produced by anti-suffragists presented angelic nurses forced to deal with the disorderly and unruly crone." (Barbara Green. "Specular Confessions: 'How it Feels to Be Forcibly Fed.'" *The Review of Contemporary Fiction* 13:3 (1993): 71.

30. Djuna Barnes, "How It Feels to Be Forcibly Fed." 1914. Reprint in *New York*, ed. Alyce Barry, 176. (Los Angeles: Sun and Moon, 1989), 176.

31. Djuna Barnes, "Surcease in Hurry and Whirl—On the Restless Surf at Coney." 1917. Reprint in *New York*, 279.

32. See Djuna Barnes, "Dempsey Welcomes Women Fans." 1921. Reprint in *Interviews*, 283–287. Also see, Djuna Barnes, "My Sisters and I at a New York Prize Fight." 1914. Reprint in *New York*, 168–173.

33. Djuna Barnes. "The Girl and the Gorilla." 1914. Reprint in *New York*, 181.

34. See Djuna Barnes, *Ryder*. Reprint 1928. Normal: Dalkey Archive Press, 1990. Ryder views himself as "The Beast Thingumbob," a monster who can subdue an equally formidable beast woman. A composite of different animals, the lovesick Beast Thingumbob finds a faceless ten breasted female creature who vows to die for him in childbirth. Sheryl Stevenson explains that Ryder's beast woman can be defined in Bakhtinian terms as a representation of the carnivalesque grotesque body—a rendering of the human form in terms of bodily functions and deformity (Sheryl Stevenson. "Writing the Grotesque Body: Djuna Barnes' Carnival Parody," in *Silence and Power*, 90).

35. quoted in Angus Wilson. *The Strange Ride of Rudyard Kipling*. (New York: Viking Press, 1977), 155.

36. Djuna Barnes. "Djuna Barnes Probes the Soul of Jungle Folk at the Hippodrome Circus." 1915. Reprint, in *New York*, 193.

⊠ Chapter Four

1. Judith Butler articulates the relation between performance and epistemological power when discussing the connection between gender and transvestism. She argues that drag performances call into question the naturalness of conventional sex roles by ironically exaggerating "those aspects of gendered experience that are falsely naturalized" in order to support the heterosexual status quo (*Gender Trouble: Feminism and the Subversion of Identity* 137).

2. Joseph Frank goes into detail about O'Connor's resemblance to Eliot's Tiresias. Besides having "homosexual inclinations," both claim to speak from a universalizing historical perspective, and function as "father confessors" to marginalized people. (Joseph Frank, *The Widening Gyre: Crises and Mastery in Modern Literature* (New Brunswick: Rutgers UP, 1963), 43.

3. According to Eliot, Tiresias "is yet the most important personage in the poem, uniting all the rest" (quoted in Jewel Spears Brooker and Joseph Bentley, *Reading the Waste Land: Modernism and the Limits of Interpretation*. (Amherst: The U of Massachusetts P, 1990) 53. In doing so, he reflects Eliot's movement beyond Bradlean epistemology and towards the universalizing perspective of myth. As Jewel Spears Brookner and Joseph Bentley argue, Tiresias represents a mythic vantage point that supercedes the limitations of perception from only within or only outside a field of vision (53).

4. Huyssen describes "imaginary male femininity" as the attempt by nineteenth and twentieth century male writers to appropriate a "deviant" feminine subject position (45).

5. T.S. Eliot, introduction to *Nightwood*, by Djuna Barnes (New York: Harcourt, Brace & Co, 1937; reprint, New York: New Directions, 1961), xiv, xv, and xvi. .

6. Early in his career, Eliot was concerned with defining the difference between cogent and obtuse uses of rhetoric. For instance, in "Rhetoric and Poetic Drama," Eliot asserts that speeches within plays should never address the spectators directly, but exaggerate the distance between the audience and the performers:

> A speech in a play should never appear to be intended to move us as it might conceivably move other characters in the play, for it is essential that we should preserve our position of spectators, and observe always from the outside with complete understanding (T.S. Eliot, *Selected Essays*. (New York: Harcourt, Brace and Company, 1950) 28.

7. Commenting on the reclusive tendencies she developed later in life, Barnes told an interviewer, "I used to be invited by people who said, 'Get Djuna for dinner, she's amusing.' So I stopped it." (Mary Lynn Broe, introduction to *Silence and Power: A Reevaluation of Djuna Barnes* (Carbondale: Southern Illinois UP, 1991), 5–6.

8. Adrielle Anna Mitchell, "'The Plain Reader Be Damned': Confusion as Method in the Works of Djuna Barnes." (Ph.D. diss., University of California Santa Cruz, 1995), 215.

9. According to Altman, the only alternatives to such discourses were provided by organized religion and the state, both of which viewed "social deviance as a sin—a curable or punishable weakness of the will . . ." (163).

10. Schilefer, Ronald. "Yeats's Postmodern Rhetoric," in *Yeats and Postmodernism*, ed. Leonard Orr, (Syracuse: Syracuse UP, 1991), 18–19.

11. Schliefer states, "For the postmodern, the articulation of 'nothing,' in one way or another, is hardly a crises; it hardly imagines as Yeats said, that 'where there is nothing, there is God'" (19).

12. Barnes based Felix Von Volkbein on Guido Bruno, a son of a Rabbi and a closeted Jew whose real name was Curt Kisch (Herring 216). A publisher of chap books in early twentieth century Greenwich Village, Bruno tried to commodify Barnes "as a risqué lesbian poet whom tourists would do well to read and gawk at" (Herring 215). Barnes turns the tables on Bruno by satirizing his tendency to "bow down" to the dominant culture.

13. Anthony Julius explains that in "Burbank with a Baedeker: Bleistein with a Cigar," T.S. Eliot portrays upwardly mobile Jews as "effortlessly philistine" and "bogusly aristocratic" (Anthony Julius, *T.S. Eliot, Anti-Semitism, and Literary Form* (Cambridge: Cambridge UP: 1995), 99.

14. Franz Fanon ironically suggests that the West has attributed black males with such extraordinary sexual powers, that they have become "penis symbols" See Franz Fanon,

Black Skin, White Masks (New York: Grove Press, 1967), 159. Fanon also explains that the matriarchal structure of black families in the French Antilles does not produce conventional oedipalization in black male children (152). From this perspective, black males, like women, never appropriate the phallus, while they become fetishized objects.

15. Citing Michel Thevoz's analysis of the cultural significance of tatooing, Jane Marcus argues that the tattooed body represents the "primitive human grappling with the mirror stage of development and identity formation, so that human skin is humanity's 'first ground and surface of sign making." (Jane Marcus, "Laughing at Leviticus: *Nightwood* as Woman's Circus Epic," in *Silence and Power: A Reevaluation of Djuna Barnes*, ed. . Mary Lynn Broe, (Carbondale: Southern Illinois UP, 1991), 227. From this perspective, the marked body on the one hand represents "symbolic separation from the mother," yet also signifies "the return of the repressed savage and unconscious desire" (227). As a caricature of the racist projection of the phallic black male, Nikka calls into question the Western need to define itself against cultural Others. By presenting himself in terms of parody and exaggeration, he in turn, presents a mirror to the white Western unconscious.

16. The earlier Dr. Matthew O'Connor declares in his soliloquy, "I'm a woman of a few thousand gestures and a hundred words. . . ." (Djuna Barnes, *Ryder* 1928; reprint, Normal, IL: Dalkey Archive Press, 139). Also, when asked if he believes in heredity he states, "I would be an ass if didn't . . . Heredity is absolute and conclusive proof of God and the father" (201).

17. Kaja Silverman, *Male Subjectivity at the Margins* (New York: Routledge, 1992), 340. Contemporary discourses on gender have criticized this view "for its heterosexist bias [based on] its conception of homosexuality as a 'misplaced heterosexuality'" (Silverman 344).

18. Djuna Barnes, *Ladies Almanack*. 1928; (reprint, Normal, Illinois: Dalkey Archive Press, 1992), 6.

19. As Fran Michel notes, this rejection of binary logic implicitly defies essentializing discourses on gender:

> Yet if bisexual positioning is understood as one way of acknowledging the complexity of sexuality—of the interplay of desire, fantasy, behavior, social affiliation, emotional connection—then it serves as a challenge to essentializing dichotomies, a challenge evident in Barnes's works (Fran Michel, "I Just Loved Thelma: Djuna Barnes and the Construction of Bisexuality," *The Review of Contemporary Fiction* 3:3 (1993): 55.

20. Judith Lee. "The Sweetest Lie," in *Silence and Power*, 215.

21. In her interview "Who's the Last Squatter?," Barnes shows disdain for the homeless of early twentieth century New York City. After interviewing a group of squatters in Brooklyn, Barnes cannot leave the scene quickly enough:

> You give the ticket man your nickel and jump for the Park Row local, for you are due to get back to civilization (Djuna Barnes, "Who's the Last Squatter," 1913. Reprint in *New York*, ed. Alyce Barry (Los Angeles: Sun & Moon Press, 1989) 119–122.

22. Jane Marcus believes that in *Nightwood*, Barnes rivals Joyce's phallogocentrism, particularly by "giving the logos to a woman identified man" ("Laughing at Leviticus" 230). Barnes, I believe, takes to task the limits of phallogocentrism by exploring the difference and the distance between verbal transgressions and biological deviance.

23. Paul deMan, *Rhetoric of Romanticism*. (New York: Columbia UP, 1986), 80–81.

24. With reference to De Man, Cynthia Chase cites a definition of *prosopopeia* from the *Oxford English Dictionary*:

> [Prosopopeia is] a rhetorical figure by which an imaginary or absent person is represented as speaking or acting . . . De Man's translation or definition of prosopopeia is already a reading, and is in fact a giving of face. Translating *prosopon* as "face" or "mask," and not as "person," is to imply that a face is the condition—not the equivalent of the existence of the person (Cynthia Chase, *Decomposing Figures: Rhetorical Readings in the Romantic Tradition*. (Baltimore: John Hopkins UP, 1996) 83.

Chase further argues that since De Man views "face" or identity as a condition "given by an act of language," then "[p]rosopopeia, or the giving of face, is de-facement" because "face" is determined through linguistic figurations (84–85).

25. Miriam Fuchs explains that because Eliot "did not value genres that women modernists like Dorothy Richardson, H.D., Anais Nin, and Jean Rhys practiced, including diaries, journalistic memoirs, and autobiographical fiction, he worked to diminish *Nightwood's* personal and autobiographical elements, and he avoided statements that would link the narrative to Barnes's life" (Miriam Fuchs, "Djuna Barnes and T.S. Eliot: Authority, Resistance and Acquiescence," *Tulsa Studies in Women's Literature* 12.2 (1993): 293.

26. Using De Man's theories to illuminate Eliot's aesthetic values, John Paul Riquelme argues that this poet consistently called into question the notion of stable meaning and identity:

> The unstable, irresolvable ambivalences regularly evoked in Eliot's styles do not point to speech, immediacy, identity, presence, or spatial form as instances of meaning's self-presence (John Paul Riquelme, *Harmony of Dissonances: T.S. Eliot, Romanticism, and the Imagination*. (Baltimore: Johns Hopkins UP, 1991), 4).

27. Marcus notes that "the smashing of the doll is a recurrent scene in women's writing . . . For a woman who is socialized to be looked at, who even objectifies herself in the mirror, the uncanny is not figured in a symbolic castration of the eyes—for she is being gazed at—but in the fear of becoming a living doll or statue, of becoming only an object" ("Laughing at Leviticus" 243).

28. Both Barnes and Thelma Wood suffered bouts of alcoholism when living as expatriots in Paris. Constance Perry believes that *Nightwood* "reflects [Barne's] emotional exit from a cafe culture which condoned alcoholism and sexual promiscuity, a culture which, in the end, would turn her female exiles into somnambulists living a nightmare" (Constance Perry, "A Woman Writing Under the Influence: Djuna Barnes and *Nightwood*," *Dionysos: the Literarture and Addiction Quarterly* 4.2 (1992), 12.

29. Guido Von Volkbein's emotional excesses parallel contemporary diagnostic paradigms of fetal alcohol syndrome:

> Children with FAS/FAE have difficulty taking in sensory information, integrating, organizing and processing it and then developing an appropriate social response. Some sensory channels (auditory, tactile) may be overly-responsive to input (sensory defensiveness), while others (vestibular, olfactory, gusatory) may be under-responsive to input. Sensory processing deficits

Chapter Five

1. Dori Carter, *Beautiful WASPs Having Sex* (New York: Perennial, 2000), back cover.

2. See Neil Gabler, *An Empire of Their Own: How the Jews Invented Hollywood* (New York: Anchor Books, 1988).

3. Charles Higham, *Merchant of Dreams: Louis B. Mayer, MGM, and the Secret Hollywood* (New York: Dutton Books, 1993), 109–110.

4. Richard Burt comments that both fascism and Hollywood are based on an intense theatricalization which "fosters a collapse between the real and the simulated" (*The Administration of Aesthetics*, 246).

5. bell hooks, *Black Looks: Race and Representation* (Boston: South End Press, 1992), 119.

6. Gerald Frank, *Judy* (New York: Harper & Row Publishers, 1975), 72.

7. William J. Hynes and William G. Doty, "Mapping Mythic Trickster Figures," in *Mythical Trickster Figures: Contours, Contexts, and Criticisms*, eds. William J. Hynes and William Doty (Tuscaloosa: University of Alabama Press, 1993), 34.

8. John McCarty, *The Fearmakers* (London: Virgin Publishing Inc., 1995), 3.

9. Joan Berning Hawkins. "Horror Cinema and the Avant-Garde." Ph.D. diss., University of California at Berkeley, 1993.

10. David J. Skal and Elias Savada, *Dark Carnival: the Secret World of Tod Browning, Hollywood's Master of the Macabre.* (New York: Anchor Books, 1995), 302–305.

11. Robert Lang, *American Film Melodrama.* (Princeton: Princeton UP, 1989), 4.

12. Stanley Diamond, introduction to *The Trickster: A Study in American Indian Mythology*, by Paul Radin (New York: Philosophical Library, 1956), xiii.

13. Bob Thomas, *Thalberg: Life and Legend* (New York: Garland Publishers, 1984), 146.

14. Ann Douglas, *The Feminization of American Culture* (New York: Knopf, 1977), 74–76.

15. Alison M. Parker, *Purifying America: Women, Cultural Reform, and Pro-Censorship Activism, 1873–1933* (Chicago: University of Illinois Press, 1997). Parker explores the dominance of women's reform and censorship movements from 1873 to 1933.

16. Douglas presents a detailed analysis of the ways in which patriarchy drove moral feminization of America during the nineteenth century. Within this cultural context, male authority constructed the ideal woman as a saint, a consumer, and a mother whose role was to enforce bourgeois morality as she engaged in conspicuous consumption (60).

17. *The Unholy Three*, VHS, directed by Tod Browning (1925; Silent Screen Movie Classics, n.d.).

18. Susan Stewart explains that the "capacity of objects to serve as traces of authentic experience is, in fact, exemplified by the souvenir" (135). According to Stewart, the souvenir "represents not the lived experience of its maker but the 'secondhand' experience of its possessor/owner" (135). In one sense, Echo, whose "lived" experience and

identity are constantly shifting, can only pretend to capture it in a kitschy souvenir. In another, the souvenirs may also be viewed as objects that authentically represent Echo's tendency to live in language.

19. Janet Beizer, *Ventriloquized Bodies: Narratives of Hysteria in Nineteenth Century France* (Ithaca: Cornell UP), 48.

20. Lynn Kirby, "Male Hysteria in Early Cinema" in *Male Trouble*, eds. Constance Penley and Sharon Willis, 78 (Minneapolis: University of Minnesota Press, 1993).

21. During the 1930's, the Catholic church also began to exert considerable influence as a censor of films. By this time, the Women's Christian Temperance Union, an influential Protestant censorship group, found an ally in the Catholic Legion of Decency. While the former lobbied for the "federal regulation" of film content, a measure which the film industry loathed, the latter promoted public bans on films it deemed inappropriate, "perhaps out of a greater concern for the separation of church and state" (Parker 155). Thus the Catholic church found an opportunity to gain political power, by trying to prove it was less theocratic than popular opinion held it to be.

22. *The Unknown*, videocassette, directed by Tod Browning, (1927; Silent Screen Movie Classics, n.d.).

23. Lewis Hyde, *Trickster Makes This World: Mischief, Myth, and Art* (New York: Farrar, Straus, and Giroux, 1998), 220–221.

24. *New York Herald Tribune*, June 19, 1927 (quoted in Skal and Savada 296).

25. Gregory A. Waller, "Tod Browning's *Dracula*." 1897, edited by Nina Auerbach and David J. Skal, 382 (New York: W.W. Norton & Company, 1997).

26. Cesare Lombroso (1836–1909), an Italian Jewish criminologist and physician, believed that criminals are born with the atavistic tendency to "[revert] to more primitive stages of evolution," and he consistently argued that such reversion is evident in their facial structures. Lombroso thus produced a complex system of evaluating and categorizing the physiognomies of society's wrong doers, and he framed his finding with racist ideologies (*Faces of Degeneration* 126).

27. Halberstam notes that the medallion worn by Browning's Dracula resembles the Star of David, as did the medallion worn by Count Chocula, a figure on the box of a contemporary children's cereal. In 1897, the Anti-Defamation League sued General Mills for displaying a seemingly parodic version of this Jewish religious symbol. To avoid legal battles, General Mills complied to alter the figure. See Judith Halberstam, *Skin Shows: Gothic Horror and the Technology of Monsters*. (Durham: Duke UP, 1995), 86–88.

28. See Joyce Carol Oates, "Dracula: the Vampire's Secret," *Southwest Review* 76 (4): (1991): 498–510.

29. Stephen Arata. "The Occidental Tourist: Dracula and the Anxiety of Reverse Colonization." *Dracula*. 1897. Eds. David J. Skal and Nina Auerbach. (New York: W.W. Norton & Company, 1997), 463.

30. Freud to Flies, Vienna, 21 September 1897, in *The Freud Reader*, ed. Peter Gay (New York: W.W. Norton & Company, 1989), 112. Freud confesses that his early theory was particularly troublesome because it places the onus of hysteria on all fathers:

> Then came surprise at the fact that in every case the father, not excluding my own, had to blamed as a pervert—the realization of the unexpected

frequency of hysteria, in which the same determinant is invariably established, though such a widespread extent of perversity towards children is, after all, not very probable.

According to contemporary psychoanalytic feminist critics, Freud's revised theory suggests not only that the child fantasizes that she has been seduced, but that "the oedipus complex is mutual: the desire of the parent is transitional to the desire of the child; these desires are reciprocal, and may spill over into acting out." See Dianne Hunter, introduction to *Seduction and Theory: Readings of Gender, Representation, and Rhetoric*. Ed. Dianne Hunter. (Chicago: University of Illinois Press, 1989), 5.

31. Freud defines transference as a process during which the patient projects "some earlier person" into the psychiatrist, in order to re-experience past episodes. See Sigmund Freud, "Fragment of an Analysis of a Case of Hysteria ("Dora"), in *The Freud Reader* 234).

32. See Martha Noel Evans, "Hysteria and the Seduction of Theory," in *Seduction and Theory*, 77. Evans states, " As the phenomenon that marks a limit to science, the major issue hysteria poses to the analyst as a theorist is the question of who, between the analyst and the hysteric, knows what."

33. *Rob Wagner's Script*, quoted in *Dark Carnival*, 305.

34. The loss of teeth is a familiar Freudian symbol of castration.

35. See Sigmund Freud, "The Uncanny." in *The Standard Edition of the Complete Psychological Works of Sigmund Freud*, trans. James Strachey (London: The Hogarth Press, 1955), 235.

36. Mikita Brottman, *Offensive Films: Towards an Anthropology of Cinema Vomatif*. (Westport: Greenwood Press, 1997), 30.

37. Ronald V. Borst, "Re-Evaluating a Screen Classic," *Photon* 23 (1973):34.

38. Skal and Savada note that the carny talker in *Freaks* is dressed in a manner strangely similar to the way that Browning appears in a number of publicity photographs (*Dark Carnival* 175).

39. Browning's reactions to Esper's prologue are unavailable. Skal and Savada emphasize that "audiences and critics have assumed [the prologue] is some kind of position statement by Tod Browning himself, instead of a distributor's cynical attempt to position the picture with a moralistic, 'educational' defense . . ." (223).

40. Joanne Berning Hawkins views Phroso's comment mainly in terms of its sexist implications, particularly in light of Cleopatra's mutilation at the end ("Horror Cinema and the Avant-Garde" 163).

41. Eli Savada, "The Making of Freaks," *Photon* 23 (1973): 172.

42. Joan Hawkings, "One of Us: Tod Browning's Freaks," in *Freakery*, 267.

43. *Bright Lights Film Journal*, http://www.brightlightsfilm.com/32/freaks.html (Accessed November 16, 2001).

Chapter Six

1. Leslie Fiedler, "Adolescence and Maturity in the Modern Novel," in *An End to Innocence: Essays on Culture and Politics* (Boston: The Beacon Press, 1955), 202.

2. See Lori U. Kenschaft. "Homoerotics and Human Connections: Reading Carson McCullers as a Lesbian" in. *Critical Essays on Carson McCullers*, ed. by Beverly Lyon Clark and Melvin J. Friedman (New York: G.K. Hall), 220–233.

3. See Virginia Spencer Carr. *The Lonely Heart: A Biography of Carson McCullers.* (New York: Anchor Books, 1976), 158. Carr explains that Edward Newhouse, a short story writer who came to know McCullers at Yaddo, saw a connection between her transvestism and possible lesbianism:

> . . . I was not very good at recognizing a homosexual when I met him. . . . I was not surprised when Carson told me about herself. She sometimes wore a man's trousers and often a man's jacket, and even I was able to make the connection.

4. Lori J. Kenschaft points out that McCullers frequently uses terms such as "queer," "odd," "strange," "offbeat," "gay" and "lavender" to signal homosexual characters and themes.

5. See Sander Gilman, *Smart Jews: The Construction of the Image of Superior Jewish Intelligence* (Lincoln: U of Nebraska P, 1996).

6. Gilman notes that in a public forum about the significance of IQ scores, Charles Murray, a coauthor of *The Bell Curve*, conflates the notion of Jewish intellectual ability with Jewish artistic creativity, a practice that "adds a greater complexity to the meanings associated with Jewish superior intelligence" (*Smart Jews* 29).

7. An egregious example of such prejudice occurred in the early 1950's in Farmington, Connecticut, when the residents of the (then) rural New England community vehemently protested the construction of a theater that would have been designed by Frank Lloyd Wright. Current commentary on the incident cites anti-Semitism and homophobia as prime reasons for the objection, since the residents of Farmington associated the arts with Jews and gays. See Jenifer Frank, "Missed Chances: Three Case Studies of the Lost Art of Connecticut," in *Northeast Magazine*, supplement to the *Hartford Courant*, July 10, 1988, 10–13.

8. Among these narratives are biographies of Zelda Fitzgerald, Margaret Sargeant, and Sylvia Plath.

9. Carson McCullers. "Wunderkind." 1936. *Collected Stories of Carson McCullers.* (Boston: Houghton Mifflin Company), 65.

10. Carson McCullers. *The Ballad of the Sad Café.* 1936. *Collected Stories of Carson McCullers,* 202.

11. Oliver Evans. *The Ballad of Carson McCullers: A Biography* (New York: Coward-McGann, Inc., 1966), 126.

12. Carson McCullers, "Poldi." 1941. *Collected Stories of Carson McCullers,* 21.

13. Richard Gray. "Moods and Absences," in *Modern Critical Views: Carson McCullers*, ed. By Harold Bloom (New York: Chelsea House Publishers, 1986), 84.

14. Carson McCullers, "Court in the West Eighties."1935 or 1936. *Collected Stories of Carson McCullers,* 16.

15. Robert Philips, "Freaking Out: The Short Stories of Carson McCullers," in *Critical Essays on Carson McCullers*, ed. by Beverly Lyon Clark and Melvin J. Friedman. (New York: G.K. Hall), 175.

16. Carson McCullers, "The Aliens." 1935 or 1936. *Collected Stories of Carson McCullers,* 72.

17. Carson McCullers, "The Jockey." 193?. *Collected Stories of Carson McCullers,* 109.

18. Michiko Kakutani, 1987. "Books of the Times." *New York Times,* 14 July, p. C20, quoted in Judith Giblin James, *Wunderkind: The Reputation of Carson McCullers, 1940–1990* (South Carolina: Camden House), 168.

19. Carson McCullers, *The Heart is a Lonely Hunter* (New York: Houghton Mifflin, 1940; reprint, New York: Bantam Books, 1967), 11.

20. Lawrence Graver, "Penumbral Insistence in McCullers's Early Novels," in *Modern Critical Views: Carson McCullers*, 55.

21. Barbara A. White, "Loss of Self in Member of the Wedding," in *Modern Critical Views: Carson McCullers*, 135.

22. Gayatri Spivak, "A Feminist Reading: McCullers's *Heart is a Lonely Hunter*, in *Critical Essays on Carson McCullers*, 133.

23. In *Smart Jews*, Sander Gilman emphasizes that the image of Jewish intellectual superiority exists in relation to the myth of Black inferiority. The most recent example of this ideology occurs in *The Bell Curve* (1995), Charles Murray and Richard Hernstein's treatise on the relation between intelligence quotient and social class (8). Gilman attributes the academic and professional success of American Ashkenazi Jews to the focus on education within their culture (184–186). Gilman discusses Mariana DeMarco Torgovnick, a writer from a working class Italian American background who identified early on with the stereotypical Jewish emphasis on education: "Her sense of the positive nature of Jewish superior intelligence is that it may be copied, for her own academic success is proof positive that anyone following the 'Jewish' model can become an intellectual" (186).

24. Carson McCullers, *Clock Without Hands* (New York: Houghton Mifflin Company, 1961; reprint, New York: Houghton Mifflin Company, 1998), 7.

25. Richard Burt, "Degenerate 'Art': Public Aesthetics and the Simulation of Censorship in Postliberal Los Angeles and Berlin," in *The Administration of Aesthetics: Censorship, Political Criticism, and the Public Sphere*. Ed. by Richard Burt (Minneapolis: U of Minnesota P, 1992), 248.

26. Delma Eugene Presley, "Carson McCullers and the South," *Georgia Review* 28 (1974): 20–23.

27. Virginia Spencer Carr demonstrates some of McCullers's friends have speculated that some of her illnesses may have had a psychosomatic basis (303).

28. Carson McCullers, *The Member of the Wedding*, 1946; (reprint, Boston: Houghton Mifflin Company, 1987), 272.

Conclusion

1. Sally Banes notes that by the mid 1970's, performance art became a mainstay of New York City's alternative art scene. While it was based primarily on esoteric themes and allusions during the 1970's, in the 1980's it engaged more fully with popular culture. During this time, performance artists used elements from television and rock music, and performed as often in dance clubs as they did in museums. See Sally Banes, *Subversive Expectations: Performance Art and Paratheater in New York, 1976–1985*. (Ann Arbor: The University of Michigan Press, 1999), 9.

2. It is now well known that in 1990, the National Endowment For the Arts took away funding from Karen Finley, John Fleck, Holly Hughs and Tim Miller, four controversial artists whose work was filled with sexual and scatological content. Carr, C. "'Telling the Awfullest Truth': An Interview With Karen Finley," in *Acting Out: Feminist Performances*, eds. Lynda Hart and Peggy Phelan. (Ann Arbor: U of Michigan P), 155.

3. Patricia Bosworth, *Diane Arbus: A Biography* (New York: Alfred A. Knopf, 1984), 234–235.

4. Susan Sontag, *On Photography* (New York: Anchor Books, 1977), 40.

5. Catherine Lord, "What Becomes a Legend Most: the Short, Sad Career of Diane Arbus," in *A Contest of Meaning: Critical Histories of Photography*, ed. Richard Bolton (Cambridge: MIT Press, 1989), 117.

6. Lord emphasizes that Bosworth fails to do justice to the complexity of Arbus's life and art by focusing exclusively on her angst and alienation: "The photographs are 'explained' by constructing Arbus herself as a freak, and their power, from which derives their value as art, is legitimated by her suicide" (8). In an interview, performance artist Karen Finley has a similar bone of contention with stereotypes that insist on pigeon holing artists as "freaks" who must suffer:

> . . . I really can't stand the way the life of the artist is identified with "*suffering.*" I don't have to "suffer" with my art—I've suffered in my own personal life just being sensitive to things that seemed "wrong," and just from the fact of being "born a woman." So I don't need to suffer in my leisure time by drinking 2 gallons of bourbon while hanging out in some cafe—I don't buy that. See Andrea Juno and V. Vale, *Angry Women* (San Francisco: Re/Search Publications, 1991), 48.

7. Doon Arbus and Marvin Israel, eds., *Diane Arbus: An Aperture Monograph* (Millerton: NY: Aperture, 1972), 5.

9. A.C. Coleman, interview quoted in C. Zoe Smith, "Audience Reception of Diane Arbus' Photographs," *Journal of American Culture* 8:1 (1985): 15.

Bibliography

Abraham, Julie. "'Woman, Remember You': Djuna Barnes and History." In *Silence and Power,* edited by Mary Lynn Broe, 252–270. Carbondale: Southern Illinois UP, 1991.

Adler, Kathleen. "John Singer Sargent's Portrais of the Wertheimer Family." In *The Jew in the Text,* edited by Linda Nochin & Tamar Garb, 83–96. London: Thames and Hudson,1995.

Adler, Thomas P. *A Streetcar Named Desire: The Moth and the Lantern.* Boston: Twayne Publishers, 1990.

Agee, James. "Masterpiece at 24." In *Critical Essays on Carson McCullers,* edited by Beverly Lyon Clark and Melvin J. Friedman, 26–27. New York: G.K. Hall & Co., 1996.

Allen, David. *The Fear of Looking or Scopophilic-Exhibitionistic Conflicts.* Charlottesville: University of Virginia Press, 1974.

Altman, Meyrl. "A Book of Repulsive Jews?: Rereading *Nightwood.*" *The Review of Contemporary Fiction* 3:3 (1993), 160–171.

Anderson, George Kumler. *The Legend of the Wandering Jew.* UP of New England, 1991.

Anderson, Mark M. *Kafka's Clothes: Ornament and Aestheticization in the Habsburg Fin-de Siecle.* New York: Oxford UP, 1994.

Arata, Stephen. "The Occidental Tourist: Dracula and the Anxiety of Reverse Colonization." *Dracula.* 1897. Edited by David J. Skal and Nina Auerbach, 462–470. New York: W.W. Norton & Company, 1997.

Arbus, Diane. *Diane Arbus.* Edited by Doon Arbus and Marvin Israel. Millerton, NY: Aperture Monograph, 1972.

Bakhtin, Mikhail. *The Dialogic Imagination.* Ed Michael Holquist. Trans. By Caryl Emerson and Michael Holquist. Austin: The U of Texas P, 1981.

Bannard, Darby. "The Unconditional Aesthete," http://www.sharecom.ca/greenberg/bannard.html.
Banes, Sally. *Subversive Expectations: Performance Art and Paratheater in New York, 1976–1985.* Ann Arbor, Michigan.: The U of Michigan P, 1999.
Barnard, Darby. "The Unconditional Aesthete," http://www.sharecom.ca/greenberg/bannard.html.
Barnes, Djuna. *The Book of Repulsive Women.* 1915; Los Angeles: Sun & Moon Press, 1994.
——. *Interviews.* Los Angeles: Sun & Moon Press, 1985.
——. *Ladies Almanack.* 1928; Normal, Illinois: Dalkey Archive Press, 1992.
——. *New York.* Los Angeles: Sun & Moon Press, 1990.
——. *Nightwood.* 1937; New York: New Directions, 1961.
——. *Ryder.* 1928; Normal: Dalkey Archive Press, 1990.
Barnard, Rita. *The Great Depression and the Culture of Abundance: Kenneth Fearing, Nathanael West, and Mass Culture in the 1930's.* New York: Cambridge UP, 1995.
Barish, Jonas. *The Antitheatrical Prejudice.* Berkeley: University of California Press, 1981.
Barron, Stephanie. "1937: Modern Art and Politics in Prewar Germany," in *"Degenerate Art": the Fate of the Avant-Garde in Nazi Germany,* edited by Stephanie Barron, 9–23. New York: Harry N. Abrams Inc., 1991.
Bauman, Zygmunt. "Desert Spectacular." In *The Flaneur,* edited by Keith Tester, 138–157. New York: Routledge,1994.
Beizer, Janet. *Ventriloquized Bodies: Narratives of Hysteria in Nineteenth Century France.* Ithaca: Cornell UP, 1994.
Benjamin, Walter. *Charles Baudelaire: A Lyric Poet in the Era of High Capitalism.* London: NLB, 1973.
——. "The Significance of Beautiful Semblance," in *Walter Benjamin: Selected Writings, 1935–1938, Volume 3.* Cambridge: The Belknap Press of Harvard UP, 2002.
——. "Surrealism," in *Reflections: Essays, Aphorisms, Autobiographical Writings.* Translated by Edmund Jephcott.177–192. New York: Schocken Books, 1986.
——. The Work of Art in the Age of Mechanical Reproduction." In *Illuminations,* edited by Hannah Arendt and translated by Harry Zohn, 217–251. New York: Shocken Books, 1969.
Benstock, Shari. *Women of the Left Bank: Paris 1900–1940.* Austin: U of Texas P, 1986.
Bercovitch, Sacvan. *The Puritan Origins of the American Self.* New Haven: Yale UP, 1975.
Berg, Elizabeth. "The Third Woman." *Diacritics: A Review of Contemporary Criticism.* 12 :2 (1982): 11–21.
Bernstein, Susan. "Confessing Lacan." In *Seduction and Theory,* edited by Dianne Hunter, 195–213. Urbana: University of Illinois Press, 1993.
Bettelheim, Bruno. *The Uses of Enchantment: The Meaning and Importance of Fairy Tales.* New York: Alfred K. Knopf, 1976.
Bloom, Alexander. *Prodigal Sons: The New York Intellectuals and Their World.* New York: Oxford UP, 1986.

Blyn, Robin. "From Stage to Page: Franz Kafka, Djuna Barnes, and Modernism's Freak Fictions." *Narrative* 8:2 (May 2000), 134–160.

Bogdan, Robert. *Freak Show: Presenting Human Oddities For Pleasure and Profit*. Chicago: U of Chicago P, 1985.

———. "The Social Construction of Freaks." In *Freakery: Cultural Spectacles of the Extraordinary Body*, edited by Rosemarie Garland Thomson, 23–27. New York: New York UP, 1996.

Borst, Ronald V. "Re-Evaluating a Screen Classic." *Photon*. 23 (1973): 29–35.

Bosworth, Patricia. *Diane Arbus: A Biography*. New York: Alfred A Knopf, 1984.

Bradley, F. H. *Collected Essays*. Oxford: Clarendon Press, 1935.

Brand, Dana. *The Spectator and the City in Nineteenth Century American Literature*. New York: Cambridge UP, 1991.

Brennan, Matthew C. "The Novel as Nightmare: Decentering of the Self in Bram Stoker's Dracula." *Journal of the Fantastic in the Arts*. 7 (4(28) (1996): 48–59.

Bright Lights Film Journal, http://www.brightlightsfilm.com/32/freaks.html (Accessed November 16, 2001).

Britt, David, translator. "Facsimile of the *Entartete Kunst* Exhibition," in *Degenerate Art*, 356–390.

Brooker, Jewel Spears, and Bentley, Joseph. *Reading the Waste Land: Modernism and the Limits of Interpretation*. Amherst: The U of Massachusetts P, 1990.

Brottman, Mikita. *Offensive Films: Towards an Anthropology of Cinema Vomatif*. Westport: Greenwood Press, 1997.

Buck-Morss, Susan. *The Dialectics of Seeing: Walter Benjamin and the Arcades Project*. Cambridge: MIT Press, 1997.

Burt, Richard. "Degenerate 'Art': Public Aesthetics and the Simulation of Censorship in Postliberal Los Angeles and Berlin." In *The Administration of Aesthetics: Censorship. Political Criticism, and the Public Sphere*, edited by Richard Burt, 216–259. Minneapolis: U of Minnesota P, 1992.

Burton, Stacy. "Paradoxical Relations: Bakhtin and Modernism." *Modern Language Quarterly: A Journal of Literary History* 61:3 (September 2000), 519–543.

Bush, Ronald. *T.S. Eliot: A Study in Character and Style*. New York: Oxford UP, 1993.

Butler, Judith. *Gender Trouble: Feminism and the Subversion of Identity*. New York: Routledge, 1990.

Carr, C. "'Telling the Awfullest Truth': An Interview With Karen Finley" in *Acting Out: Feminist Performances*, eds. Lynda Hart and Peggy Phelan. Ann Arbor: U of Michigan P, 153–160.

Carr, Virginia Spencer. *The Lonely Hunter: A Biography of Carson McCullers*. New York: Anchor Books, 1976.

Carter, Dori. *Beautiful Wasps Having Sex*. New York: Harper Collins, 2000.

Chaberlin, Edward J. and Gilman, Sander L., eds. *Degeneration: The Dark Side of Progress*. New York: Columbia UP, 1985.

Chase, Cynthia. *Decomposing Figures: Rhetorical Readings in the Romantic Tradition*. Baltimore: Johns Hopkins UP, 1996.

Chenieux-Gendron, Jacqueline. *Surrealism (European Perspectives)*. New York: Columbia UP, 1994.
Cheyette, Bryan, ed. *Between Race and Culture: Representations of "the Jew" in English and American Literature*. Stanford: Stanford UP, 1996.
Cohen, Margaret. *Profane Illumination: Walter Benjamin and the Paris of Surrealist Revolution*. Berkeley: University of California Press, 1993.
Commerchero, Victor. *Nathanael West: The Ironic Prophet*. Syracuse: Syracuse UP, 1964.
Connor, Stephen. "'I . . . AM. A': Addressing the Jewish Question in Joyce's *Ulysses*," in *The Jew in the Text*, ed. By Linda Nochlin and Tamar Garb. 219–237. New York: Thames and Hudson, 1995.
Cook, Richard. "Reflections in a Golden Eye." In *Modern Critical Views: Carson McCullers*, edited by Harold Bloom, 69–76. New York: Chelsea House Publishers, 1986.
Davis, Thadious. "Erasing the 'We of Me' and Rewriting the Racial Myth: Carson McCuller's Two *Member(s) of the Wedding*." In *Critical Essays on Carson McCullers*, edited by Beverly Lyon Clark and Melvin J. Friedman, 206–219. New York: G.K. Hall & Co., 1996.
Dazey, Mary Ann. "Two Voices of the Single Narrator in *The Ballad of the Sad Cafe*." In *Critical Essays on Carson McCullers*, 117–124.
de Man, Paul. "Autobiography as De-Facement." *Rhetoric of Romanticism*. New York: Columbia UP, 1986.
———. *Rhetoric of Romanticism*. New York: Columbia UP, 1986.
Debord, Guy. *The Society of Spectacle*. 1968. Trans. by Donald Nicholson Smith. New York: Zone Books, 1995.
Dijkstra, Bram. *Evil Sisters: the Threat of Female Sexuality and the Cult of Manhood*. New York: Knopf, 1996.
———. *Idols of Perversity: Fantasies of Feminine Evil in Fin-de-Siecle Culture*. New York: Oxford UP, 1986.
Doane, Mary Ann. "Film and Masquerade: Theorising the Female Spectator." *Screen* 23. 3.4 (1982): 74–87.
Doughty, Ann. C. M. *Travels in Arabia Deserta*. New York: Heritage Press, 1953.
Douglas, Ann. *The Feminization of American Culture*. New York: Knopf, 1977.
Dracula, VHS. . Directed by Tod Browning. 1932; MCA Universal, 1991.
Eissler, Benita. *O'Keefe and Stieglitz: An American Romance*. New York: Penguin Books, 1991.
Eliot, T.S. *Collected Poems: 1909–1962*. New York: Harcourt, Brace and World, Inc., 1970.
———. *Selected Essays*. New York: Harcourt, Brace and Company, 1950.
Ellman, Richard. *James Joyce*. New York: Oxford UP, 1959.
Emerson, Ralph Waldo. *Nature*. 1836. Ed. Jaroslav Pelikan. Boston: Beacon, 1985.
Erdman, Harley. *Staging the Jew: The Performance of An American Ethnicity, 1860–1920*. New Brunswick: Rutgers UP, 1997.

Evans, Martha Noel. "Hysteria and the Seduction of Theory." In *Seduction and Theory*, 73–85.
Evans, Oliver. *The Ballad of Carson McCullers: A Biography*. New York: Coward-McGann, Inc., 1966.
Eysteinsson, Astradur. *The Concept of Modernism*. Ithaca: Cornell UP, 1990.
Fanon, Franz. *Black Skin, White Masks*. New York: Grove Press, 1967.
Fergusson, Priscilla Parkhurst. "The *Flaneur* On and Off the Streets of Paris." *The Flaneur*, edited by. Ketih Tester, 22–42. New York: Routledge, 1994.
Feld, Ruth. "[Review of] *Reflections in a Golden Eye*." In *Critical Essays on Carson McCullers*. 28–29.
Fiedler, Leslie. "Adolescence and Maturity in the American Novel." In *An End to Innocence Essays on Culture and Politics*, 191–210. Boston: The Beacon Press, 1955.
———. *Freaks: Myths and Images of the Secret Self*. New York: Simon and Schuster, 1978.
Freaks, VHS. Directed by Tod Browning. 1932; MGM/UA Home Video, 1990.
Foucault, Michel. "Nietzsche, Genealogy, and History." *The Foucault Reader*. Ed. Paul Rabinow. New York: Parthenon Books, 1984. 76–100.
———. *The Order of Things: the Archeology of Human Sciences*. New York: Vintage Books, 1973.
Frank, Gerald. *Judy*. New York: Harper & Row Publishers, 1975.
Frank, Jennifer. "Missed Chances: Three Case Studies of the Lost Art of Connecticut," in *The Northeast Magazine*, supplement to *The Hartford Courant*, July 10, 1988, 10–13.
Frank, Joseph. *The Widening Gyre: Crises and Mastery in Modern Literature*. New Brunswick: Rutgers UP, 1963.
Freud, Sigmund to Flies, Vienna, 21 September 1897, in *The Freud Reader*, 112. Edited by. Peter Gay. New York: W.W. Norton & Company, 1989,
———. "Fragment of an Analysis of a Case of Hysteria" ("Dora"), in *The Freud Reader*, 172–239.
———. "The Uncanny." *The Standard Edition of the Complete Psychological Works of Sigmund Freud*, 219–251. Translated by James Strachey. London: The Hogarth Press, 1955.
Fried, Michael. *Absorption and Theatricality: Painting and Beholder in the Age of Diderot*. Berkeley: U of California P, 1980.
Fuchs, Mirian. "Djuna Barnes and T.S. Eliot: Authority, Resistance and Acquiescence." Tulsa Studies in Women's Literature 12:2 (1993) .
———. "Dr. Matthew O'Connor: The Unhealthy Healer of Djuna Barne's *Nightwood*" Literature and Medicine 2 (1983): 126–134.
Gabler, Neil. *An Empire of Their Own: How the Jews Invented Hollywood*. New York: Anchor Books, 1988.
Garber, Marjorie. *Vested Interests: Cross Dressing and Cultural Anxiety*. New York: Routledge, 1997.

Gardiner, Michael. "Bakhtin's Carnival: Utopia as Critique." In *Critical Essays on Bakhtin*, edited by Caryl Emerson, 252–276. New York: G.K. Hall, 1999.

Geller, Jay. "The Aromatics of Jewish Difference; or Benjamin's Allegory of Aura." In *Jews and Other Differences: The New Jewish Cultural Studies*, edited by Johnathan Boyarin and Daniel Boyarin, 202–256. Minneapolis: U Minnesota P, 1997.

———. "(G)nos(e)ology: The Cultural Construction of the Other." In *People of the Body: Jews and Judaism From an Embodied Perspective*, edited by Howard Eilberg-Schwartz, 243–83. Albany: State University of New York Press, 1992.

Genova, Pamela. "How Modern is the Surreal? Surrealism, Modernism, Postmodernism." *West Virginia University Philological Papers* 39 (1993): 83–93.

Gerber, David A. "The 'Careers' of People Exhibited in Freak Shows: The Problem of Volition and Valorization." In *Freakery: Cultural Spectacles of the Extraordinary Body*, 38–54.

Gerstenberger, Donna. "Modern (Post)Modern: Djuna Barnes Among Others." *The Review of Contemporary Fiction* 3.3 (1993). 33–40.

Gilbert, Sandra M. and Gubar, Susan. *No Man's Land: The Place of the Woman Writer in the Twentieth Century. Volume 2: Sexchanges*. New Haven: Yale UP, 1989.

Gilman, Sander L. *Difference and Pathology: Stereotypes of Sexuality, Race, and Madness*. Ithaca: Cornell UP, 1985.

———. *Franz Kafka: The Jewish Patient*. New York: Routledge, 1995.

———. *The Jew's Body*. New York: Routledge, Chapman and Hall, Inc., 1986.

———. *Jewish Self-Hatred: Antisemitism and the Hidden Language of the Jews*. Baltimore: The Johns Hopkins UP, 1986.

———. *Smart Jews: The Construction of the Image of Jewish Superior Intelligence*. Lincoln: U of Nebraska P, 1996.

Glover, David. "Bram Stoker and the Crises of the Liberal Subject." *New Literary History* 23 (1992): 983–1002.

Goffman, Irving. *Stigma: Notes on the Management of Spoiled Identity*. New York: Simon and Schuster, Inc., 1963.

Graver, Lawrence. "Penumbral Insistence in McCuller's Early Novels," 53–67, in *Modern Critical Views: Carson McCullers*.

Gray, Richard. "Moods and Absences." In *Modern Critical Views: Carson McCullers*, 77–85.

Green, Barbara. "Spectacular Confessions: How it Feels to Be Forcibly Fed." *The Review of Contemporary Fiction* 13.3 (1993): 70–88.

Greenberg, Clement. "Abstract, Representational and So Forth."1954. *Art and Culture*. New York Beacon Press, 1961. 133–145.

———. "Avant-Garde and Kitsch." 1939. *Clement Greenberg: The Collected Essays and Criticism: Volume I: Perceptions and Judgments, 1939–1944*. 5–22. Chicago: University of Chicago Press, 1986.

———. "Kafka's Jewishness." 1956. *Art and Culture*, 266–273.

———. "Surrealist Painting." 1944. *Clement Greenberg: The Collected Essays, Volume I*, 225–231

———. "On Paul Klee." 1941. 65–73.
———. "Review of Exhibitions of Joan Miro, Fernand Leger, and Wassily Kandinsky." 1941. 62-65.
———. "Under Forty: A Symposium on American Literature and the Younger Generation of American Jews." 1944. 176–179.
Grosz, Elizabeth. "Lesbian Fetishism?" In *Fetishism as Cultural Discourse*, ed. Emily Apter and William Pietz, 101–115. Ithaca: Cornell UP, 1993.
Halbertstam, Judith. *Skin Shows: Gothic Horror and the Technology of Monsters*. Durham: Duke UP, 1995.
Haller, Mark. *Eugenics: Hereditarian Attitudes in American Thought*. New Brunswick: Rutgers UP, 1963.
Hanson, Ellis. *Decadence and Catholicism*. Cambridge: Harvard UP, 1997.
Hawkins, Joan. "'One of Us': Tod Browning's *Freaks*." *Freakery: Cultural Spectacles of the Extraordinary Body*. Ed. Rosemarie Garland Thomson. New York: NYU Press, 1996. 265–276.
———. "Horror Cinema and the Avant-Garde." Ph.D. diss., University of California at Berkeley, 1993.
Hennelly, Mark M. "Dracula: The Gnostic Quest and the Victorian Wasteland." *English Literature in Translation: 1880–1920* 20 (1977): 13–26.
Herring, Philip. *Djuna: The Life and Work of Djuna Barnes*. New York: Penguin Books, 1995.
Hetherington, Kevin. *The Badlands of Modernity: Heterotopia and Social Ordering*. New York: Routledge, 1997.
Hewitt, Andrew. *Political Inversions: Homosexuality, Fascism, & the Modern Imaginary*. Stanford: Stanford UP, 1996.
Higham, Charles. *Merchant of Dreams: Louis B. Mayer, MGM, and the Secret Hollywood* New York: Dutton Books, 1993.
hooks, bell. *Black Looks: Race and Representation*. Boston: South End Press, 1992.
Huyssens, Andreas. *After the Great Divide: Modernism, Mass Culture, Postmodernism*. Bloomington: Indiana UP, 1986.
Hyman, Stanley Edgar. *Nathanael West*. Minneapolis: U of Minnesota P, 1962.
Hyde, Lewis. *The Trickster Makes This World: Mischief, Myth, and Art*. New York: Farrar, Straus, and Giroux, 1998.
Hynes, William J. and Doty, William G. "Mapping Mythic Tricksters." *Mythical Trickster Figures: Contours, Contexts, and Criticisms*. Tuscaloosa: University of Alabama Press, 1993.
James, Judith Giblin. *Wunderkind: the Reputation of Carson McCullers, 1940–1990*. Columbia, SC: Camden House, 1995.
Jameson, Frederic. "Postmodernism and Consumer Society." *Postmodernism and Its Discontents*. Ed. Ann Kaplan. New York: Verso, 1990.
———. *Postmodernism: The Cultural Logic of Late Capitalism*. Durham: Duke UP, 1991.
Jay, Karla. "The Outsider Among the Expatriates: Djuna Barnes' Satire on the Ladies of the Almanack." In *Silence and Power*, 184–193.

Jay, Martin. *Downcast Eyes: The Denigration of Vision in Twentieth-Century Thought*. Berkeley: U of California P, 1994.
Julius, Anthony. *T. S. Eliot, Anti-Semitism and Literary Form*. Cambridge: Cambridge UP, 1995.
Jumonville, Neil. *Critical Crossings: The New York Intellectuals in Postwar America*. Berkeley: U of California P, 1991.
Juno, Andrea and Vale, V. *Angry Women*. San Francisco: Re/Search Publications, 1991.
Kafka, Franz. "The Metamorphosis," in *The Penal Colony: Stories and Short Pieces*. Translated by Willa and Edwin Muir. New York: Schocken Books, 1977. 67–132.
——. "Josephine the Singer, or the Mouse Folk." 256–277.
Keller, Johanna. "The Called Him Ugly, and the Pain is In His Music," *New York Times* (9 June 2002): sec. AR, p. 30.
Kenschaft, Lori. "Homoerotics and Human Connections: Reading Carson McCullers as a Lesbian." In *Critical Essays on Carson McCullers*, 220–233.
Keveles, Daniel J. *In the Name of Eugenics*. Cambridge: Harvard UP, 1995.
Kime Scott, Bonnie. "Barnes Being 'Beast Familiar': Representations on the Margin of Modernism." *Review of Contemporary Ficiton* 13.3 (1993): 41–52.
Kirby, Lynn. "Male Hysteria and Early Cinema." *Male Trouble*. Eds. Constance Penley and Sharon Willis. Minneapolis: U of Minnesota P, 1993. 67–85.
Kristeva, Julia. *The Powers of Horror: An Essay in Abjection*. New York: Columbia UP, 1982.
Kuhlman, Susan. *Knave, Fool, and Genius: the Confidence Man as He Appears in Nineteenth Century American Fiction*. Chapel Hill: U of North Carolina P, 1973.
Kumler, George Anderson. *The Legend of the Wandering Jew*. UP of New England, 1991. Lang, Robert. *American Film Melodrama*. Princeton: Princeton UP, 1989.
Lagerkvist, Par. *The Dwarf*. Translated by Alexandra Dick. New York: L.B. Fischer, 1945.
——. *The Death of Ahasuerus*. Translated by Naomi Walford. New York: Random House, 1962.
Lanser, Susan Sniader. "Speaking in Tongues: Ladies Almanack and the Discourse of Desire." In *Silence and Power*, 156–159.
Lee, Judith. "The Sweetest Lie." In *Silence and Power*, 207–18.
Levine, Nancy. "'Bringing Milkshakes to Bulldogs': the Early Journalism of Djuna Barnes." In *Silence and Power*, 27–34.
Levine, Nancy and Marian Urquilla. "Introduction." *The Review of Contemporary Fiction*. 13.3 (1993): 7–15.
Locklin, Gerald. "The Day of the Painter, the Death of the Cock: Nathanael West's Hollywood Novel." In *Los Angeles in Fiction: A Collection of Essays From James McCain to Walter Mosley*, edited by David Fine, 67–82. Albuquerque: U of New Mexico P, 1995.
Long, Robert Emmet. *Nathanael West*. New York: Frederick Ungar Publishing Company, 1985.

Lord, Catherine. "What Becomes a Legend Most: the Short, Sad Career of Diane Arbus." *A Contest of Meaning: Critical Histories of Photography*, edited by Richard Bolton, Cambridge: MIT Press, 1989. 111–123.
Lynes, Barber Buhler. *O'Keefe, Stieglitz and the Critics, 1916–1929*. Ann Arbor: UMI Research Press, 1989.
McCarty, John. *The Fearmakers*. London: Virgin Publishing Inc., 1995.
McCullers, Carson. "The Aliens." 1935 or 1936. *Collected Stories of Carson McCullers*. Ed. Virginia Spencer Carr. Boston: Houghton Mifflin Company, 1987. 71–79.
———. *The Ballad of the Sad Café*. 1936. _____. 197–253.
———. *Clock Without Hands*. New York: Houghton Mifflin Company, 1998.
———. "Court in the West Eighties." 1935 or 1936. *Collected Stories*. 11–19.
———. "The Jockey." _____. 104–109.
———. *The Member of the Wedding*. 1946. _____. 255–295.
———. "Poldi." 1941. _____. 20–26.
———. *Reflections in A Golden Eye*. Boston: Houghton Mifflin Company, 1968.
MacDonald, Beth E. "The Vampire as Trickster Figure in Bram Stoker's Dracula." *Extrapolation* 33.2 (1992): 128–144.
McHale, Brian. *Postmodernist Fiction*. New York: Methuen, 1987.
Madden, David. "The Shrike Voice Dominates *Miss. Lonelyhearts*," in *Critical Essays on Nathanael West*, ed. Ben Siegel. New York: MacMillan, 1994.
Marcus, Jane. "Laughing at Leviticus: *Nightwood* as Woman's Circus Epic." In *Silence and Power*. 221–251.
Martin, Jay. *Nathanael West: the Art of His Life*. New York: Farrar, Straus, & Giroux, 1972.
McGee, Daniel. T. "Dada Da Da: Sounding the Jew in Modernism," ELH 68:2 (2001), 501–27.
Meisel, Perry. *The Myth of the Modern: A Study in British Literature and Criticism After 1850*. New Haven: Yale UP, 1987.
Merish, Lori. "Cuteness and Commodity Aesthetics: Tom Thumb and Shirley Temple." *Freakery: Cultural Spectacles of the Extraordinary Body*, 185–203.
Meliville, Stephen W. *Philosophy Beside Itself: On Deconstruction and Modernism*. Minneapolis: U of Minnesota P, 1986.
Michel, Fran. "All Women Are Not Women All: *Ladies Almanack* and Feminine Writing." In *Silence and Power*, 170–182.
———. "'I Just Loved Thelma': Djuna Barnes and the Construction of Bisexuality." *The Review of Contemporary Fiction* 3:3 (1993): 55.
Mitchell, Adrielle Anna. "*The Plain Reader Be Damned*": *Confusion as Method in the Works of Djuna Barnes*. Ph.D. diss., University of Santa Cruz, 1995.
Mollon, Phil. *Multiple Selves, Multiple Voices: Working With Trauma, Violation, and Dissociation*. Chichester, New York: Wiley, 1996.
Morawski, Stefan. "The Hopeless Game of Flanerie." In *The Flaneur*, 181–197.
Morson, Gary Saul and Emerson, Caryl. *Mikhail Bakhtin: Creation of a Prosaics*. Stanford: Stanford UP, 1990.

Mosse, George L. "Beauty Without Sensuality: The Exhibition *Entartete Kunst*," in *Degenerate Art*, 25–32.

Mulvey, Laura. "'Afterthoughts on Visual Pleasure and Narrative Cinema': Inspired by Duel in the Sun." In *Psychoanalysis and Cinema*, edited by Ann Kaplan. New York: Routledge, 1990.

———. "Visual Pleasure in Narrative Cinema." In *Art After Modernism: Rethinking Representation*, edited by Brian Wallis, 361–374. New York: Museum of Contemporary Art, 1984.

Murray, Charles and Hernstein, Richard. *The Bell Curve: Intelligence and Class Structure in American Life*. New York: Free Press, 1994.

Murray, Gale B. "Toulouse Lautrec's Illustrations For Victor Joze and Georges-Clemenceau and Their Relationship to French Anti-Semitism of the 1890's." In *The Jew in the Text*, 57–82.

Nadel, Ira. *Joyce and the Jews*. Iowa City: University of Iowa Press, 1989.

Nietzsche, Friedrich. *The Genealogy of Morals* and *Ecce Homo*. Ed. Walter Kaufman. New York: Random House, 1967.

Nochlin, Linda and Garb Tamar. *The Jew in the Text*. New York: Thames and Hudson, 1996.

Nordau, Max. *Degeneration*. New York: D. Appleton, 1895; Lincoln: Reprint, University of Nebraska Press, 1993.

Northeast Consultation and Training Center, http://www.taconic.netseminars/fas-b.html (Accessed December 25, 2004).

Oates, Joyce Carol. "Dracula: the Vampire's Secret." *Southwest Review*. 76 (4): (1991): 498–510.

Owens, Craig. "The Discourse of Others: Feminists and Postmodernism." *The Anti-Aesthetic*. Port Townsend: Bay Press, 1993.

Parker, Alison M. *Purifying America: Women, Cultural Reform, and Pro-Censorship Activism, 1873–1933*. Chicago: University of Illinois Press, 1997.

Paulson, Suzanne Morrow. "Carson McCuller's *The Ballad of the Sad Cafe*: A Song Half Sung, Misogyny, and 'Ganging Up.'" *Critical Essays*. 187–205.

Perry, Constance. "A Woman Writing Under the Influence: Djuna Barnes and *Nightwood*." *Dionysos: the Literature and Addiction Quarterly*. 4.2 (1992): 3–14.

Philips, Robert. "Freaking Out: The Short Stories of Carson McCullers, in *Critical Essays on Carson McCullers*, 172–178.

Pick, Daniel. *Faces of Degeneration: A European Disorder, c. 1848–1918*. Cambridge: Cambridge UP, 1989.

Pickens, Donald K. *Eugenics and Progressives*. Nashville: Vanderbilt UP, 1968.

Presley, Delma Eugene. "Carson McCullers and the South." *Georgia Review* 28 (1974): 19–32.

Radin, Paul. *The Trickster: A Study in American Indian Mythology*. New York: Philosophical Library, 1956.

Readings, Bill and Schaber, Bennet. *Postmodernism Across the Ages: Essays For a Postmodernity That Wasn't Born Yesterday*. Syracuse: Syracuse UP, 1993.

Reizbaum, Marilyn. "A Nightmare of History: Ireland's Jew and Joyce's Ulysses," in *Between Race and Culture*, 102–113.
Riquelme, John Paul. *Harmony of Dissonances: T.S. Eliot, Romanticism, and the Imagination*. Baltimore: Johns Hopkins UP, 1991.
Joan Riviere. "Womanliness as Masquerade." In *Formations of Fantasy*, eds. Victor Burgin, James Donald, and Cora Kaplan, 35–44. New York: Metheun, 1986.
Rose, Margaret. *Parody: Ancient, Modern, and Postmodern*. London: Cambridge UP, 1993.
Rowe, Joyce. *Equivocal Endings in Classic American Novels: The Scarlet Letter; The Adventures of Huckleberry Finn; The Ambassadors; The Great Gatsby*. Cambridge: Cambridge UP.
Rubenfeld, Florence. *Clement Greenberg: A Life*. New York: Scribner, 1997.
Savada, Eli. "The Making of Freaks." *Photon*. 23 (1973): 25–29.
Schliefer, Ronald. "Yeats's Postmodern Rhetoric," in *Yeats and Postmodernism*, ed. Leonard Orr. Syracuse: Syracuse UP, 1991.
Sedgwick, Eve. *Epistemology of the Closet*. Berkeley: U of California P, 1990.
Shattuck, Roger. *The Banquet Years: the Arts in France, 1855–1918*. New York: Anchor Books, 1961.
Silverman, Kaja. *Male Subjectivity at the Margins*. New York: Routeledge, 1992.
——. *The Subject of Semiotics*. New York: Oxford UP, 1983.
Simon, Richard Keller. "Between Capra and Adorno: West's *Day of the Locust* and the Movies of the 1930's." *Modern Language Quarterly* 54.4 (1993): 513–34.
Skal, David J. and Savada, Elias. *Dark Carnival: the Secret World of Tod Browning, Hollywood's Master of the Macabre*. New York: Anchor Books, 1995.
Smith, C. Zoe. "Audience Reception of Diane Arbus' Photographs." *Journal of American Culture* 8:1 (1985): 13–28.
Sontag, Susan. "Notes on Camp," 1964. 105–119. *A Susan Sontag Reader*. New York: Vintage Press, 1983.
——. *On Photography*. New York: Farrar, Strauss, and Giroux, 1978.
Spivak, Gayatri Chakravorty. "A Feminist Reading: McCuller's *Heart is a Lonely Hunter*." In *Critical Essays on Carson McCullers*, 129–142.
Stallybrass, Peter and White, Allen. *The Politics and Poetics of Transgression*.
Stevenson, Sheryl. "Writing the Grotesque Body: Djuna Barnes' Carnival Parody." *Silence and Power: A Reevaluation of Djuna Barnes*. Ed Mary Lynn Broe. Carbondale: Southern Illinois UP, 1991.
Stewart, Susan. *On Longing: Narratives of the Miniature, the Gigantic, the Souvenir, the Collection*. Baltimore: the Johns Hopkins UP, 1984.
Stoker, Bram. *Dracula*. 1897. Edited by Nina Auerbach and David J. Skal. New York: W.W. Norton& Company, 1997.
Tabachnick, Stephen Ely. *Charles Doughty*. Boston: Twayne Publishers, 1981.
Tester, Keith, ed. *The Flneur*. New York: Routledge, 1994.
Thomas, Bob. *Thalberg: Life and Legend*. New York: Garland Publishers, 1984.

Thomson, Rosemarie Garland. "Introduction: From Wonder to Error—Genealogy of Freak Discourse in Modernity." In *Freakery: Cultural Spectacles of the Extraordinary Body*, 1–19.
——. *Extraordinary Bodies: Figuring Physical Disability in American Culture and Literature*. New York: Columbia UP, 1997.
Trillling, Lionel. "On the Modern Element in Literature." In *Literary Modernism*, edited by Irving Howe. Greenwich: Fawcett Publications, Inc., 1967.
The Unholy Three. Directed by Tod Browning. 1925; Videocassette. Silent Screen Classics, 1990.
The Unknown. Directed by Tod Browning.1927; Videocassette. Silent Screen Movie Classics, 1990.
Vidal, Gore. "Carson McCullers *Clock Without Hands*. In *Modern Critical Views: Carson McCullers*. 17–19.
Von Luttichau, Mario-Andreas. "*Entartete Kunst*, Munich 1937: A Reconstruction," in *Degenerate Art*, 45–81.
Walden, Daniel. "Nathanael West: A Jewish Satirist in Spite of Himself." In *Critical Essays on Nathanael West*, edited by Ben Siegel, 203–212. New York: MacMillan Library Reference, 1994.
Waller, Gregory A. "Tod Browning's Dracula." *Dracula*. 1897. Edited by Nina Auerbach and David J.Skal, 382–389. New York: W.W. Norton & Company, 1997.
Weber, Nicholas Fox. *Patron Saints: Five Rebels Who Opened America to New Art, 1928–1943*.
West, Nathanael. *A Cool Million*. 1934. *The Complete Works of Nathanael West*. New York: Farrar, Straus, and Giroux, 1957. 143–155.
——. *The Day of the Locust*. 1939. _____. 259–421.
——. *The Dream Life of Balso Snell*. 1931. _____. 3–62.
——. *Miss. Lonelyhearts*. 1933. _____, 65–140.
Westling, Louise. "Carson McCullers's Amazon Nightmare." In *Modern Critical Views: Carson McCullers*. 109–116.
——. "Tomboys and Revolting Femininity." In *Critical Essays on Carson McCullers*, 155–165.
White, Barbara. "Loss of Self in *The Member of the Wedding*."*Modern Critical Views: Carson McCullers*. 125–142.
Williams, Tennesseee. "*This Book: Reflections in a Golden Eye*." _____. 11–16.
Wilson, Angus. *The Strange Ride of Rudyard Kipling*. New York: Viking Press, 1977.
Wilson, Deborah Sue. *Lost Boundaries: Kenneth Burke, Nathanael West, Djuna Barnes, and the Disorder of Things*. Ph.D. diss, University of California at Irvine, 1987.
Woolf, Virginia. "Street Haunting," 1927, in *The Virginia Woolf Reader*, edited by Mitchell A. Leaska. New York: Harcourt, Brace, Jovanovich, 1984. 246–259.
Zuschlag, Christoph. "An 'Educational Exhibition': The Exhibition of *Entartete Kunst* and its Individual Venues," *Degenerate Art*, 83–97.

Index

Aguglia, Mimi, 59
alleumeuse, 96
Anglo-Americans, 3, 15, 25, 27–28, 30, 34, 35, 36, 44, 45, 59, 81, 82, 83, 87
anti-Semitism, 11, 15, 19, 26, 29, 49, 50, 78, 94, 115–116, 157n7
anti-theatrical prejudice, 10
Arbus, Diane, 133–137
aura, 22–23

badouds, 43
Bakhtinian carnival, 6–7, 140n12, 150n34
Barnes, Djuna, 49–80; journalism, 49–64; *Ladies' Almanack*, 71–72; *Nightwood*, 65–80; *Ryder*, 63, 70, 72
Baartman, Sartje, 3
Belasco, David, 53–54
Benjamin, Walter, 1, 21–23, 26, 29, 74, 123, 126, 143n3
Bogdan, Robert, 6–7
Browning, Tod, 81–108; *Devil Doll*, 108; *Dracula*, 93–97; *Freaks*, 97–108; *Unholy Three*, 88–91, 93; *Unknown*, 91–93
Butler, Judith, 65, 150n1

castration, 35, 50, 92, 107

Catholicism, 27, 53–54, 75, 155n21
Chaney, Lon, 88

dadaism, 13–14
Davenport, Charles, 34
degenerate art (*entartete kunst*), 11–15
degeneration, 2, 4, 9–15
DeMan, Paul, 75–77
Dempsey, Jack, 62
doubling, 92
Douglas, Ann, 88, 154n16
Doughty, C.M., 28, 30

Eliot, T.S., 4, 15–16, 33, 54, 66, 76
Emerson, Ralph Waldo, 26
enfreakment, 9, 10, 13, 136, 140n1
eugenics, 3–4

Fanon, Franz, 151n14
fascism, 31, 126
fascist aesthetics, 11–13, 15, 82
Faulkner, William, 110, 123
femme fatale, 51–52, 81, 82, 147n6
female fetishist, 49, 50, 55, 58, 62, 64, 77, 78, 147n5
fetishism, 1, 2, 30, 120, 133–134, 136, 144n11
Fiedler, Leslie, 8, 110–111

Index

flâneur (Benjaminian), 16–17, 26–27, 67, 76, 82, 109, 118, 121, 122, 123, 125, 129, 148n16

flâneur colonizer, 30, 34, 37, 38, 47, 55, 56, 66, 69, 74, 77, 79, 82, 87, 95, 99–100, 106

Foucault, Michel, 1, 5, 140n14

freakish *flâneur*, 29, 30, 40, 42, 54, 56, 57, 58, 65–67, 70, 72,80, 83, 87, 100, 109, 119, 135, 137

freak show, 6–8, 13, 139n8

Freud, Sigmund, 50, 56, 65, 72, 92, 95, 99, 144n11, 149n19, 155n30–32

Galton, Sir Francis, 34

Gilman, Sander, 4, 11, 29, 35, 113, 157n6, 158n23

Goffman, Irving, 35–36

Great Depression, 3, 44, 118

Greenberg, Clement, 13–15, 20–22

Halacha, 21, 142n42

heredity, 68

heterotopia, 6–8, 17, 18, 19, 47–48, 72, 140n12 and n14

high modernism, 2, 5, 15, 31, 32, 33, 43

horror films, 84–88

Huyssen, Andreas, 2, 66

hysteria, 89–90, 97, 104, 108, 128, 130

Ibsen, Henrik, 10

James, Henry, 110, 123

Jews, 3, 11–23, 26, 32, 53, 54, 57, 58, 59, 82–83, 111, 113, 115–116, 118–119, 124–125, 134–136, 143n48, 144n14, 147n2

Joyce, James, 16, 17–18, 27, 32, 33 *Portrait of the Artist as a Young Man*, 18; *Ulysses*, 18

Kafka, Franz, 5, 16, 18; "Josephine the Singer," or "the Mouse Folk," 20; *Metamorphosis*, 19–20

kitsch, 13, 14, 20, 22, 38, 40, 41, 42, 53, 119, 145n23

Kristeva, Julia, 49–50

Lacan, Jacques, 28, 29–30, 56, 149n21

Lagerkvist, Par, 5, 16, 18–19; *Death of Ahasuerus*, 19; *Dwarf*, 18–19

Lombroso, Cesare, 94, 155n26

Mallarmé, M. Stéphane, 10

Mann, Thomas, 5

masquerade, 51, 147n6

Mayer, Louis B., 81–3, 88, 101, 107

McCullers, Carson, 109–131; "Aliens," 118–119; *Ballad of the Sad Cafe*, 115–116; *Clock Without Hands*, 124–125; "Court in the West Eighties," 117–118; *Heart is a Lonely Hunter*, 109, 120–124, 125–128; "Jockey," 119; *Member of the Wedding*, 109, 112, 128–131; "Poldi," 114, 116–117; "Wunderkind," 114–116

Melville, Herman, 110, 123

melodrama, 85–86, 97, 101, 104

modernist abstraction, 14–15, 142n47

Mulvey, Laura, 50, 62, 144n15

Nazism, 9, 12, 13, 15

New York Intellectuals, 14, 25–26

Nietzsche, Friedrich, 27

Nordau, Max, 9–11

Partisan Review, 14, 25–26

performance art, 133, 158n1

phallogocentrism, 71, 75, 152n22

Picasso, 31

postmodernism, 10, 146n35, 151n11

Porter, Katherine Ann, 112

pre-mirror stage *flaneur*, 29–30, 42, 70, 73

profane illumination, 22

progress narratives, 2, 4–5

reform movements, 88, 90–91, 154n15, 155n21

Riviere, Joan, 51, 148n7

Sedgwick, Eve, 145n23

Semites, 28, 30

Sontag, Susan, 133–134, 135

Stewart, Susan, 6, 83, 154n18

Stieglitz, Alfred, 56–58, 149n25

Stoker, Bram; *Dracula*, 93–94

superego, 88
surrealism, 13–14, 23, 31–32, 144n12

Tiresias, 65–67, 71
Thalberg, Irving, 86–88
transvestism, 67, 68, 76, 88, 90
trickster, 83–84, 86, 91, 128, 136

uncanny, 56, 64, 75, 78, 79, 92

Verlaine, Paul, 10
Voetglin, Arthur, 50, 52–53, 56

Weininger, Otto, 18
West, Nathanael, 25–48; *Cool Million*, 40–45; *Day of the Locust*, 26, 40–41, 43, 45–48, *Dream Life of Balso Snell*, 26–35; *Miss Lonelyhearts*, 26, 35–40
White Anglo-Saxon Protestants (WASPS). *See* Anglo-Americans
Wilde, Oscar, 10
Williams, Tennessee, 112
Woolf, Virginia, 4, 16–17

Ziegfield, Florence, 50, 51–52, 56, 148n12

Yoshinobu Hakutani, *General Editor*

The books in this series deal with many of the major writers known as American realists, modernists, and post-modernists from 1880 to the present. This category of writers will also include less known ethnic and minority writers, a majority of whom are African American, some are Native American, Mexican American, Japanese American, Chinese American, and others. The series might also include studies on well-known contemporary writers, such as James Dickey, Allen Ginsberg, Gary Snyder, John Barth, John Updike, and Joyce Carol Oates. In general, the series will reflect new critical approaches such as deconstructionism, new historicism, psychoanalytical criticism, gender criticism/feminism, and cultural criticism.

For additional information about this series or for the submission of manuscripts, please contact:

>Peter Lang Publishing
>P.O. Box 1246
>Bel Air, MD 21014-1246

To order other books in this series, please contact our Customer Service Department at:

>800-770-LANG (within the U.S.)
>(212) 647-7706 (outside the U.S.)
>(212) 647-7707 FAX

Or browse online by series at:

>www.peterlangusa.com